US RESPONSE TO SOVIET INVASIONS

HUNGARY AND CZECHOSLOVAKIA

A CRITIQUE OF LIBERATION POLICY

US RESPONSE TO SOVIET INVASIONS

HUNGARY AND CZECHOSLOVAKIA

A CRITIQUE OF LIBERATION POLICY

ABU NASAR SAIED AHMED

AKANSHA PUBLISHING HOUSE
NEW DELHI - 110 002

AKANSHA PUBLISHING HOUSE
4649-B/21, Ansari Road
Darya Ganj, New Delhi - 110 002
Email: ektabooks@yahoo.com
Ph. : 23263193 / 09435116718

US Response to Soviet Invasions: Hungary and Czechoslovakia

First Published 2007
ISBN 81-8370-095-0

PRINTED IN INDIA

Published by M.P. Misra for Akansha Publishing House, New Delhi and Printed at Aryan Enterprises, Delhi.

TO

RUBY

MY STRONGEST CRITIC

CONTENTS

PREFACE

Five decades have passed since the Soviet army marched into Hungary with the twin objectives of putting down the revolt in Budapest and consolidating Moscow's control over Eastern Europe, which had came under its sphere of influence during the latter phase of World War II. The invasion not only demolished the myth of American policy of liberation of the region, the core of America's foreign policy in the Eisenhower era, but also paved the way for similar surgical action in the Soviet zone of influence twelve years later to crush a reformist and peaceful movement spearheaded by a section of the ruling elite within the communist echelon in Czechoslovakia. Three decades later the people of the 'satellite' countries broke the chain of captivity taking advantage of the inherent, palpable and profound weaknesses of an over-extended empire. This time the might of an ageing and hence a fading superpower could be seen nowhere. The controversial doctrine of limited sovereignty of the submissive socialist countries under the orbit of Soviet sphere of influence too evaporated under the heat of the democratic urge of the freedom loving 'enslaved people'. Moscow could not dare to crush the popular urge of the people of East Europe for freedom of action in internal and international affairs. All this had happened without any external aid and inducement.

Historians, experts and critics of US foreign policy face an overwhelming task of putting together the vast stockpile of documents and analyses of the two stifling events in the post-World War II history of Eastern Europe – Hungarian revolution and Prague experiment of communism with a human face. They are often baffled by the kind of measured and limited response that the United States showed despite its professed position of encouraging the 'captive peoples' to achieve independence of Moscow's control. There were compulsions set by the Cold War - the national interest and intervening factors which encircle a great power making it too confused and weak to respond in a manner expected of it within the framework of its declared foreign policy goals. Such compulsions were not addressed properly and dispassionately at the time of public pronouncements leaving enough scope for false expectation and senseless incitement, which eventually exposed the people to ruthless consequences. Politicians make promises to gain a mileage in the race for capturing power, leaving the common masses to suffer for taking such promises seriously.

The present work is an attempt to understand the US liberation policy in the backdrop of the two major military incursions in Eastern Europe committed by the Soviet Union along with some other minor but relevant developments inside the Soviet sphere of influence. It is the result of my research done in the University of Illinois at Urbana-Champaign, USA, as a Fulbright Visiting Scholar during 1981-1982. While some of my earlier publications are the product of my research on various issues of America's foreign policy, the major task of putting an enormous quantity of data in the form of a book remained incomplete for all the years for several reasons, which need an explanation to escape criticism that it naturally deserves. Certain inadequacies/data gaps in the first draft held me back and to handle it from this part of India is too daunting a task to accomplish. I set a deadline to publish the present work by October 2006 commemorating fifty years of the historic Hungarian revolution of 1956.

A number of institutions, scholars and individuals helped me in writing this book. The Council for International Exchange of Scholars, Washington DC, offered me the prestigious Fulbright Post-Doctoral Fellowship, the University of Illinois at Urbana Champaign offered me a placement and Dibrugarh University (India) granted me the necessary leave to undertake my journey to the USA. Omeo Kumar Das Institute of Social Change and Development, where I have been working since June 1999, extended me the infrastructural facilities. Those who deserve special mention with profound gratitude are Professor Stephen P. Cohen, now a Senior Fellow at the

Brookings Institution, Professor Richard L. Merritt, the then Head of the Department of Political Science at University of Illinois at Urbana-Champaign, Professor Roger E. Kanet, with whom I had discussed many issues on Moscow's uneasy relations with the East European Countries, Professor Henry Hart, Professor Louis Dupree and Professor Myron Weiner (who was one of the examiners of my Ph. D thesis). Roberta Cohen (Bobby) took interest in my work during my stay at the University of Illinois and extended courteous hospitality more than once. My two esteemed friends Professor Adil-ul-Yasin of Dibrugarh University and Professor Dipankar Purkayatha of Assam University offered critical comments on an earlier draft of the book. Professor Anuradha Dutta, my teacher at Gauhati University and now a colleague at the Institute, inspired me to complete the book. Ratna Bhuyan, Research Associate at the Institute, did the painstaking copy-editing task meticulously. Mr. M.P. Misra took the trouble of bringing out the book quickly. Needless to state, the final responsibility for the facts, analyses and the content of the book remain my own.

I wish to express my appreciation to the Librarians of University of Illinois at Urabana-Champaign, US Library of Congress, Dibrugarh University, Jawaharlal Nehru University, American Information Resource Center, New Delhi, and Indo-American Centre for International Studies, Hyderabad, for giving me an easy access to their Libraries and the facilities.

I have dedicated this book to my wife Ruby, who not only stands before me as the strongest critic but also as a source of tremendous inspiration. My children Sazhiv and Rosa offered their encouragements and hence tender pat of thanks to them.

October 2006 **ABU NASAR SAIED AHMED**

CHAPTER I

US POLICY TOWARDS EASTERN EUROPE

American foreign policy towards Eastern Europe in the Cold War era was fraught with an illusory and unresolved question. Did the military strategy of the Allied powers during World War II lead to Western acquiescence to the ultimate Soviet advantage in that region? There is no quick answer to the question. As the war was drawing to an obvious end with the Allied victory in sight and as the Soviet forces were liberating East and Central Europe from the Nazi occupation, it became clear that the former Nazi satellites would now fall within the Soviet sphere of influence. The available documents as well as the exhaustively analyzed books on the post-war arrangements and agreements convincingly present the fact that at the critical moment of historic transition, the United States remained uncertain about its future relations with the countries entering the Soviet sphere of influence. The Roosevelt Administration was still ambivalent over the course of American policy towards the newly gained Soviet sphere of influence. For example, on November 21, 1944 when Cordell Hull, Secretary of State, handed over his office to Edward Stettinus, he recorded that the "question of our future relations with satellite countries are still under discussion"[1]. President Roosevelt gave priorities to the maintenance of the unity of purpose among the partners of the grand alliance at least till

1. *The Memoirs of Cordell Hall* (New York: Hodder and Stoughton, 1948) p. 1461.

the end of the War and also to the success of the efforts towards the establishment on an international organization over the need to frame a meaningful policy towards the future course of American policy towards Eastern Europe. The Administration felt that the Soviet participation in the War was an imperative to its successful end. The fear of the West of the reemergence of Germany within a foreseeable future coincided with the historically proved Soviet fear for the future use of Eastern Europe as a corridor of invasion. All these eventually facilitated the Soviet advantage in the region.[2] While the Soviet Union was clear about its position in the region, the United States had nothing better than a policy of appeasement. Hans Morganthau wrote that the US was "slow to recognize that its victory in the Second World War eliminated one threat to its security, opened the door for a new threat more dangerous than the one against which the Second World War had been fought"[3].

The realization that US vacillating position to promote its national interest in Eastern Europe had resulted in the full and complete domination of the Soviet Union over the region was immediately felt after the death of President Roosevelt. However, the Truman Administration could not afford to renounce the US commitment to the war-time agreements, more particularly, the Yalta agreement, as President Truman had the moral obligation to carry out the policy of his illustrious predecessor. Therefore, he told the US Congress:

> The Government does not regard the treaties as completely satisfactory. Whatever their defects, however, I am convinced that they are as good as we can hope to obtain by agreement among the principal wartime Allies. Further

---

2. Documents now available testify that the United States tacitly recognized the Soviet interests in Eastern Europe which were 'more direct' than that of the West. One of such documents is the US Department of State, *Foreign Relations of the United States*, 1945: *The Conferences at Malta and Yalta* (Washington DC, 1955).

3 Hans J. Morganthau, *American Foreign Policy: In Defense of the National Interest* (London: Mathuen, 1952), p. 91.

disputes and delay [in ratifying the agreements] would gravely jeopardize political stability in the countries concerned for many years.[4]

The Truman Administration decided to confront the Soviet Union and check the 'communist thrust' in Asia and Europe. This resulted in a series of developments beginning with the pronouncement of the Truman Doctrine and followed by the Marshall plan. But the whole spectrum of American foreign policy neither threw any light on the possibility of US intervention to liberate the peoples of Eastern Europe nor did it indicate the American position on the post-war *status quo* in Europe. In between the two, the Administration showed clear hostility to the governments in the region by reducing its trade relations and by gearing up the propaganda machine against the Soviet domination.

The US Government considered that the anti-communist propaganda, and not merely the trade restrictions, could serve as a moral force generating ideas of freedom among the peoples of the region. As the normal channels of contact between the United States and the East European countries were almost eliminated by the Soviet backed governments and as the operation of the western information services was almost completely stopped by an active Soviet vigilance, the United States found that only through radio anti-communist propaganda could be effectively communicated to the peoples of the region. The Voice of America (VOA) as well as the BBC's East European services were found to be the only alternatives. In 1948, the VOA propaganda was accelerated to convey to the 'captive peoples' the message of democracy and freedom.[5] The Radio Free Europe (RFE) went on air on July 4, 1950. The aim of the propaganda was to help "those trapped behind the iron curtain" to prepare themselves for the day of liberation.

4 World Peace Foundation, ***Documents on American Foreign Relations*** (Princeton: Princeton University Press, 1949), p. 2.

5 Council on Foreign Relations, *The United States in the World Affairs, 1948-1949* (New York: Harper, 1949) pp. 23-24.

These agencies were glorified as 'prophets of early liberation' and officially unofficial media of the US Government.[6] Later on it was found that these agencies had encouraged the peoples of Eastern Europe against the Soviet Union and had given them the implicit idea that at the event of their rebellion, peaceful or otherwise, the United States would extend substantial help leading to their eventual liberation from the Soviet domination.

THE CAMPAIGN FOR LIBERATION:

The 1952 US Presidential election ushered in a great foreign policy debate. Although the containment policy spearheaded a diplomatic offensive against the Soviet-led socialist world, a strong group of critics launched a hostile attack on the efficacy of the policy. Besides the New Left, an articulated section of the American public including the isolationists offered a strong criticism of the policy on its 'defensive and immoral' foundation as it had apparently accepted the *status quo* in Europe. Such criticism gave birth to an alternative formula for the US policy makers. It was Walter Lippmann who initiated an academic debate on the viability and soundness of the containment policy. His criticism originated in his misreading of George Kennan's recommendations. His argument was that the US foreign policy could not be shaped on an erroneous assumption that the inherent weakness in the Soviet system would eventually lead to its natural collapse.[7] A negative approach to foreign policy could not be expected to produce a positive result, and hence, miracles would not happen unless the United States took a positive stand to contribute effectively to the collapse of the 'Soviet empire'. A number of developments like the communist take over of power in Czechoslovakia in February 1948, the Berlin Blockade and Soviet A-bomb test in September 1949,

---

6 For details of the US sponsored mass media like the VOA and the RFE see Allen A. Michie, *Voices through the Iron Curtain: The Radio Free Europe Story* (New York: Dodd and Co. 1963), Robert T. Halt, *Radio Free Europe* (Minneapolis: University of Minnesota Press, 1958) and also for an early account see Brutus Coste, "Propaganda to Eastern Europe", *Public Opinion Quarterly*, 14 (Winter, 1950/51) pp. 643-58.

7 Walter Lippmann, *The Cold War* (New York: Harper, 1947).

Mao Zedong's victory in China and the outbreak of the Korean War provoked the American public to question the vitality of the containment policy. Serious criticism on the policy leveled by conservative-isolationists like Senator Robert A. Taft and Alexander Wiley turned an academic debate on the subject to a political campaign. They rejected the policy as merely 'pantywaist' diplomacy and urged upon the Government to encourage the peoples of Eastern Europe to revolt against the Soviet domination. Senator Wiley suggested that the United States should sponsor a "commando-type program of psychological and revolutionary penetration, including the use of 'silver bullets' – money",[8] without making a thorough assessment of the objective situation in Eastern Europe. Such proposals were advanced without considering the fact that a military adventurism would be not only ineffective in the face of the presence of about 14 million Soviet troops but also would expose the common people to ruthless destruction.

There was a tearing hurry in seeking liberation of Eastern Europe. Testifying before the House Committee Republican Congressman Charles J. Kersten advanced an idea to overthrow the Soviet system failing which, he argued, "will bring us war". He suggested that the United States should withdraw the recognition of the Soviet Union and the Soviet-backed governments in Eastern Europe. He went a little further to make an unrealistic suggestion, which hardly received any attention of the US Congress that the United States should work to force the expulsion of these countries from the United Nations. Nonetheless, his proposal to accord political asylum to the dissidents in Eastern Europe did receive support. He argued emotionally:

> . . . let the people behind the iron curtain know that we will do *everything* we can to work for the eventual liberation...and when time is opportune we should actively assist the people behind the iron curtain to liberate themselves[9]. [Emphasis added]

---

8 For details of Senator Wiley's extension remarks entitled "Penetration of Program against Communism" see *Congressional Record: Appendix*, 82nd Congress, 1st Session, 1951, pp. A7975-77.

9 US Congress, House Committee on Foreign Affairs, *The Mutual Security Program: Hearings*, 82nd Congress, 1st Session, 1951, pp. 1106-09.

The Kersten proposals, later on came to be known as Kersten Amendments, were approved on October 10, 1951 as an integral part of the Mutual Security Act, that led to the allocation of $100 million as a military assistance fund for organizing an armed force with the escapees from Eastern Europe to strengthen US military objectives in Europe.[10] After the approval of the Act, Kersten justified the aggressive overtone of his proposals saying that, "In this cold war against communism, we must do more than merely try to contain it". He believed that "offensive in the cold war" would create "some trouble for Jeo Stalin in his backyard".[11]

In the UN General Assembly the Soviet Union sharply assailed the Kersten Amendments as 'aggressive acts' and interference in the domestic affairs of other countries.[12] To most Americans these proposals generated optimism among the people in Eastern Europe who had been seeking US support for their liberation. The 1953 report on the Mutual Security Act also added that the President had "authorized the use of Kersten Amendment funds to help provide better facilities for the flood of escapees, and their training and rehabilitation would eventually lead to the formation of the bulk of the liberation forces".[13]

The Truman Administration was happy with these exercises, but refrained from demonstrating an aggressive posture threatening the very foundation of Soviet sphere of influence. There are reasons for this. The presence of the Soviet force, an estimated 14 million in number, greatly reduced the possibility of US military option for upsetting the *status quo* in Europe. For the United States, the Soviet advantage in Eastern Europe did not pose a direct threat to its security,

---

10 *New York Times*, October 14, 1951.

11 US Congress, *Congressional Record*, 82nd Congress, 1st Session, 1951, pp. 1351, A6950-51.

12 Council on Foreign Relations, *The United States in World Affairs, 1951* (New York: Random, 1952), p. 399

13 US Congress, Senate, Committee on Foreign Relations, *The Mutual Security Act 1953*, 83rd Congress, 1st Session, 1953, p. 61.

mainly because of the geographical situation, and therefore, the question of the fate of the 'captive peoples' became a moral platitude rather than a serious challenge to the US interests in international power structure and diplomacy. The reliance on moral force gave an easy device to cover up an unpleasant reality, i.e. the impossibility of using the military might to liberate these peoples. Added to this, in 1949 the Soviet Union demolished the US atomic monopoly by exploding it's A-bomb. Close on the heels of this development, Mao Zedong captured power in China. Later on, the Korean War demonstrated that even with its great military strength, the United States was unable to crush communism. All this testified to the limits of a great power in waging a war for others' buried cause.

These developments presented the *foci* of the great debate of 1952 which eventually planted the roots of an alternative to the containment policy. President Truman's last year in office had experienced an all out attack on the containment policy for its tacit acceptance of Soviet hegemony in Eastern Europe. He tried to convince his critics that his Administration had been conveying the hope of good days to the peoples of the region and wished that in future too the message would be carried to them. In his last address to the Congress he said:

> During the coming year, we must not forget the suffering of the people behind the Iron Curtain. In these areas, minorities are being suppressed, human rights violated, religion persecuted. We should continue and expand the activities of the Voice of America, which brings our message of hope and truth to these peoples.[14]

Such a vague statement could hardly convince the critics and the general public who found the newly christened liberation policy more appealing. The name of John Foster Dulles was prominently associated with the liberation theory as a logical alternative to the old concept of containment. While still serving as a consultant of the Truman Administration, Dulles argued, as early as 1949, in favour of adopting a policy to ensure liberation of Eastern Europe.[15] This argument was

14 *New York Times*, January 10, 1952.

15 *ibid*, December 14, 1949.

expanded in his book published a year later.[16] Deploring the alleged negligence to the cause of the people of Eastern Europe, he wrote that a moral offensive against the Soviet Union would incapacitate its leaders to consolidate the hegemony in the region. Taking the core of George Kennan's thesis of inherent weaknesses of the Soviet Union, he contended that the "communist structure is over-extended, over-rigid, and ill-founded. It could be shaken if difficulties that are latent were activated". He defined the nature of activation in the following manner:

> "Activation" does not mean open revolt. The people have no arms, and violent revolt would be futile. It would be worse than futile, for it would precipitate massacre...we have no desire to weaken the Soviet Union at the cost of those who are primary concern.[17]

Two years later he made a comprehensive statement on the policy of liberation, which eventually replaced the containment policy as the Republican President moved to the White House. In his famous election-year article entitled "A Policy of Boldness", Dulles advanced two characteristic alternatives to the containment policy: (i) the military preparedness capable of resorting to instant and massive retaliation, and (ii) political offensive against the Soviet Union. He wrote:

> *There is only one solution and only one: that is the free world develop the will and organize the means to retaliate instantly against open aggression by Red armies, so that, if it occurred anywhere, we could and would strike back where it hurts, by means of our choosing.*[18]

His second alternative was the political offensive of a propaganda nature to be guided by a spirit of moral assumption that "the dynamic prevails over static" that the "non-material forces are more powerful than those that are material". He wrote, "We shall let these truths work in and through us. We should be dynamic, we should use *ideas* as weapons, and these

16 John Foster Dulles, *War or Peace* (New York: Macmillan, 1950).

17 *ibid*, p. 247.

18 John Foster Dulles, " A Policy of Boldness", *Life*, May 19, 1952, p.151.

ideas should conform moral principles". He, however, conceded that secret works within the basic objectives of liberating the 'captive peoples' might have been going on. But to him these were not adequate:

> As a matter of fact, some highly competent work is being done, at one place or other, to promote liberation. Obviously such activities do not lent them to public explosion. But liberation from the yoke of Moscow will not occur for a very long time, unless the United States makes it publicly known that it wants and expects liberation to occur. The mere statement of that wish and expectation would change, in an electrifying way, the mood of the captive peoples. It would put heavy burden on the jailors and create new opportunities for liberation.[19]

The two-fold Dullesian policy to liberate Eastern Europe eventually leading to the collapse of the Soviet Union included a programme of action, *viz*, declaration to the effect that the liberation as a peaceful objective of American policy, creation of a political 'task force' of the dependable escapees from Eastern Europe who would develop a freedom programme for each of the satellite countries, coordination of freedom programmes of the RFE with VOA, snapping of the diplomatic relations with the existing communist governments in the region if and when the freedom programme progressed, and cultivation of international support of the 'free world' for such a programme. He, however, tried to convince that such a programme had not been designed to instigate the 'captive peoples' to armed revolt. He wrote:

> We do not want a series of bloody uprising and reprisals. There can be peaceful separation from Moscow, as Tito showed, and enslavement can be made so unprofitable that the masters will let go his grip. Such results do not come to pass overnight. But we can know, for history proves, that the spirit of patriotism burns unquenched in Poles, Czechs, Hungarians, Romanians, Bulgarians, Chinese and others, and we can be confident that within two, three or 10 years substantial parts of the present captive world can peacefully regain national independence, that will mark the beginning

19 *ibid*, p. 154.

> of the end of the Soviet despotism's attempt at world conquest.[20]

To Dulles, a Tito-type arrangement in Eastern Europe could be a satisfactory replacement of the captive status, which, he was convinced, could be attained by peaceful means.

As the 1952 Presidential election was approaching, a series of important events took place. Dulles resigned in March as the foreign policy adviser to President Truman marking thereby the end of the bipartisan commitment to the foreign policy of the Administration. He assumed the responsibility as the foreign policy planner of the Republican Presidential candidate. In the tussle for the Republican Party nomination between the isolationist Taft faction and the internationalist faction, General Dwight D. Eisenhower became victorious indicating thereby the general acceptance of the liberation policy. The foreign policy plank of the Republican Party adopted on July 10, 1952 was a thorough and severe assault on the Administration for having "abandoned friendly nations such as Latvia, Lithuania, Estonia, Poland and Czechoslovakia to fend for themselves against the communist aggression which soon swallowed them."[21] The party platform pledged to end the "negative, futile and immoral policy" of the Truman Administration and entrust the VOA with a positive programme of carrying the message of liberation to the captive peoples. It further stressed:

> The policy we espouse will revive the contagious, liberating influence, which are inherent in freedom. They will inevitably set up strain and stresses within the captive world which will mark the beginning of the end.

The Republican platform incorporated another dose of popular rhetoric by way of promising the voters to repudiate "all commitments contained in secret understandings such as those of Yalta which aid communist enslavements" and by charging the Democratic party for associating itself in the enslavement process. It is, however, noteworthy that just after the Presidential elcction when a move was initiated to repudiate

---

20 *ibid*, p. 157.

21 US Congress, *Congressional Almanac*, 1952, p. 490.

the Yalta agreements, President Eisenhower and Dulles opposed it.

There was basically no difference between the Republican platform and the Democratic one on the issue of liberation. The Democratic plank also pledged not to "abandon the once free peoples of Central and East Europe who suffered under the Kremlin tyranny in violation of the Soviet Union's most solemn pledge at Tehran, Yalta and Potsdam". It further stated:

> We look forward to the day when the liberation of Poland and other oppressed Soviet satellites including Czechoslovakia, Rumania, Bulgaria, Albania, Lithuania, Estonia and Latvia and other nations of Asia under Soviet domination will be restored to them and they can again take their rightful place in the community of free nations.
>
> We will carry forward and expand the vital and effective program of the Voice of America for preparation of the "Iron Curtain" bringing truth and hope to all the people subjugated by the Soviet empire.[22]

Although the Democratic Party pledged not to abandon he people of Eastern Europe, an aggressive Republican commitment to secure the liberation proved to be more effective vote-catching device. The campaign for liberation was designed to enlist the support of the ethnic voters of East and Central European origins who had strong concentration in a number of cities and urban centers of Northeast and Midwest. A year before the 1952 electioneering, the Republican Party created an Ethnic Origins Division headed by Arthur Bliss Lane, the former US Ambassador to Poland, with a view to mustering support of this segment of the American society for the party. A number of studies later on revealed that Lane had urged Dulles not merely to internationalize the liberation issue but also make it politically profitable.[23] Lane was reportedly to have mobilized the ethnic support by distributing two

---

22 *ibid*, p. 496.

23 Louis L. Gerson, *The Hyphenate in Recent American Politics and Diplomacy* (Lawrence: University of Kansas, 1964) p. 183 and Arthur G. Theoharis, *The Yalta Myth: An Issue in US Politics, 1945-1955* (Colombia: University of Missouri Press, 1970) pp. 17-148.

pamphlets, one entitled "Betrayal: Over 100, 000,000 East Europeans by the Democratic Administration" and the other "Republican Policy of Liberation or Democratic Policy of Containment". But Eisenhower, with an outstanding military background had realized the hollowness of liberation ideas, and therefore, appeared to have been reluctant to make liberation speeches during the campaign.[24] He carefully avoided the propagation of armed revolt in the Soviet zone of control. In his speeches he vaguely mentioned about the US support for 'peaceful liberation'. For example, at the American Legion Convention in New York, he said: "...the American conscience can never know peace until the millions in Soviet satellites are restored again to be masters of their own fate."[25] His speech carried emotions but not a programme of action:

> We can never rest – and we must inform all the world, including the Kremlin – that until the enslaved nations of the world have the fullness of freedom, the right to choose their own path, that then, and then only, can say that there is a possible way of living peacefully and permanently with communism in the world.
>
> We must tell the Kremlin that never shall we desist in our aid to every man and woman of these slacked lands who seek refuge with us, any man who keeps burning away his own people the flame of freedom or who is dedicated to the liberation of his fellows.

The emotional statements and rhetoric gave the Republicans an edge over the Democrats, which eventually brought the victory of a less known in politics General Eisenhower over a political heavy weight Adlai Stevenson. The fact remains that both Eisenhower and Dulles maintained ambiguity in their statements on the nature of support for the cause of the liberation. Political propaganda without a concrete promise created an air of false hope in Eastern Europe, encouraged the 'captive peoples' to revolt and exposed them to Soviet military intervention.

On August 27, 1952, while addressing the annual meeting of the American Political Science Association in Buffalo, Dulles

---

24 Louis L. Gerson, *The Hyphenate, ibid*, pp. 189-191.

25 *New York Times*, August 26, 1952.

spelt out the plan for the liberation of Eastern Europe.[26] He said that the incoming administration should encourage a peaceful revolution using 'quiet' methods like passive resistance, non-cooperation, discontentment, slowdown and industrial sabotage. The VOA and other agencies would begin to stir up resistance behind the 'Iron Curtain', letting the peoples know that they had the *moral* support of the US Government. Dulles was convinced that the resistance movement would spring up among the patriots. They could be supplied information and also integrated through airdrops and other private organizations like the Committee for a Free Europe (CFE). Consequently, he predicted that the Soviet Union would disintegrate and its leaders would not be able to hold together the huge country with the newly acquired sphere of influence.

The liberation theory did not go unopposed. Averill Harriman, the Mutual Security Director, who also addressed the Association, argued objectively that the 'liberation' policy would spread tension in Europe and it was a trap prompting revolt in the satellite states resulting in a massacre. Dulles sharply reacted to the comment of Harriman:

> It is nonsense for Harriman to say that General Eisenhower's liberation policy is a trap and would lead to premature uprising and more Warsaw massacres. There was nothing premature about Warsaw uprising. What was wrong was that the Russians double-crossed the Poles. To suggest any analogy between this treachery and General's idea is unthinkable. The only trap I see is that the Democratic platform, which says, they look forward to liberation of all these peoples but they aren't willing to do anything about it. It is a trap to get votes, but I don't think it will work.[27]

President Truman launched a severe frontal attack on the exponents of liberation policy. He accused them of playing 'gutter politics' in foreign policy betraying willingness to risk an atomic war in Europe in delusive effort and yet was willing to increase the risk of it to gain victory in the Presidential election. "To try to liberate these enslaved people at this time,"

---

26 *New York Times*, August 28, 1952.

27 *idem.*

he argued, "might will mean turning lands into atomic battlefields". He further stated:

> Nothing could be worse than to raise false hopes of this [liberation] in eastern Europe...Nothing could be worse than to incite uprisings that can only end by giving a new crop of victims to the Soviet executioners. All Europe knows quite well that insurrection in the Soviet borderlands these days could only be successful with armed support from outside...If the Republicans don't mean to give armed support – I am sure they don't – they are trying to deceive their fellow citizens at home and playing cruel, gutter politics with lives of countless good men and women behind the Iron Curtain.[28]

Dulles responded to President Truman's criticism without clarifying the nature of Republican support for the cause of liberation. He only accused the Administration of following an appeasement policy towards the Soviet Union. He said: "We can trust a man who won peace rather than the man who lost it." Dulles believed that even without waging a war against the Soviet Union, liberation of Easter Europe was possible. He argued:

> It is, of course, absurd to suggest that General Eisenhower anticipates invoking wholesale insurrection by armed slaves. Premature revolt would expose the patriotic people to liquidation. There are countless peaceful ways by which the task of Russian despots can be made unbearably difficult that they will renounce their rule. This was shown in Yugoslavia.[29]

Secretary of State Dean Acheson defended the containment policy and rejected the Dullesian rhetoric as a "positive prescription for disaster."[30]

Despite the vagueness in the content of the liberation policy, certain conclusions can be drawn from the pronouncements made by Dulles: (i) the United States would continue to encourage through mass media the anti-communist sentiments to grow inside the Soviet sphere of influence and also to form underground armed units capable of fomenting

---

28 *ibid*, September 3, 1952.

29 *ibid*, September 4, 1952.

30 *ibid*, September 12, 1952.

large scale violent revolt against the Soviet domination of Eastern Europe; (ii) instead of killing the vast majority of people the Soviet authorities would give up their control over Eastern Europe; and (iii) the moral support of the United States for such a revolt would be a deterrent factor against the possible Soviet suppression of such a revolt. In this way the Soviet domination of the region would come to a logical end.

The Dullesian rhetoric on 'peaceful liberation' left a number of questions unanswered. How could the people of Eastern Europe stage a peaceful revolution against Moscow when the Soviet forces in massive strength were stationed in the region to protect and defend the Soviet interests? What would be the nature of US response to the Soviet suppression of 'peaceful revolution' in any part of the region? Unfortunately, no serious debate was engaged on such issues, and therefore, there was no plausible answer to them.

Theories may appear to be more romantic than practice. Dulles too was not unaware of the practical consequences of US induced massive rebellion in Eastern Europe and also US limitations in taking recourse to military options against a conventionally preeminent power in Europe, and therefore, he propagated in an ambivalent way a 'peaceful liberation' in the Tito's mould. But the situation obtaining in Yugoslavia at the time of Tito's parting with Moscow was different from the one in Eastern Europe in the early 1950s when the Soviet Union fully consolidated its hold in the region politically and militarily with remarkable rapidity and effectiveness. Dulles himself admitted later on that he had not seriously subscribed to some of the electioneering statements. As a platform writer he had merely exposed the failure of the Truman Administration. He had been aware of the over-simplification of the liberation issue.[31] Therefore, he carefully avoided the explanation regarding the extent of the American involvement in the actual act of liberation. Herman Finer, of course, did not like to question the sincerity of Dulles in his advocacy of the collapse of the Soviet Union and felt that the seed of the disintegration

31 Sherman Adams, *Firsthand Report* (New York: Harper, 1961) p. 88; Dulles to Richard Rovere in John R. Beal, *John Foster Dulles 1888-1959* (New York: Harper, 1959) p. 139.

could be planted in Eastern Europe.[32] All what he spoke was a part of the psychological warfare against the Soviet Union and to that extent it remained as an abstract goal without any concrete plan to back it up.

Despite its vagueness, the liberation polemic gained popularity during the Presidential electioneering. At the initial stage, the Democratic party candidate, Adlai Stevenson, warned against the liberation ideas because he felt that the United States would not be able to extend any concrete help in the near future to the cause of liberation. Therefore, instead of advancing false hope, the US Government should "negotiate and initiate negotiation" on the basis of "give and take" on the fate of Eastern Europe.[33] But later on, being sensitized about the election wave centering around 'liberation' thesis, he changed his content to woo the ethnic voters of Eastern European origins and declared that the question of liberation "should never be an issue among the Americans for we are all united in our desire for their liberation from oppression and in confidence that freedom will once again be theirs."[34]

The West European reaction to the liberation theory was of anguish and apprehension.[35] The *Economist* (London) could make a correct assessment of the campaign. "Unhappily 'Liberation' applied to Eastern Europe, it commented, "means either risk of war or it means nothing."[36] Just before the election it observed that the liberation ideas "sent shivers down every European spine and seemed to confirm insidious propaganda that paints the clumsy Americans as the chief threat to peace."[37]

---

32 Herman Finer, *Dulles over Suez* (Chicago: Quadrangle, 1964) p. x./ and Abu Nasar Saied Ahmed, "Dulles and Eastern Europe: A Retrospection", *Journal of Politics*, Vol. IV, March 1997, pp, 95-105.

33 *New York Times*, August 26, 1952, for details see Adlai Stevenson, *Major Campaign Speeches* (New York: Random, 1953) pp. 74, 92, 119.

34 See Norman A. Graebner, *The New Isolationism* (New York: Ronald, 1956) p. 104.

35 *Life*, September 22, 1952, p. 30.

36 *Economist*, August 30, 1952.

37 *ibid*, October 18, 1952.

New York Times reported the reaction of the Chief of Allied Headquarters. In an interview, General Alfred M. Gruenther said that it was necessary to keep up the hope of liberation of the captive peoples, but he argued, "I do not believe that could liberate them without war. There is no question of launching such a war."[38] From time to time *New York Times* reported the skeptical response of the Western Europe to the liberation propaganda and observed that the Republicans were "offering a new American policy no European statesman could follow."[39] Similarly, *Washington Post* commented that Europe "will discover that Mr. Eisenhower cannot change the grim facts of international life and therefore cannot appreciably change foreign policy of the United States."[40] Most of the West European states had gained out of the US assistance under the Marshall Plan, and therefore, saw the dynamism in the Republican foreign policy as a calculated risk. They could understand the impracticability of such ideas with a military confrontation with the Soviet Union. They probably felt that the issue became more alarmingly an election issue rather than a serious foreign policy option. The emotion associated with electioneering would evaporate soon after the election. One can easily notice the contradictions between the liberation campaign and Eisenhower's pledge to go to Korea to bring an honourable armistice. When the incoming Administration was not prepared to prolong the war in Korea in which the United States got deeply involved as a part of its roll back communism strategy, it would not definitely risk a major war with the Soviet Union, and that too in the European theatre, in order to liberate the 'captive peoples' of Eastern Europe. Therefore, the liberation campaign remained a 'moral' and abstract issue. When the new Administration began to work, pragmatism prevailed over theoretical romanticism.

It would be unfair to state that the Americans did not see the hollowness of the idea of liberation. Critics like Walter Lippmann wrote that the Republican campaign to liberate

38 *New York Times*, September 12, 1952.

39 *ibid*, September, 7, 1952.

40 *Washington Post*, November 9, 1952.

Eastern Europe was dangerously misleading and vague. It was an incitement to revolt by unarmed people who could be easily crushed by the Soviet armies. Without making a comparative assessment of the ground realities in Yugoslavia in 1947 and the one prevailing in Eastern Europe in the 1950s, he, however, subscribed to an idea of encouraging Titoism in the region.[41]

POST-ELECTION LIBERATION PROGRAMME:

The liberation ideas continued to constitute the core of the foreign policy statements of the new Administration. The President-elect, Dwight D. Eisenhower, said in his New Year Message:

> I want to assure them [the people of Eastern Europe] they are not forgotten. I know that many of them fought bravely in the underground against Nazi tyranny and they tried to build up representative governments after the war. So long as the spirit of freedom lives in the youth, the future is one of promise.[42]

Some of the statements of Eisenhower and Dulles on liberation policy deserve attention here in the context of subsequent developments to be focused and analyzed in the next Chapter. As a step towards liberation, the President reiterated his commitment to repudiate the Yalta agreements, which were alleged to have given away Eastern Europe to the Soviet Union. In his first address to the US Congress he said:

> Our policy, dedicated to making the free world secure, will envisage all peaceful methods and devices – except breaking faith with our friends. We shall never acquiesce in the enslavement of any people in order to gain for ourselves. I shall ask the Congress at a later date to join in an appropriate resolution making clear that this Government recognizes no kind of commitment contained in the secret understandings of the past with foreign governments, which permits this kind of enslavement.[43]

Similarly, in his statement before he Senate Committee on Foreign Relations in connection with his nomination as the

41 *New York Times*, September 9, 1952.

42 *ibid*, January 1, 1953.

43 Department of State, *Bulletin*, February 9, 1953, p. 208.

Secretary of State, Dulles maintained a consistent stand on liberation ideas. In his reply to a question of the Chairman of the Committee as to the replacement of the containment policy by a more 'dynamic and positive policy', he said:

> . . . we shall never have a secured peace or a happy world so long as Soviet communism dominates one-third of all of the peoples that there are, and is in the process of trying to extend its rule to many others.
>
> These people who are enslaved are people who deserve to be free, and who, from our own selfish standpoint, ought to be free because if they are servile instruments of aggressive despotism, they will eventually be wedded into a force, which will be highly dangerous to ourselves and to all of the free world.[44]

Assailing the containment policy as a 'defensive policy' he argued in favour of peaceful liberation:

> It is only by keeping alive the hope of liberation, by taking advantage of that whenever opportunity arises, that we will end this terrible peril which dominates the world, which imposes upon us such terrible sacrifices and so great fears for the future. But all of this can be done and must be done in a way which will not provoke a general war, or in ways which will not provoke an insurrection which would be crushed with bloody violence.

He was confident that the liberation of Eastern Europe could be accomplished by peaceful means, and argued "those who do not believe that results can be accomplished by moral pressures, by the weight of propaganda, just do not know what they are talking about." In this connection he referred to Yugoslavia's example. He said that he did not admire the rule of Tito but "it illustrates that it is possible to disintegrate this present monolithic structure." In his testimony, some basic issues relevant to the liberation of the region did not receive adequate attention. The Committee did not discuss the possibility of Soviet suppression of a peaceful or violent rebellion. It ignored a pertinent point as to the extent of

---

44 US Congress, Senate, Committee on Foreign Relations, *Nomination of John Foster Dulles Secretary of State-Designate*, 83 Congress, 1st Session, 1953.

possibility of severing the region so closely linked with the Soviet Union ideologically, militarily and geographically and remoteness of the success in encouraging Titoism there.

As the new Administration began to function, the conservative Republicans in the US Congress introduced five separate resolutions urging the repudiation of secret treaties causing the 'enslavement' of the people of Eastern Europe. This would be the first step towards liberation of the region.[45] But both Eisenhower and Dulles did not agree to the repudiation ideas despite their earlier commitment to it. President Eisenhower wrote a letter to the President of the Senate and also to the Speaker of the House of Representatives on February 20 enclosing a draft resolution cleverly dropping the question of repudiation for the adoption in the Congress. The draft resolution states that "the United States rejects any interpretations or applications of any international agreements or understandings, made during the course of World War II, which had been perverted to bring about the subjugation of free peoples."[46] It, however, hoped that these 'captive' people would "again enjoy the right to self determination" and would have the right to choose their own forms of government. In support of the resolution Dulles made a comprehensive statement before the House Committee on Foreign Affairs on February 26, 1953. Reiterating the commitment to liberation of Eastern Europe he said that the resolution was aimed at looking forward to the future rather than the past. He said:

> The resolution is no call to bloody and senseless revolution. On the other hand, it is no idle gesture. It is an act of great historical importance and many consequences will stem from it. As its purpose becomes more and more widely understood, it will over coming years, revive the inherent longing for freedom which persists within the captive peoples so that longing becomes a mounting spiritual power which will eventually overcome the material power of Soviet dictatorship to rule what it has, or to subjugate more.[47]

---

45 US Congress, *Congressional Record*, 83rd Congress, 1st Session, 1953, pp. 67,68,318 and 438.

46 Council of Foreign Relations, *Documents on American Foreign Relations: 1953* (New York: Harper, 1953) pp. 187-188.

47 *ibid,* p. 191.

Dulles tried to bury the 'realm of controversy' over the secret treaties of the past and requested the Congress not to debate on the issue but to "unitedly move on to mould the future" in which the United States would "do what we peacefully can do, in order to revive the hopes of those now enslaved."

Why did the new Administration try to bury the 'realm of controversy' associated with the by putting off the 'repudiation' pledge? Eisenhower wrote in his autobiography that he "refused to do what the extremists asked: repudiate in their entirety the Yalta agreements and thus endanger United States rights in Vienna and Berlin, affirmed at Yalta."[48] It is an irony of history that forgetting his own electioneering pronouncements, Eisenhower now denounced those Congressmen as 'extremists' who tried to pilot resolutions to repudiate the Yalta agreements.

At any rate, the captive nations resolution did not come through the US Congress because of the tussle between the conservatives Republicans who wanted to denounce the containment policy of the Truman Administration and the Eisenhower Administration, which wanted to tame the electioneering rhetoric. The issue remained unresolved till March 5, 1953 when the death of Joseph Stalin reached the United States. Sherman Adams wrote that the death of Stalin led to the end of the debate over the repudiation controversy, and thus, it offered immense relief to both Eisenhower and Dulles.[49]

Although the 'repudiation' resolutions met their natural death, an impression, however, was left that the liberation of Eastern Europe continued to remain the core of the American foreign policy and it worked as an encouragement to the people of East Berlin, Poland and Hungary who took the earliest opportunity to revolt against the Soviet domination during the Eisenhower Administration. Events testify that as the 'captive peoples' revolted thrice in the 1950s, the US Administration's inapt gestures buried the hope for liberation. Hence, the

---

48 Dwight D. Eisenhower, *Mandate for Change* (New York, Garden City: Doubleday, 1963) p. 211.

49 Sherman Adams, *Firsthand Report*, n. 31, p. 93.

liberation policy, as Bennett Kovig comments, was "never really translated into operational policy, survived and endured as a dangerous myth."[50]

EAST BERLIN UPRISING: THE FIRST TEST:

The East Berlin uprising took place in the first year of the Eisenhower Administration, and stood as the first test case of the United States commitment to the liberation policy.

It is not easy to state precisely the reasons for the outbreak of the East Berlin riot of June 17, 1953. The Western accounts on the uprising hold a number of factors responsible for the sudden outbreak of violence, *viz*, the failure of the Soviet model of voluntary collectivism, cultural russification and lower benefits to the workers. There was dissatisfaction of the workers over the Soviet domination in East Berlin and their number was estimated to be 58,000 in March 1953. Those who hoped the unification of Germany were also unhappy about the failure of the latest round of negotiations.[51] The death of Stalin caused some uneasiness in the Soviet leadership, and therefore, they could not handle the situation in East Germany where simmering discontentment among the workers had already surfaced. Vladimir Semeonov, the Soviet political adviser in East Germany, held a series of discussion with SED (Sozialistische Einheitspartei Dautschlands) i.e. Socialist Unity Party of Germany formed as a result of the amalgamation of the Communist Party and the Social Democratic Party in the Soviet zone of Germany. The Politburo adopted a resolution on June 9, 1953 admitting a "series of errors" on the part of the Government, which were responsible for the current discontentment looming large over the sky of East Berlin. It announced a number of measures to ease the situation, such as, shifting of emphasis from heavy industry to consumer goods, relaxation of travel restrictions, normalization of relations with

---

50 Bennett Kovig, *The Myth of Liberation: East Central Europe in US Diplomacy and Politics since 1941* (Baltimore: The John Hopkins University Press, 1973) p. 125.

51 For details of the East Berlin uprising see Stefan Brant [*pseud*], *The East German Rising* (London: Thames and Hudson, 1955) and also Eugene Davidson, *The Death and Life of Germany* (New York: Alfred A. Knopf, 1959).

the Evangelican Church, amnesty for 'economic criminals', restoration of ration cards to large section of the middle class and the return of confiscated farms to those owners who wanted to return back to their respective places. Although these measures appeared to be acceptable to a large section of East Germans, who were unhappy with the Soviet domination, one contentious issue remained unsettled. The Central Committee adopted a resolution on May 14 recommending an average increase of 10 per cent in the working norms beginning on June 1, 1953. While the workers opposed the resolution, the Committee stood firm on its implementation. This precipitated into a crisis leading to the June 17 outburst.

The long-standing grievances and discontentment of the workers suddenly took the turn of an open revolt spearheaded by the workers of the prestigious Stalinalle project on East Berlin. The 'elite brigade' of the Stalinalle project brought out a procession carrying banners reading, "We demand a reduction of norms". They decided to confront the Government staging a general strike. The propagandists approached one of the ministers. As he appeared to address the agitated workers, they demanded not only the reversal of the working norm but also free election by secret ballots at all levels and threatened a countrywide general strike. They shouted slogans denouncing Walter Ulbricht, SED General Secretary, and Grotewohl and their leadership. As the situation was slipping out of the Government control, on the night of June 16 and 17 the mobile units of Volkspolizei and the Soviet armor divisions moved into East Berlin. On the morning of June 17, thousands of workers gathered in front of the Government buildings and subsequently clashed with the police. After a brief encounter with the police the agitated processionists held a massive meeting in the Marx-Engels Plaza, but they were dispersed by the Soviet backed forces. The demonstrators then gathered at the Brandenburg Gate, tore down the red flag and shouted anti-Soviet, anti-Ulbricht and anti-communist slogans. A series of clashes took place in different sectors of the city. The number of casualty was 22, which, of course, indicated the restrained exercised by the *Vops*, the Red army and the demonstrators. By the end of the day the uprising was quelled and the situation was brought under full control of the Government.

The brief account of the East Berlin uprising is a preface to an analysis of the West's response to the crisis. A thorough review of the West's reaction, more particularly of the United States, tells of total dismay and of testimony of impotence, a negation of the commitment to the cause of liberation. A naïve argument could be advanced that the uprising was so sudden and that the West caught unaware and hence could not offer any help to the participants of the short-lived rebellion. But there are accounts, which reveal that the western powers were not unaware of the economic crisis in East Berlin and the explosive situation obtaining at that time. James B. Conant, the US High Commissioner for Germany, foresaw the eruption of the explosive situation gradually built up by the factors best known to the West.[52] The US sponsored Radio in the American Sector (RIAS), without having a well-defined role to play at the time of grave crisis, had been inciting the workers to revolt. The RIAS had been broadcasting programmes for the workers in East Berlin with high dose of inducement to revolt.[53] On June 16, a delegation of Stalinalle workers went to RIAS headquarters with a request to broadcast a programme favouring their demands. The request was turned down. It, however, did broadcast the workers demands including the payment of wages according to the old norms, steps for lowering the cost of living and free elections.[54] Early in the morning of June 17, Gordon Ewing, the RIAS Director, allowed the station to broadcast a message from Ernest Scharnowski, a union leader of West Berlin, calling for a general strike in East Berlin, which was nothing short of gasoline pouring on the flame, although there was no clear message as to what aid would be forthcoming if the rebellion were dealt with a heavy hand.[55]

The RIAS broadcasts made the East Berliners to believe that the United States, being present across the dividing line

---

52 James B. Conant, *My Several Lives* (New York: Harper & Row, 1970).

53 For details see Edmond Taylor, "RIAS: The Story of an American Psychowar Outpost" in William Daugherty (ed), *A Psychological Warfare Casebook* (Baltimore: John Hopkins University Press, 1958).

54 Stefan Brant [pseud], *The East German Rising*, n. 51, pp 67-8.

55 Edmond Taylor, n. 53, pp. 145-150.

and committed to liberation pledges, would definitely do something to their aid in view of the speedy measures taken by it during the Berlin Blocade by taking recourse to massive airlift during 1948-49. This instance had left a tremendous psychological impact on the people of East Berlin. The rioters, however, ignored a number of important realities. The massive airlift was possible in an area where the airspace was made operationally free. Nonetheless, there was no guarantee that this could be repeated in an area fully under the Soviet Control. Secondly, the RIAS and the VOA did broadcast the ideas of liberation throughout the period but did not spell out the nature of American aid. The East Berliners resorted to a rebellion without securing any concrete commitment from any quarters. In other words, the American sponsored radio broadcasts carried rhetoric of liberation, inciting the defenceless and unorganized people to revolt against a militarily powerful state without realizing the consequences for such an uprising.

At the time of the Berlin uprising James Conant was testifying before the hearings of the Senate Appropriation Committee in connection with his budget for a psychological warfare against the Soviet domination of Eastern Europe. Three days later he was back in West Berlin. He recounts the nature of the West's response to the Berlin uprising:

> By the time I got to Berlin three days later, nothing had been done and said by the Allied powers. As concession to American opinion, I wrote a public letter to General Chuikov protesting the complete closing of all crossing points between the United States and Soviet sectors. Reaffirmation of the right of free circulation through all of Berlin was at best a mild gesture. And it came from only one of the three representatives of the Allies. Washington would have vetoed anything more drastic. A three-power statement was out of question. London and Paris had little sympathy with the uprising. The British High Commissioner returned in a worried state from an interrupted vacation. He suggested that if the East Berliners were encouraged to insult the Soviet occupation forces, some of the West Germans might start making riotous protests against the American or the British or the French. Equating the legality of all occupying forces in Berlin may have been formally correct, but in no way

> corresponded with the mood of the Berliners or the Americans in Berlin.[56]

Besides the accounts of Conant, some other post-rebellion developments testify to the correctness of an assumption that the Western capitals had made up their mind not to react sharply to Berlin-type-movements inside the Soviet sphere of influence. As the East Berlin riot had been quelled by the Government with a marked speed, the Allied Commandants in West Berlin dispatched a 'message' to the Representatives of the Soviet Control Commission on the day after the uprising expressing grave concern over the events and condemned the "irresponsible killing or serious wounding of a considerable number of citizens of Berlin." The Allied Commanders protested against the repressive measures taken by the Soviet authorities. The statement considered that the Soviet authorities along with the Allied powers jointly shared the "responsibility of guaranteeing the well being and the freedom of the people of Berlin."[57] The 'message' in the form of mild protest was reacted by the Soviet authorities with a serious allegation that the East Berlin riot had been the handiwork of the groups pushed from West Berlin.[58] Except rejecting the Soviet charges the Allied Commandants had nothing to do as a reaction to the uprising.[59] Among the West European countries, West Germany was most immediately concerned with the June 17 uprising, and therefore, it was natural the reaction of this part of Germany should have been strong and sharp. But its attitude to the events was of caution and of mere sympathy. The West German leaders thought that a massive rebellion in East Germany could be a dangerous step provoking the Soviet retaliation, and therefore, they were not prepared to offer the Soviets any more pretext to say that a Western plot against them had originated in Bonn. They were not sure about the American attitude to such a situation. They had to be cautious to see their statements in no way imperil

---

56 James B. Conant, *My Several Lives*, n. 52, p. 601.

57 Department of State, *Bulletin*, June 29, 1953, pp. 897-898.

58 For details see the letter from the Soviet Commandant to the Allied counterparts, *ibid*, July 6, 1953, pp. 8-9.

59 *ibid*, p. 9.

Germany's relations with the United States as they had to heavily depend upon the latter's military and economic support. In the absence of the US initiative or guidelines at this critical moment, which concerned them directly, the West German Government did not dare to aggravate the situation. Any such adventure without the US support might have led to the transformation of the newly constructed country to a devastating battlefield. Four days after the abortive uprising, Chancellor Konrad Adenauer urged the US President to do everything in his power to reinforce the violated human rights.[60] Like all other European leaders, Chancellor Adenauer was engrossed with the reconstruction of his country's war-ravaged economy and defence, and had a little interest to show in a situation like East Berlin uprising, which was not only premature but also carried dangerous implications to the security of his own country.

Just as Chancellor Adenauer took four days after the uprising had been put down to appeal to the United States for restoration of human rights, President Eisenhower took five more days to issue a statement as reply to the former's appeal. The reply in the form of message was merely a testimony of optimism:

> This inspiring show of courage has confirmed our belief that years of oppression and attempted indoctrination cannot extinguish the spirit of freedom behind the Iron Curtain. It seems clear that the repercussions of these events will be felt throughout the Soviet satellite empire.[61]

Expressing his conviction in the "justified inspirations of the German people for freedom and unity, and for the restoration of fundamental human rights in all parts of Germany", President Eisenhower concluded: "I trust that the people of East Germany will know that their call for freedom has been heard around the world." Needless to say, the statement did not spell out the nature of the US response to such an adventure in future in search of freedom.

---

60 *Public Papers of the Presidents: Dwight D. Eisenhower*, 1953, p. 458.

61 *ibid*, p. 457.

US Secretary of State, Dulles, was equally uncertain about the future role of his country in similar type of anti-Soviet uprising. Nonetheless, he argued that the East Berlin crisis demonstrated the correctness of his 'diagnosis' of the eventual collapse of the Soviet Union. His thesis was that the "communist structure is over-extended, over rigid and ill-founded' and the 'captive peoples' wanted to come out of the system. The urge for freedom would dislodge the Soviet Union. He argued:

> The unquenchable spirit of the people dramatized in East Berlin where unarmed youths tore up paving stones from the streets to hurl in defiance at tanks. Such a spirit can never be suppressed, and this love of freedom is more and more manifesting itself through the captive peoples.[62]

As the wounds of East Berlin uprising started healing with the passage of time, Dulles became more emphatic in propagating liberation of Eastern Europe. In his address before the UN General Assembly on September 17, 1953 he said: ". . . it is not in the interest of peace, or the other goals of our charter, that they can no longer live by their traditions and their faith" but the United States "does not call for exporting revolution or inciting others to violence. Let me make [the statement] more emphatic. We believe that violent changes destroy what it would gain. We put our hopes in the vast possibilities of peaceful changes."[63]

As stated already, Chancellor Adenauer was not prepared for any dangerous adventure to change the *status quo* in Europe. When he found that Soviet forces had accomplished their law-enforcing task efficiently and quickly, pragmatically enough, he requested President Eisenhower to extend food aid to the East Berliners. The President responded to it favourably to alleviate the acute food shortage in East Berlin. The United States offered 200 tons of flour, 1000 tons of lard, 1000 tons of beans and 500 tons of dried milk. The Soviet Foreign

---

62 Department of State, *Bulletin*, July 13, 1953, p. 40.

63 Council on Foreign Relations, *Documents on American Foreign Relations*, 1953, p. 40.

Minister Vyacheslav Mikhailovich Molotov rejected the offer as a mere propaganda stunt.[64]

President Eisenhower's reaction to the East Berlin uprising was spelt out in his letter of July 23 to Chancellor Adenauer. He derived five conclusions out of the developments in East Berlin crisis: (i) the revolt against communism was spontaneous, (ii) the uprising was the climax of the long standing urge for freedom, (iii) the rioters were not 'bourgeois reactionaries'or 'capitalist warmongers' but workers whom the Soviet authorities killed as they had risen in rebellion, (iv) the revolt gave all out indications of complete bankruptcy of the SED, and finally (v) the rebels wanted free elections which showed their "yearning for alleviation of their grievances and sufferings". He expressed his optimism at the reunification of Germany through free elections and the "United States will continue to lend the full force of its political, diplomatic and moral support" to the realization of that basic objective.[65]

In the US Congress the Senators strongly advocated in favour of shipment of food and medicine to East Berlin in order to help the suffering people. Senator Hubert H. Humphry initiated the debate on the uprising and contended that the events in East Berlin indicated that the "Soviet empire was breaking up from within." He urged the Government to extend 'some help' such as offering bread and butter. He said:

> . . . no weapon is more important than the weapon of food, and any delay in the utilization of the food and fiber which we have can lead to nothing but real trouble for us in future...The Soviets will make terrible efforts to try to put down the uprising. It would be wonderful if America should send some of its abundance of surplus food and fiber this day...Let us send also a little of the butter in shortage and utilize it to relieve the suffering in the satellite country to show the people behind Iron Curtain that America is not only

64 *Documents on American Foreign Relations*, 1953, pp. 170-176. Several million food parcels were distributed through private channels in East Berlin some of these were confiscated by the Soviet authorities saying that German Democratic Republic was their friendly country and its needs had been well looked after by Moscow.

65 *Public Papers of the Presidents*, n. 60, pp. 516-520.

a nation of military might, but also a nation with heart and compassion. This is what is needed now.[66]

The Senate adopted a concurrent resolution hailing the East Berlin uprising for courageously demonstrating "their strong devotion to the principles of freedom and justice by their historic resistance to the Soviet controlled East German regime", and commending and encouraging the "valiant struggle of these captive peoples for freedom." It expressed 'sympathy' for the tragic victims of East Berlin and firm conviction of having a unified Germany.[67] The resolution avoided the reference to the US Commitment to liberation because its authors knew well that any active aid to the rebels would lead to a military confrontation with the Soviet forces, and the American land forces were no match to the 275,000 strong Soviet forces stationed in and around East Berlin. No one underestimated the Soviet capability in restoring order in a disturbed area within its sphere of influence. Further, the United States was not prepared to have a military confrontation with Soviet Union for the cause of a sudden and unorganized uprising at a time when the Korean War proved to be extremely costly.[68]

The East Berlin crisis proved that even with the military preponderance, the United States would not risk a major war with the Soviet Union for an East Berlin type crisis. Immediately after the uprising had been crushed there was an atmosphere of relief and relaxation. The East German Government under Walter Ulbricht became more confident of securing the Soviet support in a moment of crisis. Chancellor Adenauer expressed his satisfaction over the fact that the revolt did not export any trouble to his country. The US propagators of liberation of Eastern Europe were happy to find an

---

66 US Congress, *Congressional Record*, 83rd Congress, 1st Session, July 8, 1953, pp. 8178-79.

67 Department of State, *American Foreign Policy, 1950-1955: Basic Documents*, Vol. II (Washington DC, 1957) pp. 1749-1750.

68 Coinciding the Berlin uprising the Korean armistice was signed. The US President told the nation on July 26, 1953: "For this Nation the cost of repelling aggression has been high. In thousands of homes it has been incalculable. It has been paid in terms of tragedy." *Public Papers of the Presidents*, n. 60, p. 520.

immediate example of anti-Soviet unrest in the region and found validity in the thesis that the 'captive peoples' were longing freedom. The Soviet leadership could be sure that the US response to a similar rebellion would be nothing more than verbal condemnation. This indication gave a free hand to them to retain their sphere of influence by taking recourse to military intervention.

John Foster Dulles made an important statement before the House Committee on Foreign Affairs at the Hearings on the Mutual Security Act of 1954. Clarifying the Administration's latest stand on the "enslavement of the satellite countries behind the Iron Curtain", he said:

> It is a very clear and continuing policy of this Administration not to accept as definitive the rule of the Soviet Union over their captive peoples. We are, through various media, principally through Voice of America, and private agencies such as Radio Free Europe, carrying on a very active campaign of education, bringing news, bringing hope to these peoples...I may say there is no relaxation of the feeling of the United States Government that there cannot be real peace for the United States as long as the captivity exists.[69]

Similarly, the Assistant Secretary of State for European Affairs addressed a letter to the Central East European Committee of exiled East European officers reaffirming the continued US support for the liberation of Eastern Europe:

> Americans are firmly convinced that the captive peoples of Eastern Central Europe have every right to equal and honorable membership in the community of free nations...An alien domination now separates some of the most courageous and talented people of that community from their brother in the free world...It is, therefore, the firm and abiding purpose of the United States to encourage the creation of conditions under which the captive countries of Europe can reestablish their independence and take their rightful place in a European community of free peoples dedicated to the unselfish solution of common problems.[70]

---

69 US Congress, House of Representatives, Committee on Foreign Affairs, *Hearings of the Mutual Security Act 1954*, 83rd Congress, 2nd Session, 1954, p. 17.

70 Department of State, *Bulletin*, August 10, 1953, p. 184.

These and frequently issued statements of the US officials unmistakably made it clear that the United States would continue to encourage the people living in the Soviet sphere of influence to revolt against the foreign domination and thus achieve liberation. All these had direct and indirect role to play in the outbreak of two massive revolutions Eastern Europe in the Cold War era. Both these revolts were crushed by the Soviet and the Warsaw Pact troops. In response to the Soviet military invasions on these two occasions the United States had nothing to do except issuing verbal condemnation of the Soviet action and placing the matters before the United Nations.

The Soviet sphere of influence collapsed in the late 1980s on its own weight. The United States had no role to play in the collapse. It was a silent spectator from a safe distance.

CHAPTER II

AMERICA'S HUNGARIAN DILEMMA

The Eisenhower Administration showed caution by exercising prudence rather than pursuing 'dynamism' in the US policy towards Eastern Europe. The idea of 'rollback communism' was going to be replaced by a seemingly reconciliatory approach. After the Korean armistice and avoidance of a military intervention in Indo-China, the US simultaneously opted for a programme of strengthening the non-communist world militarily and for conference diplomacy having the potentiality of delivering diplomatic gains. That is why the SEATO came into being, and also CENTO at the instance of the United Kingdom. Yet, the psychological preparation for the acceptance of the realities in Eastern Europe was not reflected in the propaganda programmes, at the same time the American desire to liberate the region was expressed in vague and abstract terms. Richard Rovere, an eminent journalist, while recording the palpably confusing situation in 1955, observed that "it is not unreasonable to say that it has long since been less militant – in practice if not preachment – than the Truman Administration. The world does not seem to be aware of this, the American people are manifestly aware of it."[1] Rames Reston noted that the liberation of Eastern Europe continued to remain a part of the 'psychological gimmick'. He wrote: "The tendency of this Administration is to do less than their public statements imply,

1 Richard Rovere, *Affairs of the State: The Eisenhower Years* (New York: Farrar, Straus, 1956) p. 168.

and this is particularly true when Eisenhower is in charge of the 'doing' and Dulles in charge of 'talking'".[2] The talking part of the liberation of Eastern Europe continued to dominate the US foreign policy statements until it proved to be too dangerous.

The West European leaders attached more importance to the problems of divided Germany. For them the reunification through the process of free elections might be a desired goal of the bulk of the people of Europe but rearming of Federal Republic of Germany preceded the question of reunification. The Soviet leaders rejected the idea of free elections as a part of reunification because they argued that Hitler too came to power by means of such free elections, and therefore, favoured the formation of a coalition government with equal representation of both the German states, leading to the eventual neutralization of a reunified German state. The Soviet proposal was unacceptable to the Western leaders; for them free elections should precede the formation of a unified Germany.[3] Further, the reunification issue became less important than rearmament of Federal Republic of Germany.[4] The Soviet leaders were less worried about the rearmament initiatives, as the remilitarization programme could hardly pose any formidable threat to their security interests in Eastern Europe. However, the British Foreign Secretary Anthony Eden successfully formulated a plan for West European Union, joined by Italy and West Germany in October 1954, which was placed under the NATO. This prompted the Soviet Union to change its stand on Austria, eventually leading to its initiatives for a dialogue on the long-stalled problem of Austria. The successful conclusion of the Austrian State Treaty on May 15, 1955 led the Soviet Union, in return of permanent neutrality of Austria, to give up a forward military base in Central Europe. The symbolic Soviet retreat from the post-War military salient in

2 James Reston, "An Inquiry into Foreign Policy", *New York Times Magazine*, January 16, 1955, p. 62.

3 Royal Institute of International Affairs, *Documents on International Affairs, 1954* (London: Oxford University Press, 1957) p. 75.

4 Harold Macmillan, *Tides of Fortune, 1945-1955* (London: Macmillan, 1969) pp. 529-530.

its occupation of a portion of Austria in return of Austrian neutrality was well paid off, as a neutral zone of 500 miles was created between West Germany and Italy, affecting a split of the Western defence system into two fronts, and also creating a buffer zone between the West and the Soviet Union in this region.[5] Simultaneously, the Soviet Union made another significant move on May 14, one day before signing the Austrian State Treaty in Vienna, by concluding the Warsaw Pact with six East European countries. Apparently, it was a diplomatic counter-measure, but it provided the legal foundation for stationing Soviet troops in Hungary and Rumania.[6]

The conclusion of the Austrian State Treaty paved the way for the Geneva summit conference in July 1955. The idea of the conference was first advanced by Winston Churchill in May 1953. The Soviet Union, under the new leadership, was adopting a conciliatory approach as reflected in its *rapprochement* with Tito. The Belgrade declaration and the recognition of 'several road to socialism', the Soviet willingness to sit at a conference with the West with a view to reversing the military buildup of the NATO created an atmosphere congenial for a summit conference. Further, there was mounting pressure in the West for such a conference which might lead to the relaxation of international tension.[7] Both Eisenhower and Dulles valued the idea of a conference as a response to the Soviet call for peaceful co-existence, because such a conference might leave an encouraging impact on the development of a liberal political environment in Eastern Europe.[8] Dulles too appeared to have been optimistic about

5 For an excellent and well documented analysis of the Austrian State Treaty see William Lloyd Stearman, *The Soviet Union and the Occupation of Austria* (Bonn: Siegler and Co., 1960).

6 Thomas W. Wolfe, *The Evolution of the Warsaw Pact*, a RAND Corporation Memorandum, December 1965, also see "The Evolution of Warsaw Pact", *ADELPHI PAPERS*, No. 58 (June 1969) pp. 1-25 and its appendix containing the text of the Treaty.

7 *Khrushchev Remembers*, Vol. 1 (Harmondsworth, Middlesex, Penguin Books, 1977) p. 420.

8 Paul C. Davis, "The New Diplomacy: The 1955 Geneva Summit Meeting" in Roger Hilman and Robert C. Good (eds), *Foreign Policy in the Sixties* (Baltimore: John Hopkins Press, 1965) pp. 165-168.

the outcome of the Austrian State Treaty. He told before the House Committee on June 10, 1955 that the new status of Austria created a "new frontier of freedom" and put additional pressure on the Kremlin leaders to relax their control over Eastern Europe.[9]

President Eisenhower favoured US participation in the summit conference and insisted that the question of Soviet domination in Eastern Europe be put at the top of the agenda for discussion.[10] The Administration had no alternative but to raise the 'satellite question' in view of the strong clamor in the country favouring a discussion in the conference. There was a deep rooted feeling in the country that failure to raise the issue would mean US recognition of *status quo* in Europe, and hence, the conclusion of another Yalta. But the United States was not prepared to pursue the matter at the expense of the conference itself. As the preparation for the Geneva conference began, President Eisenhower made his position clear to all. He was asked in a press conference as to how far the US would proceed with the liberation issue. He replied: "You are not certainly going to declare war, are you? So there instantly, you fix yourself limitations on how far we as a people will go in accomplishing this thing."[11] The West European countries too were not enthusiastic about the issue of changing *status quo* in Eastern Europe. On July 17, just before the commencement of the conference, the Western participants met in Paris at the villa where President Eisenhower had been staying to discuss his address to the conference. Harold Macmillan later recorded: "No one seemed to have any particular view about it, except to ask the passage about the 'satellite' and 'tyranny' might be modified. This was done."[12] Nevertheless, President Eisenhower made a soft reference to the 'satellite' question in order to emphasize 'their importance'. In the opening statement he said:

9 US Congress, *House, Committee of Appropriation, Mutual Security Appropriations for 1956: Hearings*, 84th Congress, 1st Session, 1955, p. 1.

10 Dwight D. Eisenhower, *Mandate for Change* (New York, Garden City: Doubleday, 1963) p. 507.

11 *New York Times*, June 30, 1955.

12 Harold Macmillan, *The Tide of Fortune*, n. 4, p. 615.

> There is the problem of respecting the right of the peoples to choose the form of government under which they will live: and of restoring sovereign rights and self-government to those who have been deprived of them. The American people feel strongly that certain peoples of Eastern Europe, many with long and proud record of national existence, have not yet been given the benefit of this pledge [self-determination] of our United Nations wartime declaration, reinforced by other wartime agreements.[13]

Behind the euphoria of the 'Spirit of Geneva', the first step towards the future *détente*, a great degree of gloom was said to have cast in Eastern Europe, at least in the mind of those who had been cherishing the hope of liberation through diplomatic means. The Soviet Union used the 'spirit' as a propaganda value. The photographs of smiling Bulganin and Eisenhower were widely circulated among the people of Eastern Europe conveying them the message that a 'deal' had been reached between the two great powers at their expenses.[14] Later on Zbignew K. Brzezinski wrote that Eisenhower's handshakes with the Soviet leaders "implicitly meant the West's acceptance of the *status quo* in East Central Europe."[15]

Back home the President and the Secretary of State had to face the public reaction to the relative negligence of the captive nations issue. Recollecting the almost unanimous support of the Congress on the US participation in the Geneva Conference[16] Eisenhower gave an evasive report on the issue:

---

13 For the full text see *American Foreign Policy: 1950-1955: Basic Documents*, pp. 200-202, and for other details see *The Geneva Conference of the Heads of Government* (Washington DC: 1955).

14 Later on at the Foreign Ministers' Conference held in October Dulles avoided cameras so that similar propaganda could not be carried to the people of Eastern Europe. See *John R. Beal, John Foster Dulles: 1888-1959* (New York: Harper, 1959) p. 302.

15 Zbigniew K. Brzezinski, *The Soviet Bloc: Unity and Conflict* (Cambridge, Mass: Harvard University Press, 1971) p. 169.

16 US Congress, Senate, Committee on Foreign Relations, *Hearings on S. Res. 166 Favoring Discussion at the Coming Geneva Conference on the Status of Nations under Communist Control*, 84th Congress, 1st Session, June 21, 1955, pp 4-25.

> . . . outside the conference meetings there were numerous unofficial meetings - conferences ...very specially with the Soviet delegation. In these conversation a number of subjects were discussed, and among them the Secretary of State and I specially brought up, more than once, the American convictions and American beliefs and American concern about such questions as the satellites of Eastern Europe and the activities of international communism. We made crystal clear what were American beliefs about such matters as there.[17]

In the Foreign Ministers' Conference, which started on October 27, 1955, Dulles did not initiate any move to discuss the question of possible change of the *status quo* position in Eastern Europe. A couple of issues such as the Western support for a plan favouring free elections in two German states as already outlined by Anthony Eden, the mutual security arrangement advanced by the United States on one hand and the Soviet proposal for an all-European collective security excluding, of course, all 'foreign' troops from the continent and supersession of the NATO on the other, led to an unresolved deadlock in the Conference indicating thereby the hollowness of the 'Geneva Spirit'. The stormy meeting ended without any constructive and meaningful discussion on the problem of East and Central Europe as the Americans had seen it. Dulles attempted to raise the issue with the Soviet leader Molotov, and requested Macmillan and Pinay to agree to his proposal for inclusion of the 'satellite' question in the agenda. This did not materialize.[18] As a diplomatic manoeuvre Dulles made a trip to Brioni during the interval of the Conference to meet Tito in order to assess the latest developments in the Soviet-Yugoslav relations and to ascertain Tito's mind on the 'satellite' question. A joint communiqué was issued saying:

> The final subject of our talk was the problem of the status of Eastern Europe. We reached common accord on recognizing the importance of independence of these states, non-interference from outside in their internal affairs, and right

---

17 *American Foreign Policy: 1950-1955, Basic Documents*, Vol. I, p. 113.

18 Roscoe Drummond and Gaston Coblentz, *Duel at the Brink* (London: Doubleday, 1961) p. 155.

> to develop their social and economic order in ways of their own choice.[19]

The report of Dulles to the American nation on November 16, 1955 on the Geneva Conference contained nothing about the US pursuance of the problem of Eastern Europe. He told the nation: "the Soviet-controlled governments are facing raising pressure. Many within the satellite countries believe that the 'spirit of Geneva' means that they are entitled to more tolerance and to governments more responsive to the needs and aspiration of their own nation."[20] This is far from truth. The fact is that the so called 'spirit of Geneva' was an abstract idea which symbolized a possibility of reduction of the US-Soviet tension through summit conferences. Later on, he observed that he did not foresee "an early breakway of the satellites from Moscow", but he felt that there would be "visible signs of evolution toward governments which command more popular support than these exist, and which are markedly less the paid hirelings of Moscow."[21] Similar vague optimism could be discerned in his later statements. On December 8, 1955 he said:

> If the West European countries find, an unity, increased prosperity, there will be increasing pressure in the satellite countries for independent governments responsive to the needs and aspirations of the people. This may speed the day when the Soviet rulers will come to realize that to hold these East European nations in subjugation involves an obsolete reactionary practice, entailing costs, moral and material, far outweighing the seeming advantage.[22]

Dulles, however, was not unaware of the grim realities of the situation in Eastern Europe. He realized that liberation of Eastern Europe "would take a very long time. He could not find a formula to promote it with greater speed. But he never

---

19 Department of State, *Bulletin*, November 21, 1955, p.833.

20 *American Foreign Policy 1950-1955: Basic Documents*, Vol. I, p. 126.

21 For some details see Richard Good-Adams, *A Time of Power* (London: Weidnfeld & Nicholson, 1962) p. 206.

22 *American Foreign Policy 1950-1955: Basic Documents*, Vol. I, p. 126.

deviated from the notion that Eastern Europe would one day emerge in freedom."[23] The freedom that Dulles visualized was on the line of Titoism. He argued in a press conference on April 24, 1956 that "the important characteristics of Titoism is the fact that it recognizes that communism can be a national organization; not necessarily an international organization" and "that the view that Tito held and he broke relations with Stalin on this issue...If the Soviet communists now say that it is all right to have communism on a national basis, that offers a great prospect to the Poles, the Czechs and so forth, who would much rather have own national brand of communism than be run by Moscow."[24] He found such hopes in the anti-Stalin campaign inside Soviet Union which was considered to have brought about an atmosphere of relaxation indicating thereby a probable political change in the communist world. Commenting on de-Stalinization, Dulles said on April 3, 1956: "the fact that the Soviet rulers now denounce much of the past gives cause for hope, because it demonstrates that liberalizing influence from within and without can bring about peaceful change."[25] Although he was skeptical about the real moves of de-Stalinization, he thought that the intention of Khrushchev might be "merely to persuade the subjected peoples that the present dictatorship is good because it condemns past dictatorship."[26] His optimism of the ultimate Soviet acceptance of the 'different roads' to communism was strengthened by the visit of Tito to Moscow in June. In order to allow national communism to grow in Eastern Europe, the United States abstained from voting the membership of Albania, Bulgaria, Hungary and Romania of the United Nations.[27] The US abstention appears to be a tacit recognition of the regimes in Eastern Europe and also the *status quo* position in Europe. However, such a theory was dismissed by a number of officials in the latter part of the year. The Christmas messages of the

23 Drunnond and Coblentz, *Duel at the Brink*, n. 18, p. 141.

24 *New York Times*, April 25, 1956; also Adam Ulam, *Titoism and the Cominform* (Cambridge, Mass: Harvard University press, 1952).

25 *Documents on American Foreign Relations, 1956*, p. 202.

26 *ibid*, p. 206

27 Department of State, *Bulletin*, December 26, 1955, pp. 1067-73.

President and the Secretary of State to the peoples of Eastern Europe were broadcast over the RFE[28], which was considered to be "in no way in accord with the spirit of Geneva", and the US official reply to Khrushchev, and finally Eisenhower's message to the US Congress maintained that the liberation policy continued to remain as an enduring answer to the 'bondage of the millions'.[29]

Despite the US emphasis on retaining and improving its nuclear superiority over the Soviet Union[30] and its preparedness to use massive retaliatory power, Eisenhower's declaration at the Geneva Conference that " a nuclear war would be intolerable disaster which must not be permitted to occur[31], and the reduction of US military expenditure, more particularly on the land base forces, indicated the remoteness of the use of the American military might for the liberation of Eastern Europe, and therefore, the moral support for the peaceful liberation continued to guide the Administration's statement on the 'captive peoples'. This, however, did not mean, as David Lawrence wrote, a deviation from the original position of liberation, because, the US Administration had been consistent in encouraging the people of Eastern Europe "so that some day they will rise against their tyrannical masters and achieve their freedom."[32] The US sponsored propaganda media conveyed from time to time to the people of Eastern Europe the statements of the US officials on the hope of liberation, besides reporting the developments inside the Soviet Union after the secret speech of Khrushchev denouncing

28 *ibid*, January 16, 1956.

29 *Documents on American Foreign Relations, 1955*, p. 1.

30 Dulles argued: "All I can say is the advice we get from our military experts leads us to feel that as regards most essentials we are in a position of greater military strength than the Soviet Union, and it is very definitely my view that we should seek to maintain such position, unless and until some acceptable, dependable method of limitations of armament is worked out." See US Congress, Senate, Committee on Foreign Relations, *Hearings on Control and Reduction of Armaments*, 84th Congress, 2nd Session, February, 1956.

31 *Documents on American Foreign Relations*, 1956, p. 1.

32 *New York Herald Tribune*, January 7, 1956.

Stalin's high handed rule and the prospects of Titoism. All these were considered by the Soviet Union as acts inciting the people to revolt.[33]

REVOLT IN POLAND

Poland was regarded as a trouble spot in the Soviet backyard. Ever since the liberation of Poland by the Red Army, it has been alleged that about 1.5 million Polish citizens were forcibly deported to the interior of the Soviet Union during the period between February 1940 and June 1941.[34] Added to this, the reports on the Warsaw uprising at the close of the War that the Russian army had been allegedly watching the ruthless destruction of the civilian population of Warsaw by the retreating Germans[35] and also the reports on the Katyn forest massacre[36], generated a strong anti-Soviet feeling in the minds of the Polish people. Although the US policy towards Poland at the close of the War was nothing special and also the fact that it did not extend any help to Stanislaw Mikolajczyl to form the government, and thereby, prevent the leftists from capturing power, the US Administration in the post-World War II scenario started demonstrating its interest in Poland on an assumption that the communist hold in Poland had been visibly fragile. The publication of the aforementioned information and reports stirred anti-Soviet sentiments not only in Poland but also in America, where the American citizens of Polish origins constituted the largest segment of East European émigrés. At

---

33 *New York Times*, May 14, and June 2, 1956.

34 This is an account of an anonymous author of *The Dark Side of the Moon* (New York: Scribner, 1947). Its authenticity has been certified by poet T.S. Eliot in the Preface and by a note from the wife of General Sikorski.

35 Arthur Bliss Lane, *I Saw Poland Betrayed* (Indianapolis: Bobbs Merrill, 1948). Lane was known for his strong anti-communist antipathy, and hence, his version could not accepted as unbiased and dispassionate.

36 See Stanislaw Mikolajczyk, *The Rape of Poland* (New York: Whittlesey House, 1948). This is also anther passionate account of the Soviet 'betrayal' of Poland. For a different version see D.F. Fleming, *The Cold War and Its Origins 1917-1950*, Vol. I (New York: Doubleday, 1961) Chapter ix.

the end of the War their strength was more than five millions. They gave a solid backing to the Republican Party in the 1952 elections, and therefore, the Eisenhower Administration made it an imperative to express its profound sympathy for the 'enslaved people' of Poland. That is why on May 3, 1953, the Secretary of State Dulles issued a statement on the 162nd anniversary of the adoption of the Polish Constitution: "We join with them in the hope and faith that the Polish desire for freedom and independence will find fullest realization."[37] Similarly, he denounced the arrest of forced retirement of Cardinal Wyszynski.[38] Later on the US Government closed the Polish consulate at New York, Chicago and Detroit as they were found to be serving "no useful purpose in the conduct of relations between the United States and Poland."[39]

It is relevant to refer briefly to the way the US Congress had expressed solidarity in 1956 with the people on the occasion of the Polish Constitution Day and also in creating opinion on the alleged Soviet involvement in the Katyn forest massacre. In the House of Representatives, the Congressman Mcdonough remarked that the US would never reconcile with "Poland's subjugation by Russia".[40] Similar sentiments had been expressed in the Senate. All this in the final analysis, gave a clear impression that the United States would extend help to the Polish People to get themselves liberated from the Soviet domination. While participating in the debates on the occasion of the Polish Constitution anniversary, the question of Katyn forest massacre was discussed. The trend in the discussion left an ample scope to believe that the United States would actively support an anti-Soviet revolt. For example, Congressman Garmtz told in the House of Representative on May 3, 1956

---

37 The short-lived Constitution of May 3, 1792 was opposed by Russia which led to the adoption of the second Constitution on January 23, 1793 and the third one on October 24, 1795, and finally there was partition of Poland by Russia, Prussia and Austria. For the statement of Dulles see Department of State, *Bulletin*, May 18, 1953, p.721.

38 *ibid*, October 19, 1953, p. 529.

39 *ibid*, March, 1954, p. 352.

40 US Congress, *Congressional Record*, 84th Congress, 2nd Session, 1956, p. 7391.

that the US Government "must do something to encourage these people in their resistance and refusal to bow to their captors". He felt that since the new Soviet leadership started to denounce Stalin's regime, the US Government should take this 'advantage' to demand that the Soviet leaders release the Polish prisoners and admit their guilt in the Katyn forest massacre, and urged the Administration to "further the cause of the enslaved nations". He concluded:

> I strongly urge the administration to take advantage of this golden opportunity which would strengthen the hopes and beliefs of the captive nations and their continued resistance to Soviet rule, as nothing else could. Such action by our Government would speed the day when Poland and other enslaved nations would again join the free nations of the world.[41]

Congressman Donohue argued: "Americans must never relax our efforts to help the Polish people to reestablish their freedom under their own chosen government."[42] He considered it to be the 'obligation' of the US Government to continue its efforts to maintain and promote the Polish right to self-determination and self-government.

In an attempt to internationalize the Katyn massacre and to create strong public opinion against the Soviet Union and thereby to stir emotions in Poland, Congressman Madden introduced a resolution in the House of Representatives on May 3, 1956 urging upon the President to instruct the US Representatives in the UN to forward the testimony, evidence and findings of the House Committee to conduct an investigation into the Katyn massacre.[43] His colleague Yates observed that the "American people wish to assure the enslaved Poles that the United States has always recognized the right of any people to choose their own system of government . . . and we will continue to support in their struggle to be free."[44] In the Senate, Senator Douglas criticized Dulles and

41 *ibid*, p. 7403.

42 *ibid*, p. 7405.

43 *ibid*, p. 7466.

44 *Ibid*, p. 7471.

Eisenhower for their failure to redeem their election promises and alleged that "after the new administration came to power, it decided that it should not continue the policy of liberation."[45]

In the midst of the American hope for liberation of Eastern Europe, the Poznan riots took place on June 28, 1956. The Western accounts on the riots revealed that a large section of the Polish people were unhappy about the spillover adverse effect of over-industrialization, too much bureaucratization and militarization. The anti-Stalin speeches of Khrushchev and Tito's triumphant visit to Moscow following the 20th Congress of the Communist Party of Soviet Union in February 1956 appeared to have created a basis for hope for those who wanted a liberal political atmosphere in Eastern Europe that something positive would be forthcoming soon. Added to this, after the death of Boleslaw Bierut, the Polish Communist Party Chief, in Moscow in March 1956, a 'less dogmatic' Edward Ochab took over the charge of the Party. These developments were mistaken to be beginning of a liberalization process. The demand for more favourable working condition as well as a liberal political atmosphere finally resulted in the riots of June 28 in the industrial city of Poznan.

The trouble sparked off after a rumour that a delegation of Poznan workers sent to make a presentation of their grievances before the Party headquarters had been rounded up by the police. Hearing the news, which did not have any foundation, workers of Poznan came out to the streets, ransacked the Party office and the secret police headquarters. The riot continued for three days. After a bitter fighting between the rioting workers and the government forces, law and order was restored with the massive deployment of army, leaving 53 dead and some 300 wounded.[46]

On June 29, the day following the outbreak of the Poznan uprising, the Chief of the News Division of the State

---

45 *Ibid,* p. 7508

46 *New York Times*, July 1, 1956 and Paul E. Zinner (ed), *Nationalism and Popular Revolt in Eastern Europe; Selected Documents on Events in Poland and Hungary, February-November 1956* (New York: Colombia University Press, 1956) p. 127 and fn.4.

Department, Lincoln White, made a statement: "We believe that all free people will be watching the situation closely to see whether or not the Polish people will be allowed to a government which will remedy the grievances which have brought to them to a breaking point."[47] In another separate statement on July 2, Lincoln White rejected the 'communist charge' that the Poznan riot was instigated and financed by the United States Government.[48] Two weeks after the suppression of the trouble, Dulles expressed optimism that the Soviet Union would ultimately accord greater independence to the 'satellites'. He said at a press conference on July 11: "It is not a matter for this year or next year, but I believe that this second post-war decade...will see these new forces take charge of the situation and that we can really hopefully look forward to a transformation of the international scene."[49] Besides expressing vaguely the ideas of optimism, the US Government extended food aid to the workers of Poznan, a step similar to the one that had been taken after the East Berlin uprising to be, however, rejected by the Polish authorities.

Although the then available accounts did not give a clear picture of the Soviet involvement in the suppression of the uprising, the US Congress held that the Soviet Union was solely responsible for the Poznan crisis. Congressman Ray. J. Madden wrote to the Secretary of State requesting him to initiate necessary steps for taking the matter to the United Nations and to press for a "complete and exhaustive investigation of the Poznan uprising."[50] In the House of Representative, Congressman McCormack tabled a resolution urging upon the President to take up the matter to the world body and extend food aid to the people of Poznan. The House observed that "the peace of the world will be threatened and security of the

---

47 Department of State, *Bulletin*, July 9, 1956. p. 55.

48 *idem.*

49 *New York Times*, July 12, 1956.

50 US Congress, *Congressional Record*, 84th Congress, 2nd Session, 1956, p. 11655. Senator Thomas Dodd read out his letter to Dulles urging upon him to refer the Poznan crisis to the UN, and said: "When the uprising in East Berlin took place on June 17, 1953, we offered food and did no more." p. 13785.

United States endangered" until "people of Poland and other captive nations" had gained independence.[51] However, Congressman Machrowicz could correctly predict that the Administration would not honour the feelings of the House favouring internationalization of the Poznan trouble, just as it had "completely ignored" the issue of Katyn forest massacre.[52] Senator Hubert H. Humphry wanted that the "State Department should reiterate in strongest possible language the deep continuing commitment of the United States to the eventual freedom and independence of these nations."[53] Citing the statement of Dulles issued on July 11, he remarked: "the Secretary said that by 1966 there may be freedom in Russia. I hope and pray he is right, but I would not want to depend on it, and I would not want American policy to be based on that assumption."[54]

On June 29, two amendments to Mutual Security Acts were introduced in the Senate with a view to encouraging private organizations to engage themselves in "keeping alive the will for freedom" in Eastern Europe. Senator Dirksen proposed that a package of $5 million be expended to the discretion of the President, while the Douglas Amendment envisioned a $20 million programme named 'Freedom Agency' to distribute the largesse. While recalling the past promises of the Administration to liberate Eastern Europe the Senators were critical of its failure to respond actively corresponding to its pronounced position to the events in East Berlin and Poznan.[55] The State Department objected to the Douglas Amendment on the ground that such steps would invite Soviet reprisals and eventually affect adversely the image of private agencies conveying the message of liberation.[56] The Soviet Central Committee strongly reacted to these proposals and concluded that "the anti-Soviet popular demonstration in Poznan were financed from these agencies."[57]

---

51 *ibid*, p. 11775.

52 *ibid*, p. 11889.

53 *ibid*, p. 12437.

54 *ibid*, p. 12439.

55 *ibid*, p. 11339.

56 *ibid*, p.11359.

57 *Documents of American Foreign Relations*, 1956, p. 212.

Later developments in Poland which had led to providing a space to Wladyslaw Gomulka not only to rehabilitate himself in active politics after being released in 1956 from detention which had been slapped on him in 1949 for his alleged sympathy for Tito but to experiment with political liberalism led the US Government to erroneously believe that the nationalist communism in the form of Titoism would be a viable alternative to the present status of Eastern Europe. Gomulka was restored to party membership and was eventually elected as the First Secretary. Such a belief had been further strengthened by the post-Poznan period when the Poznan trial permitted the dissidents to speak openly about their grievances. The freedom to ventilate the problems of the workers during the fairly impartially conducted trials convinced the US decision-makers that a liberal political atmosphere in Poland was in process. The US Administration could not properly assess the rationale behind the rehabilitation of Gomulka. The Soviet leadership could not but acknowledge the fact that Gomulka was a popular face in Poland, a committed communist, of course with a strong nationalist sentiment, and was loyal to the Warsaw Pact, which induced him in a later period to play an active role in the Warsaw Pact intervention in Czechoslovakia in 1968.[58]

The Polish success in rehabilitating Gomulka in a shuttle bid to experiment with Titoism was greeted by the US Administration as a vindication of its conviction that the liberal ideas in the form of Titoism in Europe was forthcoming. It, therefore, refrained from condemning any further suppression of the Poznan uprising, but continued to take it as another symbol of hope for liberalization in Eastern Europe. In an interview with the CBS on October 21, Secretary Dulles said that the recent uprising in Poland was the beginning of its return to independence. He, however, ruled out the use of American forces to help Poland to regain its independence, for, to him the Poles themselves would not invite any outside intervention to resolve their internal problems. In the event of any uprising in future, he feared, there might be repression.

58 For some details see Nicholas Bethell, *Gomulka: His Poland, His Communism* (New York: Holt, Rinehart and Winston, 1969).

"But when you have a whole people rising up, it is unlikely that efforts will be made to put it down by means of military measures. That was never attempted before. I don't think it would succeed."[59] It did not take time to prove how wrong Dulles was in his assessment of the situation. As events rolled rapidly in the year, the Hungarians staged a massive anti-Soviet uprising. Dulles was caught in his indecisiveness and the Suez War. He, however, kept his word by not dragging the US to the hot bed of a real military showdown with the Soviet Union on the Hungarian crisis.

A passing reference to the liberation issue and the Presidential election of 1956 may not be out of context. Although unlike 1952 events the 1956 electioneering tempo was not entirely dominated by the liberation question, it was still an important issue in the context of wooing the ethnic voters. The prospect of securing ethnic support once again lured both the Democrats and the Republican platforms. The Democratic plank this time took the opportunity to charge the Administration for its failure in redeeming the liberation promises of 1952:

> We condemn the Republican Administration for its heartless record of broken promises to the unfortunate victims of communism. Candidate Eisenhower's 1952 pledges to 'liberate' the captive peoples have been disavowed and dishonored...We look forward to the day when liberties of all captive nations will be restored to them and they can again take their rightful place in the community of true nations. We shall press before the United Nations the principle that Soviet Russia withdraws its troops from the captive countries. . . .[60]

The Democratic platform assailed the Republican Administration for standing silent when the people of East Berlin and Poznan revolted against the Soviet-backed authorities. Evading the allegation, the Republican plank made a passing reference to the liberation issue in this manner:

> We shall continue to seek the reunification of Germany in freedom, and the liberation of the Satellite states. . . The

59 *New York Times*, October 22, 1956.

60 *Congressional Quarterly Almanac*, 1956, 709.

> Republican party stands firmly with the peoples of these countries in the quest for freedom. We are confident that our peaceful policies, resolutely pursued, will finally restore freedom and national independence to oppressed peoples and nations.[61]

The Republican Party distributed a pamphlet entitled *Republican Policy of Liberation to Turn the Tide Against Communism*, and reiterated its past promises not to abandon the captive millions. It, however, proved within a couple of weeks of making such promises that the US Government could not but abandon the Hungarians as they revolted against the Soviet Union.

THE HUNGARIAN REVOLUTION

Behind the polemics of liberation of Eastern Europe a well-meaning and cautious official statement revealing the actual *operational* stand of the Administration provides an interesting insight. Before the House Committee on Foreign Affairs, Under Secretary of State, Robert Murphy said:

> We can facilitate the exposure of Soviet and satellite citizens of free societies. We can keep before the satellite their ancient traditions. We can show them how the free world is able to accommodate diversity within it. It is our policy to do these things. We do not expect that they will bring the tyranny down tomorrow on the next day. But we must do what we can to promote an evolution in the USSR toward a society devoted to the welfare and national interests of its people and not expansion and domination of other nations.[62]

Murphy's statement provides a premonition to the US course of action and its practical politics in responding to Hungarian revolution of 1956 right from the preface to the uprising symbolically associated at the initial stage in the formation of the Petöfi Circle, a literary club in the city of Budapest named after a celebrated poet and a revolutionary Sandor Petöfi in March 1956, who was killed on July 31, 1848 in a battle waged against the Russian interventionist forces coming in aid of the

---

61 *ibid*, p. 785.

62 US Congress, House, Committee on Foreign Affairs, *Hearings on Foreign Policy and Mutual Security*, 84th Congress, 2nd Session, October-November, 1956, p. 191.

Austrians, till November 4 when the Soviet army took full control of the situation and installed a new government headed by Janos Kadar. The details of the Hungarian revolution are now available to the academic community. It was a massive anti-Soviet uprising in the Soviet sphere of influence, which attracted the attention of all the world leaders and also the academics. It generated a great deal of speculation about the future of the Soviet 'satellite' system and hence was most commented upon. Nevertheless, a brief narration of the happenings in the context of US response might be a useful exercise.

Unlike the Berlin riots and Poznan uprising, the Hungarian revolution was not a sudden outburst. It was a culmination of a process in the socialist world, which had started with the death of Marshal Stalin on March 5, 1953. The death of Stalin not only ended an era of socialist development but also created a vacuum in the communist movement which spilled over to a number of purges inside the Soviet Union, unrest in the Soviet sphere of influence beginning with East Berlin riots. In Hungary, the immediate effect of death of Stalin was felt in the change of leadership. On July 4, 1953 Imre Nagy replaced Matyas Rakosi as the Premier. Rakosi, however, remained as the party chief. This change cannot be presumed to be a conscious and preordained step towards an eventual revolution. On the day of his appointment as the Premier, Nagy gave a speech before the Parliament in which he was highly critical of the past economic policies, brutal collectivization, and super-industrialization which had been grievously felt by the people. He promised major innovations to bring a liberal atmosphere in the country in accordance with the desire of the people. His speech was the first expression of general unhappiness over the Rakosi regime. "His speech electrified the people", wrote Zinner, and "was popularly regarded as a fresh breeze in a fetid atmosphere. But it understandably alarmed Rakosi."[63] However, Nagy could not proceed further. He was surrounded by his opponents. In the struggle for power, Rakosi's vilification against Nagy's economic policies finally led to the Central

---

63 Paul E. Zinner, *Revolution in Hungary* (New York: Colombia University Press, 1962) pp. 164-165.

Committee's indictment of Nagy as a "right wing opportunist".[64] A six week later Nagy was dismissed for his 'anti-Marxist' and unparty-like activities. The short lived victory in dismissing Nagy could not relegate him to a political exile. In February 1956. Khrushchev delivered his famous secret speech before the Twentieth Congress of the Communist Party of the Soviet Union revealing Stalin's mistakes and misuse of power. The 'secret' denunciation, which stunned the party comrades, however, did not remain secret as the text of the speech reached the rest of the world, and thereby, created a widespread speculation about the future course of the communist movement. In Hungary, the party workers and officials responded to the development by way of opposing and denouncing the Rakoi regime known to be associated with Stalinist type of misrule and autocracy. A major shake up of the party became inevitable.

After the fall in 1953, Nagy advanced a 'New Course' to the Hungarian Communist party recommending a neutral and independent course for the internal and the external affairs of Hungary. The Nagy thesis provided the basis for an intellectual debate favouring a change in the political atmosphere of the country in the backdrop of impressive performance of Hungary's industrial economy, which registered a phenomenal growth amounting to 210 per cent during the period from 1949 to 1953.[65] The debate released an emotional wave of attack on the regime for its alleged purges of intellectuals in 1955. On

64 For details see Imre Nagy, *On Communism: In Defense of the New Course* (New York: Preager, 1957) pp. xliii and 103-04. A copy of Nagy's political testament (mimeographed) was smuggled out of Hungary in spring 1957 and was published in America. Also see Janos M. Rainer, "The Life Course of Imre Nagy" in Tery Cox (ed), *Hungary 1956: Forty Years On* (New York: Routledge, 1997) pp. 141-151.

65 For Details see Imre Nagy, *On Communism, ibid*, p. 185 and also see Zbigniew K. Brezinski, *The Soviet Bloc: Unity and Conflict*, n. 15, pp. 211-212. For some details see Rudolf L. Tökes, *Hungary's Negotiated Revolution: Economic Reform, Social Change and Political Succession* (Cambridge: Cambridge University Press, 1996) and György Litvan (ed), *The Hungarian Revolution of 1956: Reform and Repression, 1953-1963* English Translation by Janos M. Bak and Lyman H. Legters, (London: Longman, 1996).

October 18, 1955 fifty Hungarian writers issued a memorandum accusing the "despotic, anti-democratic methods of leadership in the cultural field" and demanded a tolerant and liberal atmosphere in the country.[66] The opposition to the Rakosi regime led to the formation of the Petöfi Circle in March 1956. Although the Petöfi Circle was established with the approval of the party, it later on became the hot bed of an open revolt against the party. By the end of June it organized a series of public debates and discussions on the wind of changes in the Soviet Union following the de-Stalinization process and also on the despotic rule of Matyas Rakosi. It could attract hundreds of people to such discussion, and therefore, it could successfully infuse an anti-establishment emotion in the mind of the people. The discourse on the apparently liberal political developments in the post-Stalin Soviet Union provided an intellectual base in the city of Budapest to clamour for a humane and tolerant political atmosphere in the country. In this way gradually the Petöfi Circle started playing a vital role in sowing the seeds of October revolution in Hungary.[67] Matyas Rakosi granted permission grudgingly to the Petöfi Circle to hold political discussions with an ulterior motive to allow the dissidents to get exposed fully and then to round them up at an opportune moment. Rakosi also wrongly anticipated an early fall of Nikita Khrushchev which would obviously go to his advantage. On July 16, without waiting much, he presented the politburo a detailed plan to purge all his dissidents.[68] But the move did not go in his favour. Anastas Mikoyan, acting as the

---

66 *The Truth about the Nagy Affair: Facts, Documents, Comments*, with a Preface by Albert Camus (London: Cecker and Warbur, 1957) p. 129 also see Peter Unwin, *Voice in the Wilderness: Imre Nagy and the Hungarian Revolution* (London: Little, Brown, 1991)

67 Paul E. Zinner, *Revolution in Hungary*, n. 63, pp. 208-210; and for the role of the intellectuals see Tamas Aczel and Tabor Meray, *The Revolt of Mind: A Case History of Intellectual Resistance Behind the Iron Curtain* (London: Tames and Hudson, 1960), also see Andras B. Hegeduss, "The Petofi Circle: The Forum of Reform in 1956", in Terry Cox (ed), *Hungary 1956: Forty Years On*, n. 64, pp. 108-133.

68 Ferenc A. Vali, *Rift and Revolt in Hungary* (Cambridge, Mass. Harvard University Press, 1961) p. 234.

representative of the CPSU, suddenly arrived at the Politburo meeting of the Hungarian Workers' Party on July 18 and steered the deliberation leading to the replacement of Rakosi by Enro Gerö.[69] In a move to please the party and the people, the Soviet Union granted a 100 million rubble loan to Hungary to accelerate its economic growth. But it proved to be too late. The crisis mounted up rapidly towards the eventual revolution.

The developments had an apparent tendency towards a peaceful change of leadership and eventually towards a Tito-type national communism. John MacCormac, a leading American correspondent, reported in May that the Hungarians "apparently have ceased to believe, as they believed a few years ago, that the United States was getting ready to free their country".[70] But they were hopeful about a breakthrough in their efforts to secure a more liberal and democratic political environment without the intervention of any outside support. In an interview with Enro Gerö, John MacCormac found that the country in the post-Rakosi months, was heading for democratic decentralization and predicted an improvement of relations with the United States.[71]

The replacement of Rakosi did not pacify the dissidents. On October 6, a symbolic date in the History of Hungary[72], a silent procession led by Imre Nagy and the widow of Laszb Rajak, who was one of the victims of the purges of 1949, took place in the city of Budapest. The procession was a mark of rehabilitation of Rajak and his associates. The reinternment of Rajak was turned into a silent national demonstration against the current regime. The developments in the following days became highly significant. On October 12, Mihaly Farkas, a top ranking secret police officer known for his notorious crimes and his son Vladimir, were arrested. On October 14,

---

69 Tamas Aczel and Tabor Meray, *The Revolt of the Mind*, n. 67, pp. 412-419. For a concise account see Ernest T. Anderson, *Hungary 56* (London: Solidarity, 1964).

70 *New York Times*, May 7, 1956.

71 *ibid*, August 15, 1956.

72 October 6 is the anniversary of the execution of 13 heroes of the Hungarian struggle for independence, 1848-49.

coinciding with the visit of Enro Gerö to Belgrade to patch up his differences with Tito, Nagy was reinstated as a party member. On October 22, students, writers and members of the Petöfi Circle met separately and drafted different sets of resolutions, a synthesis of which finally resulted in outcome of a Ten Point demand ranging from a public trial of Mihaly Farkas to the expulsion of Rakosi from the Central Committee, and above all the consolidation of Hungarian-Soviet friendship "on the basis of the Leninist principles of complete equality".[73] On October 23, the students of Budapest University gathered in front of the Petöfi Statute, sang nationalist songs, and a couple of hours later about 800 students of the Petöfi Military Academy, the Polytechnical University, the Agricultural University and the High School of Physical Education joined them. They adopted a seven-point programme which included full rehabilitation of Imre Nagy, equality as the basis of Hungarian-Soviet relations, free and secret ballot, and reexamination of planned economy.[74] Meanwhile, thousands of demonstrators gathered in front of the Polish Embassy to express their solidarity with the Polish reform movement. Then they pulled down and disfigured a huge statue of Stalin. In the afternoon, the crowd assembled at the statute of Bem, another hero of 1848, and thereafter proceeded to the parliament building shouting for Nagy, who finally appeared before them and made a brief speech. It was followed by harsh and truculent radio broadcast by Enro Gerö accusing the demonstrators for causing chaos in the city. The broadcast was considered as "the fuse that set off the explosion".[75]

Sporadic fighting between the demonstrators and the security forces took place in front of the Radio Budapest headquarters as the latter prevented the demonstrators, who made an abortive attempt to occupy the Radio station in order to broadcast their charter of demands and the programme of

---

73 For details see Lasky Melvin J. (ed), *The Hungarian Revolution: A White Book* (New York: Books of Libraries Press, 1957), reprinted in 1970, p. 47.

74 *ibid*, pp. 48-49.

75 Tibor Meray, *Thirteen Days that Shook the Kremlin* (London: Thames and Hudson, 1959), p. 85.

action. The demonstrators were stopped at the gate and were prevented from entering the premises.[76] The situation appeared to have gone out of the control of the security forces because of their limited strength. Therefore, on that fateful night of October 23-24, the party chief Gerö and Premier Hegedus requested for Soviet armed assistance to put down the uprising. The announcement of the request was made public over the radio next morning saying that as the Government was "unprepared for these bloody and dastardly attacks . . . [it] therefore applied for help to the Soviet formations stationed in Hungary under the terms of the Warsaw Treaty."[77] The Soviet forces appeared in the city but were uncertain about the job in the absence of a clear-cut direction from Moscow, where the Soviet leaders were observing the developments with attention and concern.

On the night of October 23-24 the Central Committee of the Hungarian Workers' Party appointed Nagy replacing Hegedus, but the announcement was not made public till 8:30 am. At 9:00 am the radio announced that the Government had requested the Soviet Union for military assistance to deal with the situation. This left an ample scope for confusion as to the role of Nagy in inviting the Soviet troops to intervene in the situation. At the early hours of October 24, Mikoyan and Suslov, members of the Soviet Presidium, arrived in Budapest to register their support for Nagy. They backed Nagy's appeal for the end of the fighting and dismissed Gerö and appointed Janos Kadar as the party Chief. Despite these prompt steps, the demonstrators continued their violence against the Government forces, and pressurized Nagy to withdraw from the Warsaw Treaty. Nagy took a few quick and historic decisions. He disbanded the infamous secret police, abolished one-party system and announced free and secret ballot. Gradually fighting receded. But on October 25, thousands of

---

76 J.G. Rkei and M. Horvath, *Soviet Military Intervention in Hungary, 1956* (Budapest: Central European University Press, 1999) pp. 15-20.

77 Tibor Meray, *Thirteen Days that Shook the Kremlin*, p. 58 also see Noel Barber, *Seven Days of Freedom: The Hungarian Uprising 1956* (London: Macmillan, 1974).

Hungarians assembled in the parliament square shouting anti-Soviet slogans and demanding the withdrawal of Hungary from the Warsaw Treaty. Chaos took place when the Hungarian security forces resorted to firing on the demonstrators. The Soviet forces watching the activities of the demonstrators from a distance mistook the firing as an act of violence committed by the demonstrators against them, and consequently, opened fire on the people killing several hundred people on the spot.[78] This aggravated the situation to the extent that violence against the Soviet troops spread all over the city despite repeated appeal accompanied by stern warning issued by Nagy. Thus, the movement, which had its origins in the anti-Rakosi sentiments, now took an anti-communist and anti-Soviet turn.

As already stated in an earlier context that the East Berlin and the Poznan riots had taken place so suddenly that the United States, despite its pronounced commitment to the cause of liberation of Eastern Europe, was caught so unaware that it could hardly do anything except extending unsuccessfully food aid to the suffering people. But this time as the Hungarian uprising took a turn towards a violent anti-communist and anti-Soviet revolution on October 25, the United States had no ground to argue convincingly that it had not got sufficient time to respond on the line of its expressed policy of liberation. The developments in Hungary since the formation of the Petőfi Circle and the onset of the continuous debates on the issue of change of leadership received adequate coverage in all the leading Western newspapers. The CIA gave a forecast to the Administration about the uprising but the latter could not visualize its early outburst. Christian Ravndal, a former American Minister of Hungary, told the reporters, when the fighting had already started on October 23, that the uprising began sooner than he had expected. "We expected something this sort around the end of the year."[79] Herman Finer wrote that the State Department got the 'winds' of the uprising as early as October 20.[80] But Robert Murphy, Under Secretary of

78 For details of the massacre on October 25, see George Mikes, *The Hungarian Revolution* (London: A Deutsch, 1957), pp. 100-110.

79 *New York Herald Tribune*, October 25, 1956.

80 Herman Finer, *Dulles over Suez* (Chicago: Quardangle, 1964) p. 338.

State, later on recorded that the Administration had "no advance information about the uprising" and therefore, had "no plan of action". He wrote:

> I must admit that I did not expect that an anti-Soviet revolution would spread through Hungary like a forest fire, but I never doubted that if a revolution did break out, the USSR would use every means no matter how brutal to suppress it.[81]

He further recollected: "The State Department had welcomed the stimulation which Tito seemed to be giving to a liberalizing trend, but nobody anticipating anything like Hungarian insurrection."[82] Later on, on November 23, 1961 Eisenhower went back to the memory lane while talking to the Colombia Broadcasting System (CBS) that the uprising "started in such a way...that everyone was little bit fooled".[83] The official contention on the suddenness of the uprising is not convincing. It is hard to believe that the State Department did not sense the premonition of the outburst while the US print media and other Western journalists had been publishing 'encouraging' reports of the Hungarian demand for liberalization.

The first reaction of Dulles on being informed at about 7:00 pm on October 23 of the outbreak of uprising in the city of Budapest was an expression of exceeding happiness claiming it to be the vindication of his hope for liberation of Eastern Europe. As Finer puts the words of Dulles:

> ...the people of Poland and Hungary, their leaders, have seen that it is possible to be independent of Moscow! We kept alive the yearning for freedom. It worked in Yugoslavia; it will work in Poland and Hungary. The great monolith of communism is crumbling![84]

As the Hungarian crisis unfolds itself day by day it proved how futile and substanceless were the boastings of Dulles.

---

81 Robert Murphy, *Diplomat Among Warriors* (New York, Garden City: Doubleday, 1964) p. 428.

82 *idem*.

83 For details see *New York Times*, November 24, 1961. There are other aspects of Eisenhower's statement, which would be discussed at a later stage.

84 Herman Finer, *Dulles over Suez*, n. 80, p. 343.

Except leaving the matter to the United Nation for verbal condemnation of the Soviet Union for its military intervention, the exponents of liberation thesis remained dumbfounded. As cited earlier, Dulles, in his interview with the CBS in the Face to the Nation programme on October 21, ruled out the possibility of pressing American armed forces to liberate Eastern Europe. Therefore, it became palpable that except condemning the Soviet intervention nothing was going to happen.

Hungarian revolution coincided with the final stage of the US Presidential election, and quite naturally, President Eisenhower seeking the second term had to make statement on the developments in Hungary. In his public speech he carefully avoided the question of liberation of Eastern Europe as well as the situation in Hungary. The State Department was 'handicapped' by the loss of contact with the American Legation in Budapest, and therefore, could not rely upon an overdosed speculation and premature conclusions of the western media. Although the Secretary of State, who appeared to be over-joyous on hearing the reports of the Hungarian uprising, had to maintain extremely cautious stand which unmistakably indicated that the US Government would remain a passive and silent spectator of the historic anti-Soviet movement in Eastern Europe.

On the morning of October 24, Dulles made a statement after having a discussion with the President on the development in Hungary that they had been "particularly interested today in Poland and Hungary."[85] At the same time the first official statement of the President was worded with striking caution:

> The United States considers the development in Hungary as being a renewed expression of intense desire for freedom long held by the Hungarian people...The United States deplored the intervention of Soviet military forces which under the Treaty of Peace should have been withdrawn and the presence of which in Hungary as is now demonstrated, is not to protect Hungary against armed aggression from without,

---

85 *New York Times*, October 25, 1956.

but rather to continue an occupation of Hungary by the forces of an alien government for its own purposes.

The heart of America goes out to the people of Hungary.[86]

The statement of the President did not indicate even implicitly any grain of the possibility of the US counter-intervention, although Robert Murphy later on criticized the President for giving an impression that the United States had been sponsoring the revolt.[87]

The US Government approached the British Government to take up the Hungarian crisis at the United Nations. Both the Governments were fraught with two unsettled questions. They were not sure whether the Soviet Union intervened at the request of the Hungarian Government and secondly it was not clear under what article of the UN Charter should the question be raised.[88] Edwin L. Dale Jr. reported that the United States consulted Britain, France and other friendly countries on "the feasibility and advisability of bringing the situation before the United Nations." Dale's concluding remarks are revealing:

> The Soviet troops are being used at the request of the Hungarian Government. There is little effort in Washington to deny the same way if there were a communist-led revolution in, say, Italy. In 1944 and 1945, for example British troops, at the request of the Athens Government, fought communist rebels in Greece. Furthermore, any possible United Nations approach is at the moment clouded by French threats to use force in Morocco and Tunisia to protect Europeans there.[89]

By October 27, it became clear that there was the remotest possibility of using the US military might in repelling the Soviet forces already in action in Hungary. There remained only two measures to be taken as a response to the crisis – to take the matter to the United Nations and condemn the Soviet military intervention, and to help rehabilitate the Hungarian escapees taking shelter in the West.

---

86 *Public Papers of the Presidents of the United States: Dwight D. Eisenhower, 1956*, pp. 1018-1019.

87 Robert Murphy, *Diplomat Among Warriors*, n. 81, p. 429.

88 *Manchester Guardian*, October 27, 1956.

89 *New York Times*, October 27, 1956.

On October 27, Lincoln White issued a statement on the meeting of Robert Murphy with the First Secretary of the Hungarian Legation, Tibor Zador, from whom Murphy wanted to have a clear picture of the developments inside Hungary as he appeared to be not posted with all the details of the situation there. Except confirming the news of the formation of the new Government headed by Imre Nagy on the night of October 23-24, Zador did not give any significant information.[90] Murphy cited the reports of violence in Budapest and the Soviet military intervention, and pressed for details. Zador simply said that the intervention "was quite legal under the Warsaw Pact." Murphy closed the conversation by lodging a firm protest that the US diplomatic representatives in Hungary were completely cut off from communication with the new Government.

While Robert Murphy was busy with his efforts to gather details of the Hungarian events, Henry Cabot Lodge Jr., US Representative in the United Nations, kept himself in touch with his counterparts from Britain and France, Sir Piersen Dixon and Bernard Conut-Gentille. They coordinated their efforts to draw the attention of the United Nations to the Hungarian uprising and the Soviet military intervention on October 23-24. On the afternoon of October 27, the Representatives of France, United Kingdom and United States addressed a joint letter to the President of the Security Council requesting him to convene a meeting of the Council under the provisions of Article 34 of the UN Charter for an urgent discussion on the situation in Hungary.[91] Ambassador Lodge Jr. issued a statement saying that the members of the United Nations "cannot remain indifferent" to the Hungarian situation in which the Hungarians were subjected to "violent repressive measures by foreign military forces." The Council met on October 28 and decided by a vote of 9-1 (USSR) with Yugoslavia abstaining, place the item on the agenda. Just before the meeting of the Security Council, Peter Kos, the Hungarian Representative to the UNO, transmitted to the members the text of the declaration of his Government that the "events took place on 22 October 1956 and thereafter, and the measures

---

90 Department of State, *Bulletin*, November 5, 1956, p. 701.

91 *ibid*, p. 75.

taken in the course of these events are exclusively within the domestic jurisdiction of the Hungarian People's Republic," and therefore, categorically protested "against placing on the agenda the consideration of any question concerning the domestic affairs of Hungary".[92] Despite his protest, the Security Council met at 4:00 pm on that day. Arkady A. Sobolev of the Soviet Union objected to the inclusion of the item in the agenda on the ground that the application of Article 34 of the Charter to discuss the Hungarian situation was improper because the Hungarian situation was essentially a matter of domestic jurisdiction and could not be regarded as a threat to international peace and security. On the other hand, such discussion would, he argued, "give further encouragement to the armed rebellion which is being conducted by a reactionary underground movement against the legal Government of Hungary."[93]

Henry Cabot Lodge Jr. challenged the contention of Sobolev and gave a detailed account of the Hungarian uprising beginning from October 23, when the first round of violence broke out.[94] The British and the French Representatives as expected supported Lodge Jr. Max Freedman of *Manchester Guardian* correctly wrote: "In view of Russian veto, which is certain to be cast against any sanctions or hostile resolution, the Security Council can do no more than express its moral condemnation of the repressive measures being applied in Hungary."[95] As the Security Council started the debate on the Hungarian situation, Radio Budapest announced a proclamation of Nagy which rejected the contention that the uprising was a counter-revolutionary one:

> The Government rejects the view that sees the present formidable popular movement as a counter-revolution...it is also undisputable that in this movement a great national and

---

92 For details of the letter dated October 28, 1956 from the Hungarian Representative to the Secretary General, see United Nations, Security Council, *Official Record*, S/3691.

93 *ibid*, S/3692.

94 Department of State, *Bulletin*, November 12, 1956, pp. 758-759.

95 *Manchester Guardian*, October 29, 1956.

> democratic movement embracing and unifying all our people unfolded itself with elementary force.[96]

The proclamation contained another significant statement: "Hungarian Government has come into an agreement with the Soviet Government that Soviet troops will immediately begin withdrawal from Budapest and simultaneously with the establishment of new security forces, will leave the city's territory." The statement, read out in the Security Council by Sir Ronald Walker of Australia, created general excitement among the members who felt that with impending withdrawal of Soviet troops, the Hungarian crisis would be over. The Council adjourned the meeting without introducing any resolution, leaving the matter at the discretion of the President for reconsideration when necessary. It was done to facilitate a smooth end of the crisis and shift the Council's attention to the Suez War. And the Soviet Union took the adjournment as a breathing space to prepare itself for a massive military onslaught on Hungary.

Eisenhower's reminiscence of the Hungarian event right from the time he had been first informed about the uprising was a clear testimony of America's preordained conclusion as to the possible US role in the crisis: not to intervene militarily to stop Soviet invasion. On Monday, October 23, President Eisenhower held as many as 23 meetings and the Hungarian crisis figured in all these discussions. On October 24, he reviewed the situation with Dulles and "wanted to explore the chance of helping to assist centrifugal, disruptive currents in the Iron Curtain countries". [97] However, the nature of the help at that crisis moment was not spelt out, rather not thought about seriously.

On October 26, Eisenhower presided over the National Security meeting in which Allen Dulles, the CIA Director, reported on the entry of Soviet troops inside Hungary. He said, as Eisenhower goes narrative, that Tito and the Chinese

---

96 Lasky Melvin J. (ed), *The Hungarian Revolution: A While Book*, n. 73, p. 115.

97 Dwight D. Eisenhower, *Waging Peace: The While House Years 1956-1961* (Garden City, New York: Doubleday, 1965), pp. 63 and 65.

"approved the Polish stand" in the matter of liberalization, but they were silent about the Hungarian situation and Soviet military intervention. Eisenhower wrote:

> "The Chinese Communists" he said [Allen Dulles] "may not be unhappy over what is happening in Hungary. If so, we might at this moment be seeing the beginning of the first rift between China and the USSR".[98]

After hearing from Allen Dulles, President Eisenhower remarked:

> I doubt that Russian leaders genuinely fear an invasion by the West...But with deterioration of the Soviet Union's hold over its satellites might not the Soviet Union be tempted to resort to extreme measures, even to start a world war? This possibility we must watch with the utmost care.

The President directed the State Department to prepare "an immediate, comprehensive analysis of the events in both Poland and Hungary, with the possible type of American action considered." The position paper was drafted accordingly with great care so as to leave no fabric of imagination to say that the US Government incited the Poles and the Hungarians to revolt. It reaffirmed on tactical grounds the American stand not to make these countries the future allies of the United States, but at the same time it declared that "if the USSR used forces to suppress the Gomulka regime or any further move toward Polish independence, the United States would be prepared to support UN action – including the use of force – to prevent the USSR from reinforcing its control."[99] The text of the position paper is clear indication that the US counter-intervention in Hungary on its own was a remote possibility, so also a UN punitive measure against the Soviet Union in view of full certainty of Soviet application of veto against such a move. Further, and interestingly enough, it was Gomulka's Poland and not Hungarian crisis that figured in the position paper, a deliberate and calculate step to leave no impression for Moscow that the US Government was behind the unrest in Hungary.

---

98 *ibid*, p. 67.

99 *ibid*, p. 86, fn. 5.

Secretary of State, Dulles, delivered a major address in Dallas on October 27 afternoon in which he gave a clear-cut idea of the American attitude towards the Hungarian uprising. He made it clear that there was no possibility of direct American action in Hungary:

> The Polish people now loosen the Soviet grip upon the land they love. And the heroic people of Hungary challenge the murderous fire of Red army tanks. These patriots value liberty more than their life itself. . . . Today our Nation continues its historic role. The captive peoples should never have reason to doubt that they have in us a sincere and dedicated friend who shares their aspirations. They must know that they can draw upon our abundance to tide themselves over the people of economic adjustment which is inevitable as they rededicate their productive efforts to the services of their own people, rather than of exploiting masters. Nor do we condition economic ties between us upon the adoption by these countries of any particular society.
>
> Let me make it clear, beyond a possibility of doubt. The United States had no ulterior purpose in desiring the independence of the satellite countries...We do not look upon these nations as potential military allies. We see them as friends and as part of a new and friendly and no longer divided Europe.[100]

This long statement suggests three significant points: the peoples of Poland and Hungary in their struggle for freedom eventually had shaken the very foundation of the Soviet Control over Eastern Europe; the United States extended its sincere sympathy for their struggle for liberation from Soviet domination and shared their aspiration; and under the circumstances, the United States could do no more than expressing sincere desire for the freedom of the 'captive peoples'. This naturally strengthened the belief of the Soviet leaders that the United States would not intervene militarily to liberate the Poles and Hungarians. Janos Radvanyi wrote later on that Khrushchev never took seriously Dulles's vague

100 For details of the address entitled "Task of Waging Peace" see Department of State, *Bulletin,* November 5, 1956, pp. 695-699, quotation p. 697.

statements on US "plans of building up and assisting East European resistance movements", but was concerned at the possibility of using American nuclear deterrence to ward off a full scale war in Europe over Eastern Europe.[101]

Dulles statement of October 27 carried certain far-reaching implications. It not only dismissed Soviet apprehension, but also strengthened its will to crush the Hungarian uprising. Secondly, it did not indicate that the US Administration was hoping to see the success of Titoism in Eastern Europe. The reference to "any particular form of society" other than the one prevalent in the region at that time implied that the US desire was circumscribed in the framework of Titoism. Thirdly, in the event of the emergence of such a society in Eastern Europe, the United States would invariably extend economic aid to the new governments that replaced the existing Soviet puppet regimes. It logically meant that the Hungarian transformation from a Soviet imposed system to 'any particular form of society' was to be accomplished without any direct American assistance.

On the next day in the Security Council, Ambassador Lodge Jr. quoted the most significant part of Dulles's speech which reaffirmed that the United States did not look at these nations as its potential military allies, and it would embark upon the UN action in the case of all out Soviet military action in Hungary.[102] Meanwhile, the State Department received a teletyped message from the American Legation in Budapest about the crossing of the Carpathian frontier by the Soviet troops to enter Hungary. Immediately Dulles announced that the American Red Cross had offered "to extend assistance to alleviate suffering on the part of the Hungarian people."[103]

Inside Hungary, Premier Nagy made frantic appeals to his countrymen to stop fighting as he could foresee that such violence would provide a strong pretext for a full-scale Soviet

---

101 Janos Radvanyi, *Hungary and the Superpowers: The 1956 Revolution and Realpolitik* (California, Stanford: Hoover Institution Press, 1972), p. 11.

102 Department of State, *Bulletin*, November 12, 1956, p. 758.

103 *ibid*, November 5, 1956, p. 700.

military invasion. As a positive response to it, the fighting receded from October 27 onwards, which created an impression that "this unfortunate civil war will be ended now".[104] Nagy's statement, as cited already, about the withdrawal of Soviet troops had a positive impact on the return of normalcy in the country. Yet tension continued to prevail, as the rebels remained adamant over the fulfillment of a number of demands, which could not be attended to by the new regime. They refused to appreciate the difficulties faced by the new Government in dealing with a superpower on one hand and the huge task of consolidation of its political position internally on the other hand. They failed to understand the basic fact – how could the newly formed Government meet all the demands in a violent situation not conducive to any constructive plan. At that critical time Nagy neither had the unquestioning support of all the party members nor had the Soviet backing which was an imperative for consolidation of his Government. The rebel were too intransigent to give Nagy sufficient time even to negotiate with the Soviet leaders to facilitate the withdrawal of their troops.

On October 28, the Workers' Council and Student Parliament of the northeastern country prepared a seven point reform programme including the withdrawal of Soviet troops "not only to their bases, but to their own country, to the Soviet Union", establishment of a new provincial government, holding of general elections in two months with several parties participating.[105] Amidst sporadic violence and street fighting, Nagy was confident about his moves to contain violence. But the Soviet leaders were worried at the developments of gravest intra-bloc crisis in the post-World War history threatening the very foundation of the Soviet hegemony in Eastern Europe. The possible loss of Hungary to the West would invariably lead to a series of spillover unrest in the Soviet sphere of influence. The Soviet leaders consulted the Chinese leaders and eventually after a great deal of discussion with Liu Shaoqi, a crystallized opinion was formed – to put down the rebellion

---

104 Melvin Lasky J. (ed), *The Hungarian Revolution*, n. 73, p.109.

105 *ibid*, p. 120.

with an iron hand and remove Nagy, who had proved to be a failure.[106] Still the Soviet leaders showed a conciliatory approach towards the solution of the crisis. On October 30, two important developments took place. Mikoyan and Suslov again arrived in Budapest and held a lengthy discussion with Nagy and Janos Kadar, and also with the leader of newly formed bourgeois Smallholders' Party, Ziltan Tildy. The Soviet leaders indicated that they did not oppose the formation of a coalition ministry and the reemergence of the multiparty system. They gave the impression that there would be a gradual withdrawal of the Soviet troops from Hungary. Nonetheless, on two issues they remained firm. The old capitalist system must not return and Hungary must not be an anti-Soviet state.[107] The Soviet Foreign Minister Shepilov made a statement on the same day that "the sooner the activities of anti-national and anti-democratic elements stop, and if there is no danger, the sooner would Soviet troops withdraw."[108] On October 30, the Soviet troops started withdrawing from Budapest ostensibly in an attempt to appease the warring rebels, who mistook it as a sign of weakness on the part of the Soviet Union. It was a calculated and deceptive move to hoodwink the rebels and the West, and to prepare for a greater assault.

The other important development that took place on that historic day was an announcement made by Premier Nagy breaking with one-party system:

> In the interest of further democratization of the country's life, the cabinet abolishes the one-party system and places the country's Government on the basis of democratic cooperation between coalition parties as they existed in 1954.[109]

106 For details of Soviet anxiety and its decision to intervene see *Khrushchev Remembers*, Vol. I n. 7, pp.164-165 and for Chinese role in the decision see Abu Nasar Saied Ahmed, "Chinese Response to Soviet Intervention in Hungary, Czechoslovakia and Afghanistan, *Indian Journal of Political Science,*Vol. 47. No.1, January-March, 1986, pp. 42-75.

107 Tibor Meray, *Thirteen Days that Shook the Kremlin*, n. 75, pp. 164-165.

108 Lasky, *The Hungarian Revolution*, p. 133.

109 *ibid*, p. 139.

On the same day, the Soviet Union also issued a significant statement upholding peaceful co-existence between the Soviet Union and other countries "on the principles of complete equality, of respect for territorial integrity, state independence and sovereignty, and of non-interference in one another's internal affairs." The declaration indicated the Soviet willingness to review the entire gamut of stationing the Soviet troops in the Warsaw Treaty member countries. It made a comment on the recent developments in Hungary, regretting the bloodshed and mentioned that the Soviet troops entered Hungary at the request of the Hungarian Government to bring order to the city of Budapest. A passage of the declaration deserves attention:

> Having in mind that further presence of Soviet military units in Hungary could serve as an excuse for further aggravation of the situation, the Soviet Government has given its military command instruction to withdraw the Soviet military units from the city of Budapest as soon as this is considered necessary by the Hungarian Government.

Reaffirming the Soviet willingness to negotiate on the question of the presence of Soviet troops, it ended with a note of warning:

> The Soviet Government expressed confidence that the people of the socialist countries will not permit foreign and domestic reactionary forces to shake the foundation of the people's democratic system, a system established and strengthened by the self-sacrificing struggle and labor of the workers, peasants and intelligentsia of each country...they will strengthen the fraternal unity and mutual aid of the socialist countries to buttress the great cause of peace and socialism.[110]

Close on the heels of the declaration, Mikoyan, who had been in Budapest at that time, appeared to have shown a conciliatory approach. On October 31, he met Zoltan Tildy, a member of the Nagy cabinet, and expressed his willingness to discuss four important issues – withdrawal of Soviet troops, Hungary's withdrawal from the Warsaw Treaty, the reestablishment of

---

110 For details of the Soviet declaration of October 30 published in *Pravda*, October 31, 1956, see the translation in *The Current Digest of the Soviet Press*, Vol. VII, No. 40 (November 14, 1956), pp. 10-11.

multiparty system and holding of free elections, and the Hungarian assertion of sovereignty and self-determination. After the meeting Zoltan Tildy reported: "He [Mikoyan] accepted everything."[111] Mikoyan's conciliatory approach testified to Soviet acceptance of Hungary's quest for a free and democratic system in the western model. Encouraging developments followed soon after with the Soviet withdrawal of troops from the city of Budapest. Violence subsided. Law and order returned. This gave an impression that the Soviet leaders wanted to give Nagy a chance to consolidate his position and stop violence in Budapest. However, the apparent conciliatory mood was reversed within a couple of hours by the reinforcement of Soviet troops as a part of the massive invasion of Hungary.

Between the days from October 28, when the Security Council session adjourned without adopting any resolution till late night of October 31, when the Soviet troops marched into Hungary, the whole show was stolen by the developments in West Asia with the outbreak of the Suez War. At that time when the world attention was on the Suez War, Hungary presented a somewhat stultifying confusion. The Soviet declaration of October 30 was an unequivocal expression of Moscow's willingness to withdraw the forces from Hungary and accordingly on the very next day the forces started withdrawing. Almost simultaneously, the Soviet military units began their massive assault on Hungary occupying airfields and other strategic positions. Budapest was quickly surrounded by the advancing troops. Imre Nagy asked the Soviet Ambassador Yuri Andropov for an explanation of the new military incursion. That was an exercise in futility. Already Moscow had decided to crush the rebellion. Nagy made some quick moves. At first he requested Marshal Voroshilov, the President of the Supreme Soviet, to hold negotiations with the Hungarian Government about the withdrawal of troops.[112] As the Soviet troops were pouring to occupy the country fully, a helpless Nagy summoned Andropov on November 1 to submit

---

111 Melvin Lasky J., *The Hungarian Revolution*, p. 147 and Tibor Meray, *Thirteen Days that Shook the Kremlin*, pp. 164-165.

112 Lasky, *ibid*, p. 181.

a strong protest against the invasion. As a last step to stall the invasion, Nagy proclaimed Hungary's neutrality and its withdrawal from the Warsaw Treaty. He immediately, notified the UN Secretary General Dag Hammarskjold about the decision and requested him to "put on the agenda of the forthcoming General Assembly of the United Nations the question of Hungary's neutrality and the defense of this neutrality by the four great powers."[113] The declaration of neutrality in the face of massive invasion was a head-on confrontation with the Soviet Union in which he alone would not be able to withstand the Soviet assault. He, therefore, appealed to the United Nations to defend and protect Hungary's neutrality. It was an erroneous calculation that the four great powers would respond actively to his request. On that day, Nagy's colleague, the first secretary Janos Kadar, announced the formation of a new party, the Hungarian Socialist Workers' Party, and surreptitiously sneaked away from the capital and later on joined hands with the Soviet Union to replace Nagy's Government.[114]

Right from taking the charge of the Government on October 24, Emre Nagy faced the deepening crisis problematically not being aware of his profound limitations in fulfilling the demands of the rebels who spearheaded an agitation successfully to his investiture as the Prime Minister. A couple of difficult and hasty steps were taken such as the withdrawal of Hungary from the Warsaw Treaty Organization without preparing himself to face the foreseeable consequences. There was no evidence of coordinated efforts from his end to enlist the support from possible sources. While he decided to face alone the future predictable onslaught from the Soviet Union, as he refused to seek any help from the West, which later on constituted the basis of America's argument for its inaction in the crisis, the rebels in a disorganized manner appealed to the western embassies for help.[115] Besides these, another important step he took was his appeal to the United Nations to protect

113 *UN Document A/3251*, November 1, 1956.

114 Lasky, *The Hungarian Revolution*, pp. 180-181 and 219.

115 See the dispatch of a Diplomatic Correspondent, *Manchester Guardian*, October 27, 1956.

Hungary's neutrality. As he frantically appealed for peace and order to save the country from the Soviet intervention, the rebels geared up their anti-communist and anti-Soviet violence, and thus provided the ground for the obvious surgical action from Moscow.[116] In an objective autopsy of the Hungarian crisis, Isaac Deutscher wrote that when Nagy had been struggling hard to contain violence, a liberal section of the Soviet leadership at the initial stage did not want to use force, just as Moscow did not use force in the case of Gomulka allowing him to consolidate his position in Poland. To quote Deutscher:

> When the army feigned a withdrawal from Budapest on October 30, it probably did so under pressure from the 'liberals' in the Presidium who hoped that this would enable Nagy to establish a national Communist regime that would, like Gomulka's regime, still remain aligned with the Soviet bloc. This hope was dashed in two and three days later, when the disintegration of Hungarian Communism became evident and Nagy denounced the Warsaw Pact.[117]

The Soviet leaders accomplished their duty in protecting the interests of socialist internationalism by resorting to a second and the final military intervention within the framework of the Warsaw Pact concluded one year earlier, while the exponents of liberation of Eastern Europe remained as silent spectators of the gravest crisis in the Soviet sphere of influence. A dozen of arguments defending the US inaction failed to cover up the truth: the US commitment to the cause of liberation of the 'captive peoples' was merely a part of the US psychological warfare against the Soviet Union.

As the Hungarian uprising started taking a violent turn, Dulles reported to President Eisenhower on October 27 that the revolt had become widespread and Imre Nagy was incapable of steering it to a logical conclusion, for, his Government included "a number of 'bad' people, associated with the Molotov school, and will have difficulty in attracting [popular] support".[118] Eisenhower was in touch with leaders

116 *The Current Digest of the Soviet Press*, Vol. VIII, No 42 (November 28, 1956) p.81.

117 Isaac Deutscher, "October Revolution, New Style", *The Reporter*, November 15, 1956.

118 Dwight D. Eisenhower, *Waging Peace*, n. 97, p. 69.

like Zoltan Tildy and Bela Kovac in order to obtain a dispassionate account of the developments. On October 31, before making a nation-wide TV-radio broadcast on the developments in Eastern Europe and West Asia, he learnt about the Soviet declaration of the preceding day about withdrawal of troops from Budapest. Therefore, he was careful enough to express his reactions on these developments so that his statements did not exacerbate the pandemic situation and Nagy's palliative efforts did not go in vein. Allen Dulles commented: "These utterances [Soviet declaration of withdrawal of troops] are one of the most significant to come out of the Soviet Union since the end of World War II" on which President made a soft remark: "Yes, if it is honest".[119] The President remained busy for the whole day working on the preparation of his address toning down Dulles's draft submitted for the purpose.[120] Without leaving any grain for speculation that the United States had been actively backing the uprising and a tangible scope for misconstruction that his Government would come to rescue the rebels and free their country from the Soviet occupation, he told the nation prophetically: "In Eastern Europe there seems to appear the dawn of a new day. It has not been short or easy coming." Expressing his rejoice in "these historic events" he said:

> We cannot, of course, carry out this policy by resort to force. Such force would have been contrary to the best interests of the Eastern European peoples and to the abiding principles of the United Nations. But we did help to keep alive the hope of these peoples for freedom...
>
> And more recently, all the world has been watching dramatic events in Hungary where this brave people, as so often in the past, have offered their very lives for independence from foreign masters. Today, it appears, a new Hungary is rising from this struggle, a Hungary which we hope from our hearts will know full and free nationhood.[121]

---

119 *ibid*, p. 79.

120 Emmet John Huges, *The Ordeal of Power* (New York: Atheneum, 1963) p. 220.

121 *Public Papers of the Presidents, Dwight D. Eisenhower, 1956*, p. 1061.

The optimistic statement of President Eisenhower did not carry any word of material help to those who were carrying on the struggle for freedom from Soviet domination. The President, nonetheless, assured America's "readiness to assist economically the new independent governments of these countries." Noting the Soviet declaration of October 30, he expressed his doubt whether "these avowed purposes will be truly carried out." Approving the content of Dulles's statement made on October 27, the President said:

> We have also – with respect to the Soviet Union – sought clearly remove any false fear that we would look upon new governments in these Eastern European countries as potential military allies. We have no such ulterior purpose. We see these peoples as friends and wish simply that they be friends who are free.[122]

On the very next day, reports pour in to say in unmistakable terms that the Soviet Union had already invaded Hungary with massive military force in a bid to suppress the revolt. The President lost no time to tell the nation that his Government would not respond to the invasion militarily. He declared that the United States:

> would never renounce the concern for these lands and peoples but would not use force in order to free these peoples: We have denounced – before the world forum of the United Nations – the Soviet use of force in its attempt to suppress these peoples' rising. And we have abstained from use of force – knowing it to be contrary to both the interests of these peoples, and to the spirit and methods of the United Nations.[123]

Therefore, on the following day he allocated $20 million from the emergency funds to be "employed for food and other relief for the alleviation of their sufferings". This and offering asylum to several thousand Hungarian escapees in the country were the only concrete steps taken by the United States in the moment of the gravest political crisis in Eastern Europe. Other steps like drawing the attention of the United Nations to the situation in Hungary and writing a letter to Bulganin protesting against the armed invasion were not material.

---

122 *ibid*, p. 1062.
123 *ibid*, pp. 1070-71.

Robert Murphy later on recorded that during the time of Hungarian uprising "everyone in the United States wanted to help the brave Hungarians, and the State Department was inundated with proposals ranging from outright military action to plan welcoming thousands of refugees."[124] The members of the US Congress and Ambassadors pleaded with the State Department for 'action' and some of them were bitter critics of the Administration for its inaction. But Murphy considered that a hasty American action as had been suggested would only "provoke the powerful Soviet armies to further massacre". Bela Fabian, an eminent émigré suggested that the US could have organized a Berlin-type airlift to provide moral and material support to the Hungarians. But such a plea could not be accepted in view of the opposition from Austria to use its air space for such a military operation. Murphy outlined the non-feasibility of such an operation on similar grounds – i.e. other East European countries such as Czechoslovakia, East Germany and Yugoslavia would not have allowed the US military planes to fly over their territories in aid of the Hungarians. Any such move in the teeth of opposition by these countries would have triggered off major military engagement with the Soviet Union, and the war would have proliferated to West European countries. The Yugoslav Ambassador, Leo Mates, pleaded with the State Department to avoid any 'provocation' that might open the preface to a war engulfing entire Europe. He told the State Department that Yugoslavia "was trembling on the thin edge of war against the Soviet Union" and urged that everything needed to be done to confine the conflict within the boundary of Hungary. Murphy commented: "American policy of promoting liberation of captive nations always stopped short of war and this was well known."[125] For all these reasons an American diplomat in Budapest reportedly advised Imre Nagy not to demonstrate

---

124 Robert Murphy, n. 81, p. 429. For details of the possible US action in aid of the Hungarian rebels see US Congress, House, Committee of UN-American Activities, *International Communism (Revolt in Satellites)*, 84th Congress, 2nd Session, 1957.

125 Robert Murhphy, *Diplomat among Warriors*, p. 430.

much friendship with the West as long as the Soviet troops remained in his country.[126]

Although the American President and his Secretary of State found ground to be happy over the anti-Soviet developments in Hungary, the pathetic silence on the part of the Administration after receiving the news of Hungary's withdrawal from the Warsaw Pact, marking the beginning of massive erosion of the Soviet advantage in Eastern Europe, was a clear and ominous premonition of US non-committal approach to the obvious consequence – the massive Soviet invasion of Hungary. President Eisenhower recorded the subsequent events in his autobiography without a word of comment.[127] Allen Dulles gave him an intelligence review of the situation: "The occurrences in Hungary are miracle. They have disapproved that a popular revolt can't occur in the face of modern weapons. Eighty per cent of the Hungarian army defected. Except in Budapest, even the troops have shown no stomach for shooting down Hungarians."[128] Allen Dulles concluded that there was no "strong guiding authority for the rebels; Imre Nagy was failing and the rebels were demanding that he resign." So Allen Dulles found Cardinal Mindszenty as a possible leader. The most pertinent question as to the Nagy's request for the protection of Hungary's neutrality mysteriously slipped out of his consideration. The US Administration did not appear to have taken Nagy seriously. Therefore, it did not do anything to give Nagy a chance to consolidate.

Between October 31 and November 4, the day when the Soviet invasion had begun and the day when the Soviet troops took full control of the situation in Budapest, American media, while reporting the developments in details, expressed grave concern at the Soviet action intended to crush the rebellion and topple the legitimate Government of Imre Nagy, and also at the security of the lives of the common Hungarians. *New York Times* reported on the speedy deployment of Soviet troops,

---

126 Edmund Taylor, "The Lessons on Hungary", *The Reporter*, December 27, 1956.

127 Dwight D. Eisenhower, *Waging Peace*, n. 97, p.81.

128 *ibid,* p. 82.

and the Administration's inability to show its superpower teeth by making movements of the strategic air command.[129] The Secretary of State advanced three arguments against US military response to the Soviet invasion. First, a limited military action by deploying American forces stationed in the southern part of Germany to thwart the invasion would not succeed in view of the presence of the massive Soviet forces in Hungary. Second, a full-scale military operation, an alternative to the first one in aid of the rebel, would invariably, as in the case of the first option, lead to a major and devastating war with the Soviet Union. This too is inconceivable. Third, any Western military action would annihilate rather than save the Hungarians.[130] Therefore, options confined to verbal condemnation of the Soviet intervention and to humanitarian aid for the Hungarian refugee.

Meanwhile on November 3, 1956, John Foster Dulles was hospitalized for an emergency operation and Herbert Hoover Jr. took over as the Acting Secretary of State. Later on, Hoover was criticized for his failure to provide strong leadership during the last and critical phase of the Hungarian Crisis. But the fact remains that Hoover followed the footsteps of Dulles and followed the policy that had been already operationalized by Eisenhower and Dulles – i.e. not to act militarily in response to the Soviet invasion of Hungary.

In Budapest, Imre Nagy was helplessly trying to consolidate his control over the situation and pacifying the rebels to end violence and restore order, and at same time he was attempting to find ways and means to facilitate the withdrawal of the Soviet troops. Meanwhile, the Soviet Ambassador to Hungary Yuri Andrpov gave an ultimatum to Nagy to reverse the renunciation of the Warsaw Pact.[131] Nagy

129 *New York Times*, November 3, 1956.

130 Roscoe Drummond and Gaston Coblentz, *Duel at the Brink*, n. 18, pp. 180-81.

131 Lasky Melvin Jr. (ed), *The Hungarian Revolution*, n. 73, p. 183. Eisenhower wrote in his memoirs that the State Department had received a cable from the British Military Attache informing of Andropov's ultimatum served on Nagy and stating that the latter's failure to honour the ultimatum would follow Soviet bombing on Budapest, see Eisenhower, *Waging Peace*, n. 97, p. 86.

insisted on immediate negotiation for the withdrawal of troops. The Soviet Union instead of paying any heed to his demand, started movement of troops heading towards Hungary. A desperate Nagy sent a message to the UN Secretary General, Dag Hammarskjold, on November 2, informing him of the movement of Soviet troops and requested for the second time to extend UN protection for Hungary's neutrality:

> I request Your Excellency to call upon to recognize the neutrality of Hungary and ask the Security Council to instruct the Soviet and Hungarian Governments to start negotiation immediately.[132]

On the next day the Soviet Union agreed to start negotiation on troops withdrawal. A mixed committee comprising the Soviet and Hungarian representatives decided to meet at late hours of November 2. The Soviet delegation promised that "no further trains carrying troops will cross the Hungarian frontier."[133] The mixed committee met accordingly as scheduled. The discussions were suddenly interrupted by a Soviet security police officer, Ivan Serov, who arrested the Hungarian delegation including the Defence Minister Pal Maletor. On that fateful night Soviet military units made the heaviest assault on Hungary. It did not take time for the Soviet army to crush the rebellion. Whatever resistance the Hungarian army having allegiance to Nagy could offer against the invasion lasted for only a few hours.[134] Nagy announced at the early morning[135] hours of November 4 about the fresh Soviet invasion:

> Today at daybreak Soviet forces started an attack against our capital, obviously with the intention to overthrow the legal Hungarian democratic Government. Our troops are fighting. The Government is in place. I notify the people of our country and the entire world of this fact.

---

132 *UN Document S/3726*, November 2, 1956.

133 Lasky Melvin J. *The Hungarian Revolution*, p. 220.

134 J.G. Rkei and M. Horvath, *Soviet Military Intervention in Hungary, 1956*, n. 76, pp. 22-28.

135 *ibid*, p. 228. Also see Peter Fryer, *Hungarian Tragedy: And other Writings on the 1956 Hungarian Revolution* (London: Index Books, 1997).

Then began frantic appeals for help over Radio Kossuth. *New York Times* and other newspapers published on the next day the reports collected by the Associated Press about the SOS message of the rebels. Meanwhile, in a few hours following Nagy's announcement, Janos Kadar formed the Hungarian Revolutionary Workers' Peasant Government with the Soviet backing.

The State Department got the news of the fresh Soviet military action in Hungary at the daybreak of November 4 and the matter was immediately communicated to the US representative in the UN for taking up the issue with the Security Council. Meanwhile, President Eisenhower hurriedly wrote to Bulganin expressing shock at the Soviet attack and urged upon him to withdraw troops from Hungary.[136] Bulganin's reply to Eisenhower did not pay importance to the events in Hungary. As a passing reference, he wrote: "I feel urged to state that the problem of withdrawal of Soviet troops from Hungary touched therein comes completely and entirely under the competence of the Hungarian and Soviet governments."[137] However, Bulganin's letter paid more emphasis on the Suez War and requested Eisenhower to join hands with the USSR to stop fighting in West Asia.[138] The White House statement on the letter of Bulganin was quite sharp and considered it as "an obvious attempt to divert world attention from the Hungarian tragedy."[139]

In conformity with the position to avoid any direct military confrontation with the Soviet Union for a cause where there was no involvement of basic American interests also to accentuate America's avoidance of any provocation that might cause further trouble leading to the massacre of civilians in Hungary, Eisenhower made humanitarian gesture. It is interesting to note that his concern for Poland (although there was neither any invasion of Poland nor was any violent

---

136 Department of State, *Bulletin,* November 19, 1956, p. 796.

137 *Documents on American Foreign Relations, 1956*, p. 260.

138 Department of State, *Bulletin*, November 19, 1956, pp. 796-797.

139 *ibid*, p. 795.

suppression of the Polish people) preceded his sympathy for the Hungarians. He said:

> . . . our hearts have gone to the people of Poland, and to Hungary, and we shall have given the promise, not only that we shall never forget them dear in our hearts, but we have made offers of economic help – food, shelter, clothing, medicines – which we sincerely hope they may be able to accept.[140]

Later on Robert Murphy ruefully recollected: "In the end, our government was reduced to the minimal policy of providing assistance to Hungarian refugees, and to impact on world opinion – whatever they may mean. On the assumption that the American people did not desire to go to war against the Soviet Union, and in Washington it was believed that they did not, there seemed no other policy to pursue."[141] Vice-President Richard Nixon made a trip to Austria to make a full assessment of the problems of Hungarian escapees and to report to the President and to the US Congress on the scope of "what is necessary and practicable and to recommend what further steps should be taken by the United States for the relief of this suffering."[142] Nixon's report was quite revealing. He wrote that it was not possible to make any accurate estimate of what could be the number of refugees and the United States would not put a ceiling of what it could do in fulfilling its "traditional mission of providing a haven of refugee for the victims of oppression."[143] He reported that already 155,000 refugees had been rehabilitated in Austria, 15,000 had gone over to the United States, 73,000 had been settled in different countries, and 37,000 wanted to be rehabilitated in some other countries. Nixon felt satisfied at the Hungarian uprising. To him it sounded "the death knell of international communism". He further wrote in the report ". . . we are not dealing with the basic question of how freedom is to be provided for Hungary. Compliance of the USSR with the resolution of the United

---

140 *Public Papers of the Presidents: Dwight D. Eisenhower, 1956*, p. 1084.

141 Robert Murphy, *Diplomat among Warriors*, p. 431.

142 *ibid*, December 24 and 31, 1956, p. 979.

143 *ibid*, January 21, 1957, p. 95.

Nations calling for the removal of the Soviet troops from Hungary is only adequate and permanent solution to the Hungarian problem."[144] Meanwhile, President Eisenhower announced that his country would offer asylum to 21,000 Hungarian escapees. The US Legation in Budapest offered asylum to Cardinal Mindszenty. This, as Murphy commented, cannot be regarded as a "glorious position for the United States."[145] However, the White House statement on granting the asylum concluded that this step gave "practical effect to the American People's intense desire to help the victims of Soviet oppression."[146] Murphy is right in expressing resentment at the inglorious gesture of a great power with matchless resources which propagated liberation of Eastern Europe. It was not a highly acclaimed step if one compares the American help in rehabilitating the Hungarian escapees with that of the one extended by Austria.

US ROLE IN THE UNITED NATIONS

As indicated earlier, on October 24, the Hungarian Government requested the Soviet Union to provide military assistance to quell the uprising in Budapest. While doing so, it invoked the Warsaw Treaty which provided for mutual help in case of foreign attack. Article 4 of the Treaty states that in the event of armed attack on any of the signatories, immediate mutual assistance including the use of armed forces of the other members of the Treaty would be provided in accordance with the spirit of "collective self defense embodied in Article 51" of the UN Charter, and the Security Council should be advised of the "measures taken on the basis of the present article." It also notes: "These measures shall be adopted as soon as the Security Council has taken the necessary measures for resorting and upholding international peace and security." The implication, thus, is that as soon as the Hungarian Government had requested the Soviet Union for military assistance, the matter should have been tabled on the floor of the Security Council in the form of information about the

---

144 *ibid*, p. 95.

145 Robert Murphy, *Diplomat among Warriors*, p. 431.

146 Department of State, *Bulletin*, December 10, 1956, p. 913.

actions taken. It appears that no one in the Security Council was either aware of the implications of Article 4 or took note of it seriously.[147] As a result the Hungarian question came for discussion only on October 27 when the representatives of France, the United Kingdom and the United States called for a meeting of the Security Council on the issue in pursuance of Article 34 of the Charter. Meanwhile, there had been a heavy pressure on the members of the Security Council to condemn and stop the Soviet invasion on the basis of Article 2 paragraph 4 of the Charter.[148] The Security Council sat to discuss the crisis despite strong protest of the Soviet representative and the Hungarian delegate. Soon the debate was postponed indefinitely in view of the Soviet declaration of October 30 and the negotiation between the Soviet and the Hungarian Governments for the withdrawal of troops. There were, however, requests from different countries such as Argentina, Austria, Ireland, Italy, Spain, Thailand and Turkey favouring UN action on the Hungarian crisis.[149] The general opinion in retrospection was that the UN functionaries should have rushed to Budapest to study the situation. Hammarskjold, however, argued: "There was certainly not a single member of the Security Council who at that stage felt that the situation was clear enough to make such a proposal or felt that it was a good idea to send the Secretary General away."[150]

As the Soviet troops rumbled through the streets of Budapest, Nagy informed the UN of the decision of his Government to withdraw from the Warsaw Treaty Organization and sought its protection of Hungarian neutrality, besides of course, requesting him to place the matter of the Soviet military incursion in the General Assembly session scheduled for November 22. The message communicated by Nagy in the early hours of November 1 came over to the UN teleprinter and was immediately placed before the office of the Secretary General. But Dag Hammarskjold was away for

---

147 For some analysis on this matter see DeWitt Copp and Marshal Peck, *Betrayal at the UN* (New York: Devin-Adair, 1961) p.80.

148 *New York Times*, October 26, 1956.

149 *UN Document S/3692-S/3699.*

150 J.P. Lash, *Dag Hammarskjold* (London: Cassell, 1962) p. 92.

lunch. Therefore, it did not reach him immediately. Consequently, no action even in the form of issuing a statement could be taken on an urgent basis.[151] In the mean time the second message reached the UN headquarters requesting the Secretary General to place the Hungarian crisis in a special session of the General Assembly to be convened on November 1 in which "Mr. Janos Szabo, First Secretary of the Permanent Mission, will represent Hungarian People's Republic".[152] The second message carried the gravity and urgency of the situation. At the same time it implied that the Hungarian Government was not interested in any discussion in the Security Council because of the obviousness of the application of a veto by the Soviet Union to stall any resolution favouring the protection of Hungary's neutrality and withdrawal of Soviet troops. The Secretary General did not try to understand the implication of the second appeal nor did he contact the Hungarian Government to get the full details of the situation, although the teleprinter was still operating. Except the Cuban delegate Elmilio Nunez Portuondo, no one seemed to be considering seriously the appeals coming from Nagy. The Cuban representative wanted that the Hungarian situation be tabled in the special session of the General Assembly scheduled for 5 pm of November 1. But this special session was convened to take up the Suez War only. He realized the problem, and therefore, wanted that an extraordinary session of the Assembly should be held under "Uniting for Peace Resolution" and urged that the Assembly could discuss the crisis by a two-thirds vote.[153] The Security Council had already taken up the matter but subsequently adjourned the discussion on October 28 with the hope that a settlement would be forthcoming out of the Soviet-Hungarian discussion. At that time Portuondo argued that there was no point in continuing the debate in the Security Council in view of impending exercise of Soviet veto, and therefore, the matter of Hungarian crisis should be referred

151 DeWitt Copp and Marshall Peck, *Betrayal at the UN*, n. 147, p. 83.

152 *ibid*, p. 84.

153 For detailed narration of the historic events see Gorden Gaskill, "Time Table of a Failure", *The Virginia Quarterly Review*, Vol. 34, No. 2 (Spring: 1958) pp. 162-190; and for Portuondo's contention see p. 170.

to the General Assembly under "Uniting for Peace Resolution". Although the first message of Nagy to the United Nations contained the request to take up the Hungarian situation and to extend its protection of Hungary's neutrality in the forthcoming session of the General Assembly, the second appeal was more categorical as it urged upon the Secretary General to place the Soviet invasion in the special session of the General Assembly on November 1. There was, therefore, no confusion as to the urgency of the matter and as to whether a special session of the Assembly was needed for discussion, and even if there was, it could have been settled by the Secretary General by contacting Budapest.

It was a moment of history when the General Assembly had been discussing the Suez War. The 'four great powers' were not certain about the best course the United Nations could take to deal with the Hungarian crisis. Two of these great powers, Britain and France, were preoccupied with the Suez War. Confusion still persisted as to whether the Security Council should resume its adjourned discussion of October 28 or should the matter be placed in the emergency special session of the General Assembly. The State Department did not have any confirmed report on the situation in Hungary because of the disruption of the contact with the American Legation in Budapest, and therefore, had reasons to believe that the reports now available on November 1 and 2 about massive Soviet invasion were "a bit exaggerated".[154] The 'Cassandra Club', which was formed with leading Hungarian exiles, in collaboration with some of the functionaries of the UN Secretariat, tried to pursue the matter of UN protection of Hungary's neutrality, and met Secretary Dulles who had come to New York to address the emergency special session of the General Assembly on the Suez war, with a hope that Dulles, as the principal exponent of liberation of Eastern Europe, would steer discussions in the world body towards adopting a suitable course of action in stopping the Soviet invasion. But the Suez War continued to gain priority in the Assembly and in the agenda of all the big powers including he United States, because of the direct involvement of two of America's great

154 *ibid*, pp. 172-173.

allied, Britain and France, and also because of the strong Afro-Asian lobby which wanted immediate termination of the War in West Asia. Further, the Suez War was already in the single item agenda of the special session of the General Assembly. Any attempt to give precedence to the Hungarian crisis over the War in West Asia would have antagonized the Afro-Asian delegates whose strength is overwhelming in the Assembly. Dulles was aware of the compulsions he had to face in the teeth of bitterness in the rift between Britain and the United States over the Suez crisis, and therefore, did not want to divert the UN attention from Suez War to Hungary.[155] That is why in his initial speech in the first sitting of the emergency special session of the General Assembly, he did not make any reference to the Hungarian crisis.[156] Dag Hammarskjold later on recollected:

> If you disregard all other aspects and look at the time sequence, I think it is perfectly clear to you that Suez had a time priority on the thinking and the policy-making of the main body in the UN. That was not their choice. It was history itself, so to say, which arranged it that way.[157]

Everyone, including Dulles, had no option but to cast priority on the Suez War, because, the special emergency session of the General Assembly had been convened for this specific purpose. Just before the commencement of the second sitting of the session of the General Assembly at 10:00 pm on the same day, November 1, a decision was taken to wait and see till the voting on the Suez crisis was over. While the debates over the Suez War was going on in the second session, a member of 'Cassandra Club' circulated among the delegates of the United Nations the copies of a dispatch of the Reuter which had given the news of the Soviet invasion. At 3:30 am of November 2, the General Assembly adopted a resolution censuring France, Israel and the United Kingdom for their combined invasion of Egypt, condemning the aggression and

---

155 Peter G. Boyle, "The Hungarian Revolution and the Suez Crisis", *History*, Vol. 90, October 2005, pp. 550-565.

156 United Nations General Assembly, *Official Records*, 561st meeting (First Emergency Special Session), 1956.

157 Quoted in J.P. *Lash, Dag Hammarskjold*, p. 93.

demanding the withdrawal of their troops from the territory of Egypt. Immediately, the Italian delegate rose on a point of order to draw the attention of the Assembly to Nagy's appeal: "I hope the United Nations – and, if necessary, the special session - will immediately take whatever is possible with regard to the request of the Hungarian people."[158] Dulles supported the move:

> I hope this mater, which is on the agenda, of the Security Council will be kept urgently before it and we shall not be pre-occupied with the Middle East to the exclusion of the state of Hungary to regain its independence.[159]

But the emergency special session did not take up the Hungarian issue on a technical ground that it had been convened to take up the Suez War. Instead of convening a fresh special emergency meeting of the Assembly, the Western powers immediately pressed for an urgent meeting of the Security Council with the full knowledge that this was a pointless exercise in view of inevitable and impending Soviet veto. At any rate, the Security Council met at 5:00 pm on November 2 and took up the adjourned agenda of October 28. It was quite appalling to see that the members including Henry Cabot Lodge Jr. were more engrossed with a less important issue i.e. the credentials of Janos Szabo, and spent the first hour in a useless and acrimonious debate on it rather than taking up the most vitally important issue - the contention of Nagy's appeal – protection of Hungary's neutrality. Henry Cabot Lodge Jr. demanded that the credentials of Janos Szabo had to be presented within 24 hours.[160] The Iranian delegate Nazrollah Entezam, however, observed that the Council's meeting was convened in a short notice and it would not be possible for a country to submit the credentials within 24 hours. The US representative made a passing reference to Nagy's appeal for UN protection but remained silent about the *modus*

158 United Nations, General Assembly, *Official Records*, 561st meeting, 1956 p. 35.

159 *ibid*, p. 39.

160 United Nations, Security Council, *Official Records*, 752 meeting, 1956, pp. 2-3.

operandi for extending a helping hand to Hungary towards realization of the objective. He said:

> Hungary sent an urgent communication to the Secretary General of the United Nations, which has now been documented and circulated to all the members...it is requested the inclusion in the agenda of the General Assembly of the Hungarian Government's neutrality and the defense of the neutrality by four Great powers.[161]

He said that the situation in Hungary was "so confused" that a true representative of Hungary could help the Security Council get a clear picture of the crisis. Lodge seemed to be unprepared for moving a resolution on the Hungarian question, of course, any such step would be doomed by the Soviet veto. He took pride of America's humanitarian gesture of offering $20 million in surplus food-stuff and medical aid. He concluded, "we in the United States want to do everything we can to ensure that Hungarian people shall not have to suffer in the winter which lies ahead of us."[162] Undoubted this falls far short of what was expected from the protagonist of liberation policy.

In the second meeting of the Security Council, the Soviet representative Arkady A. Sobolev accused the Western powers of diverting the gravity of the combined aggression committed by three powers on Egypt to an internal problem in Hungary. He tried to convince that the dialogue among the members of Soviet-Hungarian negotiation group was in progress and at that stage the Council should refrain from interfering in the matter. Meanwhile, the second letter of Nagy addressed to Dag Hammarskjold confirming the Soviet invasion of Hungary reached the UN and its copies were circulated among the members of the Security Council. As stated already it contained Nagy's declaration of his country's withdrawal from the Warsaw Treaty Organization and his appeal for the UN protection of Hungary's neutrality. It also urged upon the Security Council to "instruct the Soviet-Hungarian Governments to start the negotiations immediately."[163]

---

161 *ibid*, p. 9.

162 *ibid*, p. 23.

163 For details see *UN Documents, S/3726*, November 2, 1956.

Paradoxically enough, the United States agreed to have an adjournment of the meeting till 3:00 pm of the following day. The members of the Council apparently felt satisfied at the arguments of the Soviet representative and decided to wait and see the developments in Hungary. It was also expected that the Secretary General would be able to obtain the credentials of Janos Szabo before the Council reassembled at 3:00 pm on November 3 as scheduled. The approach to temporize a decision in the Security Council was an unwitting move to circumvent the crisis to the advantage of the Soviet Union.

Meanwhile, the Secretary General reported to the Council that he had obtained Szabo's credentials. The Security Council sat as scheduled at 3:00 pm on November 3 for the third time to discuss the Hungarian crisis. Lodge requested Szabo to give the details of the contention of Nagy to the Secretary General to whom he made a request once against to "get in touch with the Hungarian Government in order that this Council know facts." He submitted a draft resolution urging the USSR "to stop intervening, particularly armed intervention, in the internal affairs of Hungary and to make necessary arrangements with the Hungarian Government to withdraw all Soviet forces from Hungary without delay." The resolution urged upon the Secretary General to "investigate on an urgent basis the need of Hungarian people for food and medicine and other supplies and to report to the Security Council as soon as possible."[164] In the letter to the UN, Nagy did not ask for food and medicine. The need of the hour was UN protection of Hungary's neutrality. The Hungarian representative reported that the negotiations between his Government and the Soviet representatives on the withdrawal of Soviet troops had been in progress and the two sides would again meet at 10:00 pm. The Yugoslav delegate, Joza Brilej, requested an adjournment of the Security Council meeting till the outcome of the negotiation reached the Council. At the initial stage Sir Ronald Walker, Australian representative to the United Nations, was not in favour of the adjournment and urged for an UN action.

164 *UN Document, S/3730*, November 3, 1956.

Finally, he too agreed to the consensus for a wait and see approach. He, however, observed that the negotiation between the two governments might not be conducted on the basis of equality and respect for human rights. The British and the French representatives wanted the adoption of the American draft. Strangely enough, Lodge appeared to have taken a soft stand. He said:

> We believe . . . that adjournment for a day or two would give a real opportunity to the Hungarian Government to carry out its announced desire to arrange for an orderly and immediate withdrawal of Soviet troops.[165]

Sir Walker proposed that the Council should sit on the very next day, i.e. November 4, but Lodge wanted further postponement. Finally, as per the suggestion of the President of the Council, it was decided to reconvene the meeting on November 6. M.de Guiringaud of France supported Walker's plea but unable to pursue his position further he suggested that the Council should reserve its right to convene an emergency session of the Council on a short notice. The delay in responding to Nagy's request for UN and great power's protection of Hungary's neutrality was quite atrocious. Victor Zorza wrote: "By delaying its reply, even a day, the West is making easier for Moscow. It is, in effect, countenancing the march of Soviet troops in Budapest."[166]

It is understandable that Lodge did not act on his own in facilitating the postponement of the Security Council's meeting till November 6. Also it is difficult to comprehend the rationale behind such a palliative position taken by the US Administration. There was strong criticism of Lodge's alleged cooperation with Sobolev in agreeing to an unwarranted postponement of the Security Council which eventually facilitated the Soviet stranglehold of Hungary. Lodge later on replied:

> At that particular time, Washington could not be sure of all the facts of the situation. . . . Washington was confronting

---

165 United Nations, Security Council, *Official Records*, 753rd Meeting, November 3, 1956, p. 11.

166 Victor Zorza, *Manchester Guardian*, November 3, 1956.

> these things: Suez crisis; a fog of uncertainty about events in Hungary; and very real possibility of clash with the Soviet Union – with the world shattering consequences which this could entail.[167]

It is quite palpable that any move by the United States for formally taking a resolution condemning Soviet military incursion into Hungary and demanding the withdrawal of troops would have been frustrated by an obvious Soviet veto. That was the precise result of such a move on November 7. It might not appear sensible to argue that the adjournment of the engagement of the Security Council in the Hungarian crisis would have expedited the smooth withdrawal of Soviet forces from Hungary in view of the fact that there was remotest possibility of such a step from Moscow which would have led to the weakening the Soviet *status quo* in Eastern Europe. It was unbelievable that Moscow would allow this to happen at a time when the Cold War was at its height and the United States was accelerating the process of strengthening the Western defence system against the Soviet Union. At the same time it was an utter travesty of fact to argue, keeping the text of the second appeal from Nagy to the UN, that there was "a fog of uncertainty" about the events in Hungary; and that the US Administration was unaware of the Soviet troops movement in Hungary. The real reason for the adjournment of the debates in the Security Council is that the US wanted to circumvent a possible confrontation with the Soviet Union, which would imperil the US Security arrangements in Western Europe. All this restrained the US representative from actively advocating for the UN protection of Hungarian neutrality.

As stated already, while the General Assembly was busy with the Suez War, at 5:19 am (Hungarian time) of November 4, Prime Minister Nagy notified to his countrymen and the world that the Soviet troops had launched attack on his country "with the intention to overthrow the legal Hungarian democratic Government." The Radio announcement was conveyed to the United Nations by Reuters and to the rest of the world. Naturally, the Government and the people of the

---

167 Imre Kovacs (ed), *Facts about Hungary: The Fight for Freedom* (New York: Hungarian Committee, 1956) p. 209.

United States were not unaware of the announcement. Some of the Hungarian émigrés led by Msqr Varga tried to meet Ambassador Lodge at the premises of the United Nations but their entry was refused. Despite the strong plea of Sir Walker for an emergency special session of the Security Council, Lodge was not in favour of it and suggested that the meeting could be convened on the following day. At 1:00 am (New York time) Sir Walker interrupted the debates in the General Assembly and requested for an immediate meeting of the Security Council.[168] After the adjournment of the General Assembly which debated on the Suez War at 3:35 am the special session of the Security Council was possible.

As the Hungarian rebels fought desperately against the Soviet army, the Associated Press Bureau in Vienna was receiving frantic calls for Western help. Such calls continued till 10.50 am (Hungarian time) when the teleprinter line was snapped. Under the mounting pressure from Australian delegate in the United Nations, the US Ambassador initiated the discussion in the Security Council. But by that time the situation in Hungary had become quite hopeless; the Soviet troops were on the way to attain full control of the situation. Still the rebels continued to believe that the United Nations would do something.[169] Ambassador Lodge attempted in vain to pass a resolution in the Security Council condemning the Soviet Union for its invasion of Hungary and demanding its withdrawal from that country. With no UN action in sight to restrain the advancing Soviet troops, the protesting participants in the Council merely indulged in emotional bickering. Ambassador Lodge did not stand on an exception. With a high dose of emotion he said that by their "heroic sacrifice" the people of Hungary had given the United Nations a brief moment "to mobilize the conscience of the world". He said: "We are seizing that moment, and we shall not fail you."[170] He sidetracked

---

168 United Nations, General Assembly, *Official Records*, 564th meeting (First Emergency Special Session), 1956, pp. 69-71.

169 Lasky Melvin J., *The Hungarian Revolution*, n. 73, pp. 240-241.

170 United Nations, Security Council, *Official Records*, 754th meeting, 1956, pp. 1-3

the main issue – Nagy's frantic appeal for UN protection of Hungary's neutrality. He introduced a slightly modified resolution expressing anxiousness "to see the independence and sovereignty of Hungary respected", calling upon the USSR to desist from the invasion, to cease the introduction of additional forces and to withdraw forthwith all its forces from Hungary. The resolution requested the Secretary General to supply urgently needed food and medicine to the people of Hungary.[171] The motion, as every one could guess, was vetoed by the USSR. Immediately,. Lodge called for an emergency special session of the General Assembly under the "Uniting for Peace Resolution" (the USSR's being the only dissenting vote and Yugoslavia abstaining).[172] Despite Sobolev's vehement protest against the inclusion of the Hungarian situation on the agenda, the special session of the Assembly took up the matter for discussion. This time, when the Soviet troops took over the governance of Hungary and nothing could be done in aid of Nagy as well as the rebels, Ambassador Lodge found clarity of the situation. He expressed surprise at the sudden change in the Hungarian life under the leadership of Prime Minister Nagy whom the leaders of East European countries like Poland and Hungary had hailed a few days back as a sincere communist and now were vocal in branding him as "an accomplice of reactionary forces." He argued that this change of attitude was mainly due to Nagy's attempt to be independent of Moscow. He pleaded: "We must take drastic and decisive action here in this Assembly to answer the appeal of the Hungarian Government", but such actions meant unrealistic call for withdrawal of troops and constitution of an UN ineffective investigation committee to inquiry into the situation in Hungary. He called upon the Governments of Hungary and the Soviet Union to permit observers designated by the Secretary General to enter Hungary and travel freely

171 *UN Document S/3730.*

172 United Nations, Security Council, *Official Records*, 754th meeting, 1956, pp.10-13. Brzezinski argues that Yugoslavia had a deal with the Kadar Government to sacrifice Nagy and therefore decided to abstain from voting, See his *Soviet Bloc*, n. 15, p. 234. Also see *New York Times*, November 5, 1956.

therein. After a slight amendment to the draft submitted by Lodge, the resolution was adopted by 58 to 8 votes with 15 abstentions.[173] The long resolution had two parts: (i) the General Assembly condemned the Soviet invasion, demanded withdrawal of Soviet troops, no time limit was set notwithstanding the overwhelming support for the immediate withdrawal; and (ii) the Secretary General was requested to institute an inquiry committee to investigate into the Hungarian situation. Although the first part of the resolution could not be implemented, the second part, however, was materialized in a limited form.

The United States heavily depended upon the United Nations to mobilize world opinion against the Soviet invasion of Hungary. The Eisenhower Administration thought that on the lines of the General Assembly resolution, the Secretary General would take appropriate measures to send observers to Hungary and take steps to institute an inquiry committee to investigate into the Hungarian crisis. Notwithstanding the urgency of the matter and concern expressed on the floor of the General Assembly, no tangible UN action within the framework of the resolution was initiated between the period from November 4 to 8 i.e. from the adoption of the resolution to the second sitting of the special emergency session. Dag Hammarskjold apologized for this stunning inaction and promised to take steps towards the implementation of the resolution.[174] Later on Miklas Molnar wrote: "We only know that the Secretary General abstained from taking any action in favour of the Hungarian Government which appealed to him to protect Hungary's neutrality."[175] Similarly, the US Government too appeared conspicuous by not pressurizing the Secretary General to take steps towards implementation of the resolution.

On November 8, the General Assembly sat for a second emergency session. A five-power resolution submitted by Cuba,

---

173 *UN Document A/3284.*

174 *New York Times*, November 8, 1956.

175 Miklos Molnar, *Budapest 1956: A History of Hungarian Revolution* (London: George Allen & Unwin, 1968) p. 211.

Ireland, Italy, Pakistan and Peru called upon the USSR to withdraw its troops from Hungary immediately and requested the Secretary General to start investigation into the Hungarian situation.[176] On the next day, the US Ambassador made an emotional statement in support of the five-power resolution. He said:

> It is some measure of deep sadness which is in our hearts that the speeches here have had some of the quality of funeral orations. I say 'some' because, however sad we are, we cannot believe that this in fact is the end of Hungarian independence. We refuse to admit that the glorious dead of these past weeks have died in vain.[177]

Carefully avoiding the principal aspect of the Hungarian request, lodge introduced a resolution demanding the immediate withdrawal of Soviet troops and calling upon the USSR and the Hungarian authorities not to interfere in the distribution of food and medical supplies to the affected people.[178] Simultaneously, a humanitarian resolution was also moved by Austria urging international cooperation in the extending relief materials to the Hungarian people, which was adopted by 67-0 votes and 8 abstentions.[179]

By the time the General Assembly adopted these resolutions the situation in Hungary came under full control of the Soviet backed Hungarian authorities. An alternative to Nagy's Government was installed headed by Janos Kadar. Therefore, there was virtually no other move at the disposal of the United Nations to deal with the situation. The United Nations did not have any resources to flush out the Soviet troops to protect Hungary's neutrality. Similarly, the United States too did not have any intention to risk a war against the Soviet Union in aid of the rebels. Naturally, no one tried, not

176 The five power resolution was adopted on November 9 by a vote of 48 to 11 and 16 abstentions. See United Nations, General Assembly, *Official Records*, Second Emergency Special Session, Supplement No. 1, (A3355), pp.2-3.

177 United Nations, General Assembly, *Official Records*, 570th meeting, Second Emergency Special Session, 1956, p. 47.

178 *ibid*, (A/3355).

179 *ibid*, p. 3.

even the US Ambassador, to make any futile exercise by urging upon the United Nations to protect Hungary's neutrality. However, the members of the Security Council noted with concern the non-action at the crucial time from November 1 and 4. For example, M. de Guiringaud of France said that the Security Council took more than a week (from October 28 to November 4) to merely decide on a resolution, which was to be frustrated by Soviet veto. The General Assembly took five days to pass a resolution. On November 4, the matter was transferred from the Security Council to the General Assembly after the Soviet Union had cast a veto on the draft resolution tabled by the United States. The Assembly adopted a resolution on the crisis on November 9. The entire process was frightenly and disdainfully slow and sluggish as though it was premeditated to allow the Soviet invasion to go unopposed even verbally. He lamented: "It is as though we were waiting for a whole nation to be finally crushed before issuing a death certificate".[180]

By November 4, it was quite evident that the Hungarian crisis lost its urgency as the United Nations adopted a policy to wait and see. This was mainly due to the stand taken by the US Ambassador who favoured the postponement of the session of the Security Council. The American public could notice ruefully the oblique position of indecision. Therefore, Adlai Stevension, who had contested the 1952 Presidential election with the Democratic ticket, lost no time to send a cable to the President on November 4 requesting him to act immediately in order to 'activate the Peace Observation Commission' which had been created in 1950 under the 'Uniting for Peace Resolution'. This would make it possible for the United Nations to mobilize a large team of official observers and fly to Hungary to take stock of the situation there. The Eisenhower Administration rejected the idea for obvious reasons of impracticability. It shared the dilemma of Hammaskjold in concentrating UN attention on Suez crisis due to the direct involvement of two permanent members of the Security Council and thus relegating the issue of Soviet invasion of Hungary to a lost case. The US Government was

180 *ibid*, p. 47.

ensconced with its position of inaction and belittled the concern expressed by the media and the leading personalities. Almost all the leading newspapers carried the stories of the Soviet invasion with a sense of grave concern to convey the message that the Soviet action would create a precedence, which would have a far-reaching impact on the future of Soviet sphere of influence. Hammarskjold later on recollected: "On the 4th I had in my hand a request for a report of on UNEF within 48 hours. I do not think that the General Assembly would have asked me to do that and at the same time check what was going on in Budapest. They could not have done it."[181]

On November 10, the United States moved a resolution favouring the transfer of Hungarian question to the forthcoming eleventh regular session of the General Assembly. Virtually there ended, except of course the investigative role, the UN action in responding to the Hungarian crisis. The Secretary General made a futile attempt to send UN observers to Hungary in order to obtain a first hand and detailed information of the situation.[182] Ambassador Lodge later on tried to give explanation as to why the United Nations could not go beyond the paltry investigative role. He argued that while Britain and France decided to withdraw from the Suez, showed respect for the UN resolution and thus abjured the military option, the Soviet Union was not prepared to take recourse to an identical course of action. Moscow's intransigent position was heavily fortified with military consequences, which forestalled any measure to send UN troops to protect Hungary's neutrality. He said: "If you send an extraordinary force into Hungary, you'd simply making the whole situation worse and running the risk of a new war."[183] The United States and the rest of the world had no doubt about it, and therefore, preferred to pay more importance to the secondary issues and not the core one.

181 Richard I. Miller, *Dag Hammarskjold and Crisis in Diplomacy* (New York: Oceana, 1961) p. 139.

182 For details of an account of Hammarskjold's attempt to implement the UN mandate for the investigation of the crisis, see Leon Gordenkar, *The UN Secretary General and the Maintenance of Peace* (New York: Colombia University Press, 1967) pp. 204-210.

183 *New York Herald Tribune*, November 17, 1956.

On November 5, Anna Kethly, a member of the former Social Democratic Party, arrived in New York and claimed to be the special representative of Nagy's Government[184] and thus challenged position of Janos Szabo who had been holding onto his credentials. The UN could not take cognizance of her claim, for, she did not carry with her any credential letter. The matter was further complicated by the arrival of Imre Hovath, the Foreign Minister of the Kadar Government in New York on November 13 to head the Hungarian delegation. It implied that the new Hungarian Government had withdrawn the credentials of Janos Szabo. An informal committee of Latin-American representatives in the United Nations explored the possibility of challenging the credentials of both Szabo and Hovath. The United States reportedly initiated a move to give Kethly a hearing at the United Nations if some other countries were willing to extend support to it. In the absence of a concentrated move to back up Anna Kethly, the representatives of Cuba, France and the United States demanded the expulsion of the Hungarian delegation. On December 6, Ambassador Lodge distributed among the delegates a statement containing a proposal of the UN action to be taken against the Hungarian delegation led by Imre Hovath. In response to it, a seventeen-power meeting decided to adopt a strategy of wait and see till the recommendation of the Credential Committee which had been asked to examine the validity of Hovath's delegation were made available. On February 21, 1957, the General Assembly decided to accept the recommendation of the Credential Committee not to take any decision on the Hungarian delegation sent by the new Government implying thereby that the United Nations would neither admit the claim of Anna Kethly nor at the same time would accord recognition to Hungarian delegation led by Hovath. The formal recognition of the Kadar Government's delegation was withheld till 1963. The delay was effectively caused by the United States. In 1963 the State Department informed the House Foreign Affairs Committee and the Senate Foreign Relations Committee that a general amnesty was granted by the Kadar Government to

---

184 DeWitt Copp and Marshall Peck, *Betrayal at the UN*, p. 97 and *New York Times*, November 13, 1956.

all the political prisoners, an action well received by the West and there had been effective de-Stalinization in Hungary.[185] The State Department viewed the development in Hungary "objectively and in proper perspective". In view of this, it felt that it would not be possible to delay further the question of formal recognition of the credentials of the Hungarian delegation due to lack of sufficient support, and therefore, the United Stated did not block the Credential Committee's unanimous recommendation favouring recognition of the Hungarian delegation to the United Nations.[186]

Close on the heels of Soviet invasion and replacement of a legitimate Government of Hungary headed by Nagy, another humanitarian crisis was brought up by the Cuban representative, Elimilio Nunez Portuondo, alleging that thousands of Hungarians had been allegedly deported by the Soviet army. The US Ambassador promptly extended his support to a resolution moved by Portuondo condemning such a inhuman action. In the General Assembly, Lodge charged the Soviet Foreign Minister, Drimiti Shepilov, that as many as 16,000 Hungarians had been deported from their motherland. It was alleged that the act of deportation continued till November 14, 1956. Seven days later, the General Assembly adopted three resolutions. The first resolution sponsored by Cuba [Resolution No. 1127(xi)] urged upon the Soviet Union to take immediate steps to "cease the deportation of Hungarian citizens and to return promptly to their homes those who have been deported." The second one sponsored by Cylon (present Sri Lanka), India and Indonesia [Resolution 1128(xi)] called upon the Hungarian Government to permit the entry of the UN observers into Hungary "without any prejudice to its sovereignty". The third Resolution 1129(xi) sponsored by

---

185 For the transcription of the report of the State Department issued on May 9, 1963 see "Report on the Changing Situation in Hungary", *Congressional Record*, 88th Congress, 1st session, May 15, 1963, p. 8646.

186 The "Report of the Changing Congressional Situation in Hungary" was referred to as the basis for various Congressional and public inquiries made during the second half of 1963. For some of the representative comments of the US Congressmen see *Congressional Record*, 88th Congress, 1st session, 1963, pp. 10208 and 11218.

Argentina, Denmark and the USA dealt with smooth facilitation of relief operation.[187] On November 30 Dag Hammarskjold reported to the United Nations that the Hungarian Government did not respond favourably to his request for the admission of the UN observers into the its country. In this connection he had received a letter from V. Kuznetsov, Chairman of the Soviet delegation at the eleventh session of the General Assembly stating that the "allegations of deportation of Hungarian citizens to the USSR are based on slanderous rumors."[188] On December 1, 1956 Hungary informed the Secretary General that it would not admit the UN observers to investigate into its internal affairs but he would be welcomed at a later date.[189] But strangely enough, as the Secretary General prepared his visit to Hungary for a few days beginning December 16, Hungary refused to accept him.[190] A couple of days earlier, on December 4, the United States and 13 other members sponsored a resolution in the General Assembly requesting the USSR to comply with UN resolutions taken in connection with the Hungarian crisis. It expressed deep concern at the Soviet non-compliance of UN's repeated request to "desist from its intervention" in the internal affairs of Hungary and to permit the UN observers to enter Hungary.[191] There was no positive response from the Soviet Union to honour the UN resolutions. The Soviet Union opposed all these UN resolutions. Naturally, it was not expected that the Soviet Union would comply with them. Therefore, the United States tabled another resolution in the General Assembly with strong words condemning the Soviet non-compliance. The twenty-power resolution adopted on December 12 declared that "by using armed forces against the Hungarian people, the Government of the Union of Soviet Socialist Republics is violating the political independence of Hungary." It also condemned the

187 United Nations General Assembly, *Official Records*, Eleventh Session, Supplement No. 17 (A/3572), 1956, p. 63.

188 *UN Document A/3403.*

189 *New York Times*, December 4, 1956.

190 *ibid*, December 5 and 6, 1956.

191 United Nations, General Assembly, *Official Documents*, Eleventh Session, Supplement No. 17, (A/3572), 1956, pp. 63-64.

Soviet Union for violating the UN Charter, called upon it to withdraw its troops from Hungary and to permit the reestablishment of Hungary's political independence.[192]

Ever since the General Assembly took up the question of Hungary, a series of resolutions were adopted which had a few definite objectives: (i) to compel the Soviet Union to withdraw its troops from Hungary in order to ensure its political independence; (ii) to permit UN observers to enter Hungary and study the situation; (iii) to stop alleged deportation of Hungarian citizens; and (iv) to request the Government of Hungary to comply with the UN resolutions taken in connection with the crisis. All these were doomed to be an exercise in futility. All the members of the United Nations were not unaware of it. The only positive step that the UN could take was the constitution of the 'Special Committee on the Problem of Hungary'. It was a foregone conclusion that the special committee would not be permitted to enter Hungary. As such it would have to depend on the information made available from outside Hungary.

The Secretary General's report of January 5, 1957 voiced in favour of the formation of the Special Committee to investigate into the Hungarian crisis and obtain information on the situation from the Hungarian escapees.[193] Ambassador Lodge extended full support in the formation of the Committee in the hope that it would collect fullest information on Hungary and thereby it would be able to draw international attention to the problem inside the country. He piloted a resolution to that effect with the support from the representatives of Australia, Cylon, Denmark, Tunisia and Uruguay.[194] The report of the Special Committee on the Problem of Hungary, published on June 20, 1957, concluded that the Hungarian revolution "was a spontaneous national uprising, due to long-standing grievances which had caused resentment among the people."[195] Immediately, the State Department issued a statement

192 *ibid*, p. 64.

193 *UN Document A/3485.*

194 The Resolution 1132(xi) was adopted by a vote of 59 to 8 with 10 abstentions (including India and Egypt). See *ibid*, (A3572) pp. 64-65.

195 *UN Document, A3592*, "Report of the Special Committee on the Problem of Hungary", June 1957, for conclusions see pp. 137-139.

supporting the findings of the Committee.[196] The sponsors of the UN resolution of January 10, which finally led to the formation of the Special Committee, met on June 26 and opined that the report should be placed before the General Assembly for consideration.[197] On September 10, 1957, the US representative assailed the Soviet Union for committing act of armed invasion and presenting a false version of the Hungarian situation. In his lengthy speech he accused the Soviet Union for betraying the cause of peace and contended that the United States did not like to view the Hungarian situation from the point of the Cold War confrontation. It only intended to see that the people of Hungary would be given the right to "carry on their own affairs in freedom and quietness, according to the standards of the Charter and of common decency." He presented a draft resolution endorsing the report of the Special Committee, charging the Soviet Union for violating the Charter and for committing armed aggression, and also condemned the continued defiance of the UN Resolution.[198] The resolution requested the President of the Eleventh Session of the Assembly, Prince Wan Waithayakon, who was also the General Assembly's special representative on the Hungary problem, to take appropriate steps towards the implementation of the resolution of the General Assembly. But in the ultimate analysis, the United Nations became absolutely ineffective to deal with the Hungarian situation in view of the strong and determined Soviet opposition.

To recapitulate, Imre Nagy appealed twice to the Secretary General for UN protection of Hungary's neutrality, but the United Nations demonstrated a record of total negligence to the matter. Dag Hammarskjold's personal explanation of the negligence attributes to the preoccupation of the world body to the Suez crisis. The United States too subscribed to the

196 Department of State, *Bulletin*, July 8, 195, p. 62.

197 *ibid*, p. 63, fn. 4.

198 *ibid*, September 30, 1957, pp. 515-525; and for details of the Resolution 1133(xi) see United Nations, General Assembly, *Official Records*, Eleventh Session, Supplement No. 17A(A3572 Add 1), 1957 p. 1. The resolution submitted by 37 nations was adopted by 60 to 10 votes with 10 abstentions.

predilection of the Secretary General. It is difficult to argue which one of the two crises taking place at the same time was more important. The fact, however, remains that in the wisdom of the members of the United Nations, including the United States, the Suez War must get precedence over the Soviet invasion of Hungary. Dag Hammarskjold faced severe criticism for paying more attention to the Suez crisis at the expense of Hungary. It was not the Secretary General alone who is to be blamed for the slow motion of steps in activating the UN machinery for responding to the Hungarian crisis. Ambassador Lodge had to equally share the blame for favouring a policy of wait and see, a policy that was assailed by the Americans and their Western allies. Sir Enthony Eden wrote:

> Five days passed without any further Council meeting upon Hungary, despite repeated attempts by ourselves and others to bring one about. The United States representative was reluctant, and voiced his suspicion that we were urging the Hungarian situation to divert attention from Suez. The United States Government appeared in no hurry to move. Their attitude provided a damaging contrast to the alacrity they were showing in arraigning the French and overselves.[199]

In the introduction to the Secretary General's report for 1957, Dag Hammarskjold argued:

> The Assembly may recommend, it may investigate, it may pronounce judgment, but it does not have the power to compel compliance with its decision...in the case of Hungary, when compliance was refused, no delegation formally proposed a recommendation by the General Assembly to the Member States that they apply sanctions or use force to secure the withdrawal of foreign troops. The judgment of the majority of Member States as to the course to pursue...was, instead, reflected in the General Assembly's resolution of condemnation and decision to order an investigation.[200]

It is quite natural for the Secretary General to work within

---

199 Anthony Ethen, *Full Circle* (Boston: Houghton Miffin, 1960) p. 609.

200 Dag Hammarskjold, *The Servant of Peace: A Selection of the Speeches and Statements of Dag Hammarskjold* (London: Bodley Head, 1962) pp. 142-143.

the framework of the UN mandate. He was not expected to overreach the resolutions. The only valid criticism against Dag Hammarskjold is that he did not take urgent steps in drawing the attention of the world body about the situation in Hungary soon after he had received the appeal from Imre Nagy. He has his own answer to the criticism which has been cited already.

ANGER IN THE US CONGRESS: WHERE THINGS WENT WRONG

It did not take time for the US Congressmen to realize that hope for the liberation of Eastern Europe had evaporated with the Soviet invasion of Hungary and installation of the new government headed by Janos Kadar. Along with it the edifice of the liberation policy got dismantled once for all. In view of this, the US Congress scrutinized the American role and advanced damaging criticism for its inapt approach to the whole issue. It was worried to see that there was a world of difference in words and deeds. Its professed theory of and commitment to liberation of Eastern Europe evaporated in the face of strong military presence and political will of the Soviet Union. The Republican Congressmen like Alvin M. Bentley appeared to be protective of the US Administration and tried to accentuate the humanitarian role of his country in extending relief measures to the distressed people of Hungary. This could not, however, cover up the harsh reality of American failure to pursue the policy to a logical end. It is noteworthy, as cited earlier that he had requested the President as well as Ambassador Lodge to "permit international volunteers to enter Hungary in any capacity that will aid the Hungarian patriots."[201] Lodge, however, replied to Bentley's suggestion: "We are giving priority to the urgency of getting United Nations observers into Hungary...The Question of volunteers is one for the State Department to decide." Bentley cited the State Department's reply: "The United States Government cannot approve the participation of American volunteers." If that is allowed, the State Department argued, the volunteers would lose their citizenship by entering or serving armed forces in a

---

201 US Congress, *Congressional Record*, 85th Congress, 1st Session, January 7, 1957. p. 308.

foreign country, when they were not specifically authorized by the Secretary of State and the Secretary of Defense. Further, the American volunteers could not travel to Hungary without violating the neutrality of Austria.[202] Without spelling out the details, Bentley contended that the United States could have done more than extending food and medical aid to the Hungarian refugees. He said: "I believe that as a result of our inability or our inaction or both our so-called policy of liberation has to all intents and purposes gone down to drain."[203]

A barrage of criticism was hurled on Tito for his alleged approval of the Soviet invasion of Hungary.[204] It was viewed that Tito's position in support of the invasion handicapped the United States in sending its army to Hungary through Yugoslavia. An infuriated Congressman Gordon L. McDonough submitted a petition to the President urging upon him to withdraw recognition of the new Government, and to explore the "feasibility of intervention in Hungary by a police force comprised of [sic] the representatives of various members of the United Nations."[205] Robert C. Hill, Assistant Secretary of State replied: "It has been the position of the United States Government that the Hungarian situation can best be dealt with through the United Nations. It is our hope that through the joint efforts of freedom loving nations working within and through that organization a solution will be found."[206] Such an unfounded optimism was a self-deceptive. How could one expect an effective measure from the United Nations to deal with the Hungarian crisis when a permanent member of the Security Council, whose strong military presence in Eastern Europe was all-pervasion, was deeply involved in the problem?

---

202 For details of the Bentley's contention and his correspondence with the State Department see *idem*.

203 *ibid*, p. 309.

204 For details see *ibid*, pp. 619-620, and for Tito's speech in support of the Soviet military action against Hungary see Paul E. Zinner (ed), *Nationalism and Popular Revolt in Eastern Europe*, n. 46, pp. 527-530.

205 *Congressional Record*, *ibid*, p. 316.

206 *ibid*, p. 319.

Senator Neuberger had a discordant voice. He assailed the US Administration for encouraging the people of Eastern Europe to revolt and then remaining silent when the people staged a massive anti-Soviet revolt. He charged the Administration for doing nothing except sleeping over the dreams of liberation. He argued that his country should have led the western economic sanction against the USSR, organized trade boycott to back up the United Nations in the crisis.[207] Senator Neuberger considered that the US aid to the refugees was not sufficient; even smaller countries like Austria contributed more than the United States to redress the suffering of the Hungarian refugees. Giving a detailed account of the number of refugees accepted by the Western countries, he said that the United States ranked at the bottom of the list of these countries which had extended asylum to the Hungarian escapees.[208] Undoubtedly, there is a strong substance in the criticism of the Senator Neuberger.

Some of the Senators took exception to the Justice Department's announcement that the United States would shut down its programme of taking refugees, and that asylum would be granted to Hungarians who had relatives in the United States and a few people who are specialized in certain skills. Walter Lippmann articulated precisely the dissatisfaction of the Americans over the restriction. He wrote that there was a "very big gap between our emotions and our actions."[209] Senator Laueche concluded that the acceptance of 31,000 Hungarians by the United States did not "correspond with the words that United States had uttered."[210] Congressman Bentley had earlier suggested to the State Department to take steps in the UN to expel Hungary from the world body and use economic sanctions against the Soviet Union, to which Assistant Secretary of State Hill rightly replied: "the suspension or expulsion of Hungary from membership in the United Nations

207 *ibid*, p. 772.

208 *ibid*, p. 9763.

209 *Washington Post*, December 27, 1956.

210 US Congress, *Congressional Record*, 85th Congress, 1st Session, June 20, 1957, p. 9765.

would be subjected to veto in the Security Council, which means that the Soviet Union could block action on such a move."[211]

The debates in the US Congress on the Hungarian crisis and the postmortem of the role of the US Government generated a strong feeling that the utopian liberation policy should be replaced by a more pragmatic policy, an alternative one – 'gradualism'. It was a unanimous view that the US Government failed to assess its actual and potential strength – both political and strategic – before floating the idea of liberation. Consequently, one could find an uneasy gap between the brave words of liberation protagonists and their mellowed stand when rebels took up arms against the Soviet forces. The sordid show of temporizing approach to the Hungarian crisis caused a demoralizing and damaging impact on the operational aspect of US foreign policy to Eastern Europe and Soviet sphere of influence. The debates, therefore, laid the basis of a new policy called 'gradualism', as will be discussed in the next Chapter, as an alternative course to Eastern Europe. The US Congress tried to cover up its own uncritical role in sponsoring a impractical policy of the Administration. The entire range of the debate in the US Congress in 1952 on the liberation policy reveals that emotions, and not critical analysis, dominated their views on the issue. The sudden shift of stand on the matter and strong criticism of the Administration's inadequate response to Soviet invasion committed to crush the Hungarian rebellion smacks of the political immaturity of the US Congress. Now it was too late to correct the colossal mistake of the past. It was the time to reassess the US policy towards Eastern Europe and curve a more pragmatic policy and a future course of action.

There were a number of unpalatable questions before the US Government as the American public tried to review the Hungarian crisis from proper perspective. Did the United States provide any tangible ground to the rebels to believe that the United States would come to aid them in the event of any anti-Soviet uprising? Did they call for aid at the time of Soviet invasion? As had been spelt out earlier, the utterances of Dulles and Congressmen sent a message, though not in

211 *ibid*, p. 1778.

unequivocal terms, to the people of Eastern Europe that their captivity under Soviet authoritarianism was unacceptable to the United States, and therefore, it would do something to put to upset the *status quo* in Eastern Europe. That was in the interest of the United States and rest of the free world. With that impression in their mind, early in the morning of November 4, the Hungarian rebels made frantic appeals through the Hungarian radio for Western help: "Any news about help? Quickly, quickly, quickly." The Associated Press in Vienna received the teletype message: "Help! – help! – help! – SOS! – SOS! – SOS! They just brought us a rumor that the American troops will be here within one or two hours."[212] The rebels, immature and disorganized as they were, believed the US would lead the western help to liberate Hungary from the Soviet domination. Contrary to this assumption, the United States did not categorically announce the American troops would be sent to help the anti-Soviet rebels in Eastern Europe, but the way the propaganda media had conveyed the message of liberation to the people of Eastern Europe was enough to give an impression that there would be western help to the rebels. After the rebellion had been crushed, there came out a series of publications trying to establish the fact that the US propaganda media like RFE were largely responsible for the impression that American military help was forthcoming. Michael Gordey, who had been in Budapest at the time of the uprising, wrote:

> We heard a lot of false news about what was going on inside Budapest. We heard on Radio Free Europe, broadcasting from Munich toward the satellite countries, programs whose impassioned tone and desperate calls to revolt certainly did a lot of wrong. During those last days, numerous Hungarians told us: "These broadcasts have provoked bloodshed".[213]

There is no denying of the fact that the liberation campaign was carried on constantly by means of propaganda balloons, through the RFE, and it was alleged that these propaganda means had been responsible for triggering off an induced bloody

212 *Daily Telegraph* and *New York Times*, November 5, 1956.

213 *Washington Post*, November 13, 1956.

violence that eventually invited the Soviet invasion. The RFE came under severe criticism in and outside the United States. The most persistent critic of the RFE was Leslie B. Bain, an American journalist, who had been in Hungary during the outbreak of the revolution.[214] He leveled two blistering allegations against the RFE. (i) Instead of extending support to Nagy's Government it conveyed an impression to the rebels that Nagy was responsible for inviting Soviet troops, and such broadcasts had a damaging impact on the newly formed government, which had been struggling hard to consolidate in the riot-torn atmosphere. (ii) The RFE mischievously promised to the Hungarians of armed aid or intervention by the West under the American leadership.

Similar eye witness accounts testify to RFE's unwarranted misleading inducement to Hungarians to revolt. Tibor Meray revealed the details of the damaging role of RFE broadcasts.[215] Edmund Taylor narrated the indictment of a Hungarian freedom fighter:

> For eight years the United States had been telling us through Radio Free Europe and the Voice of America to resist communism but resistance finally leads to revolution, you stand by and watch Soviet tanks shoot us down without lifting a finger.[216]

John MacCormac, who had been in Budapest for nineteen days covering the revolution, wrote that "the Hungarians were thoroughly convinced that United States would help them against the Soviet Union". He recorded the comments of two non-communist leaders saying that the US sponsored broadcasts were harmful, "because they incited the Hungarians to further revolt and strikes." [217] Dean James A. Pike of Episcopal Cathedral in New York city later on said "it is immoral to encourage people and then, when they rise, have no policy except to say 'God bless you, we'll pray for you."[218]

---

214 Leslie B. Bain, "Have We Failed in Hungary", *The Reporter*, January 24, 1957.

215 Tibor Meray, *Thirteen Days that Shook Kremlin*, n. 77, pp. 78-140.

216 *Washington Post*, November 18, 1956.

217 *New York Times*, November 18, 1956.

218 *ibid*, November 19, 1956.

Robert Murphy later on wrote that the State Department was accused of having fomenting the Hungarian uprising and the US complicity in the rebellion. Such accusation had been based on the broadcasts from RFE. While denying the charges, he stated that the "American broadcast stations did help to incite some patriotic insurgents, thus giving credence to the rumor that the United States was a party to the uprising, but actually we had nothing to do with it".[219] It was difficult on the part of the US Administration to disabuse or obviate the deep-rooted impression that the USA, as the chief propagator of liberation, had instigated the rebellion and later on let down the rebels in a disgraceful manner on the pretext of its preoccupation with the Suez War.

In the US Congress, the role of the RFE and the VOA came under strong criticism. Senator Neuberger held that the broadcasts of these organizations created an impression that "a national fight for freedom would have American support against military repression by Russia's Red Army."[220] He cited a report of the *Newsweek*:

> It's not true, despite charges, that the United States propagandists have been encouraging the peoples of the Red satellites to revolt. It is true, however, that occasional broadcasts and leaflets have spoken of the eventual liberation of the satellites, and that many desperate victims of the Communists read more into these words than was intended. This is causing some deep soul searching in State Department.[221]

He supported the contention of Senator Claiborne Pell that the United States should henceforth prevent organizations like the RFE from giving an idea that "American armed aid will soon arrive, while at the same time the administration specifically informs the Soviet Union that the United States will not use those measures that include force."[222] He concluded that when the poorly armed men and women revolted against

---

219 Robert Murphy, *Diplomat Among Warriors*, n. 81, p. 429.

220 US Congress, *Congressional Record*, 85th Congress, 1st Session, January 17, 1957, p. 771.

221 *ibid*, p. 772, also see *Newsweek*, December 10, 1956.

222 *ibid*, p. 723.

the Soviet troops in "partial reliance on a mistaken impression of our policies, they face death, torture, and cruel deportation in many instance."

Although in the House of Representatives, Congressman Fulton, spoke in defence of the US propaganda means encouraging the people of Eastern Europe to revolt, the UN Report of Special Committee on the Problem of Hungary made a passing reference to the role of RFE during the period of the crisis. It concluded that it would appear from the broadcasts of RFE that an impression was created for which the rebels expected definitely positive help from the West. The Committee felt that in such circumstances "the greatest restraint circumspections are called for."[223] A survey report prepared by the International Research Associates, New York, based on interviews with 100 Hungarian refugees in Austria revealed: "Aid from West in general, and from the United States in particular, was universally expected during the uprising...One third of the refugees volunteered the view that western broadcasts and propaganda in general had led the Hungarians to believe that aid would be forthcoming."[224] In November 1956 Anna Kethly, President of the Hungarian Socialists Democratic Party, reported that fabricated accounts of torture inflicted on her was aired by the RFE. There was "absolutely no truth in the RFE report", she said, it "has gravely sinned by making the Hungarian people believe that Western aid was coming when no such aid was planned."[225]

Allen A. Michie contested the contention that the RFE did not act in a responsible manner. He argued that a massive

223 Report of the Special Committee on the Problem of Hungary, UN Document, n. 191, pp. 17-18.

224 US Congress, *Hearings on Review of United States Information Agency Operation*, 85th Congress, 2nd Session, September-October, 1958, pp. 126-127. For a recent analysis on the role of RFE see Johanna Granville, "Radio Free Europe and international decision-making during the Hungarian crisis of 1956, *Historical Journal of Film, Radio and Television*, Vol. 24, No. 4, October 2004, pp. 589-611.

225 For details see D.F. Fleming, *The Cold War and Its Origins*, Vol. II (New York, Garden City: Doubleday, 1961) p. 813 and also *New York Times*, November 30, 1956.

revolution could not be organized by thousands of people by incitement of the United States sponsored propaganda means.[226] In the wake of the allegations leveled against the RFE, the West German Government instituted an investigation of the RFE's broadcasts during the time of revolution on the ground that this broadcasting channel had been operating from the territory of this country, and therefore, it could not be permitted to act in an irresponsible manner. It was found that out of 308 programmes broadcast during the period of Hungarian uprising only 4 violated the RFE's standing policy.[227] Despite these defensive reports and arguments, the deep-rooted feeling among the Hungarians was that the RFE's broadcasts offered then a clear indication that the United States was going to liberate Hungary from the Soviet control by using its military might. Even one broadcast giving a false impression or message that the military aid from the West was forthcoming was enough to cause havoc. Istvan Bibo, one of the close associates of Nagy wrote that although the West did not promise to go to war in aid of Hungary, there was explicit pronouncement for using economic sanctions in order to bring the issue up for a satisfactory solution, at least to the extent of forcing the Soviet Union to respect the territorial sovereignty of Hungary. He wrote:

> The Western world did not promise to start an atomic war in their [Hungarians] interest, nor did it call on them foolishly to take up arms. Their encouragements, however, did say that if ever the international political situation and the attitude of these people justify it, the Western world will use its economic and moral weight to bring these issues up for consideration and satisfactory solution. The Hungarian Revolution brought about all requisite conditions and legal claims.
>
> The gravest consequences the Western World must face as a result of the defeat of the Hungarian Revolution are that a ten-year-long policy and propaganda referring to principles and morals can be now contested not only in terms of its effectiveness and true meaning, but in terms of its honesty as well.[228]

---

226 Allen A. Michie, *Voices through the Iron Curtain: The Radio Free Europe Story* (New York: Dodd, Mead, and Co. 1963) Chapter 11.

227 *ibid*, p. 257.

228 Imre Kovac (ed), *Facts about Hungary*, n. 167, pp. 159-161.

An emotionally charged polemic manufactured for electioneering purpose could not withstand the test of time due to its inherent fallibility. There was hardly any articulated critical assessment of the policy, except in the Democratic plank at the time of electioneering in 1952. This has laid an adverse bearing on the operational dynamics of the policy. Mere propaganda backing would not do enough to pursue a policy designed to confront America's powerful adversary. Lack of proper understanding of these realities led to an unmitigated disaster in 1956, which the Administration refused to acknowledge.

SELF-CRITICISM OR INTROSPECTION

There was a strong revulsion in the West, more particularly in West Berlin, at the Soviet suppression of the Hungarian revolution. However, a few days later as the revulsion receded to allow public criticism to surface, the American decision-makers started reasserting that their policy of liberation of Eastern Europe was consistent. They began to convey the message for public consumption that 'peaceful evolution of the present satellite countries' towards independence was possible. President Eisenhower, in his first news conference after the reelection, defined the US policy of liberation to fit in the operational framework as shaped by the events in Hungary:

> Nothing, of course, has so disturbed the American people as the events in Hungary. Our hearts have gone out to them and we have done everything it is possible to, in the way of alleviating suffering. But I must make one thing clear: the United States doesn't now and never had advocated open rebellion by an undefended populace against force over which they could not possibly prevail. We, on the contrary, have always urged the spirit of freedom to be kept alive, that the people do not lose hope. But we have never...urged or argued for any kind of armed revolt which could bring about disaster to our friends.[229]

President Eisenhower later on wrote that the twin problems of Hungary and Suez crisis occurring simultaneously complicated the international situation. He could not expect

229 *Public Papers of the Presidents: Dwight D. Eisenhower, 1956*, p. 1096.

the support of two major European powers, Britain and France, favouring a military response to the Hungarian request, because of two important reasons. Great Britain and France in collaboration with Israel were still deeply engrossed with the Suez War. At this crucial moment of history it could seldom afford to open another war front – that too against the mighty Soviet Union. Second, the United States had opposed the Anglo-French-Israeli invasion of Egypt. It was unthinkable that these two European powers would extend cooperation with the United States in a war in Europe in which they did not have any objectives to achieve. Eisenhower, however, contended that even without the Suez War the United States would not have gone for a war with the Soviet Union in order to liberate the Hungarians. He wrote:

> ...I still wonder what would have been my recommendation to the Congress and the American people had Hungary been accessible by sea or through the territory of allied who might have agreed to react positively to the tragic fate of Hungarian people. As it was, however, Britain and France could not possibly have moved with us into Hungary. An expedition combining West Germany or Italian forces with our own, and moving across neutral Austria, Titoist Yugoslavia, communist Czechoslovakia, was out of question. The fact was that Hungary could not be reached by any United Nations or United States units without traversing such territory ...unless the major nations of Europe would, without delay, ally themselves spontaneously with us (an unimaginable prospect), we could do nothing. Sending United States troops alone into Hungary through hostile or neutral territory would have involved us in a general war.[230]

Much later in an interview with the CBS on November 23, 1961 Eisenhower explained at length with great difficulty that his Government would have encountered in taking a military action in Hungary. A pointed question that was put to him

230 Dwight D. Eisenhower, *Waging Peace*, n. 97, pp. 88-89. For some of the critical comments on the inapt attitude of the US Government in dealing effectively with the Hungarian situation see Csaba Bekes, "The 1956 Hungarian Revolution and the Great Powers" in Terry Cox (ed), *Hungary 1956: Forty Years On*, n. 64, pp. 51-66.

was: "What reason prevented our intervention in Hungary?" To this he gave a long reply:

> The United States could have intervened only in agreement with other countries...No European country was any more ready than ours to plunge into this matter [military intervention] and liberate Hungary from Communist influence. I don't think that the United Nations would have supported our intervention, which would have been followed by an open war...The tragedy was inevitable. And even today I don't think that the United States or any other country would have risked a major war for that cause.[231]

Even after the Hungarian fiasco, Eisenhower defended the US policy of liberation of Eastern Europe and argued that it had a consistent foundation. In reply to a volley of charges of deception he had maintained about the operative part of America's policy of liberation, he maintained that he had never advocated for an armed rebellion inside the Soviet sphere of influence. He said: I was very careful in 1952 campaign; I always said, 'By every peaceful means'. I said, we will never accept the theory that these nations are be forever enslaved. But we are not going to war to liberate them." He assigned another argument for not responding militarily to the Hungarian crisis – the Hungarian Government had "never requested our intervention; in fact no contact was made until a certain revolutionary government of very short duration had been formed, from what it seems to me." This statement invoked sharp reaction from the Hungarians. Tibor Meray wrote that the Hungarians did not demand such intervention, but what the Hungarians would have been satisfied with was a clear US declaration before November 4 of its decision not to intervene in aid of the Hungarians, and secondly, restraint on the part of the American propaganda media, because that would have minimized the magnitude of the tragedy.[232] It was not easy to obliterate the deep sense of revulsion at the untenable justification of inaction at the need of the hour to save the Hungarians from the ruthless suppression. That is

---

231 *New York Times,* November 24, 1961.

232 Tibor Meray, *That Day in Budapest, October 23, 1956* (New York: Funk and Wagnalls, 1969) p.454

why uncomfortable questions were raised centering around the basic issue, was it possible to conceive a process of peaceful liberation of Eastern Europe when the Soviet Union had been accelerating its defence system moving abreast of America's military engagements with Western Europe.

At any rate Eisenhower's retrospection would provoke one to compare his 1952 election campaign speeches and promises with his argument in the post-revolution period. The content and the spirit of the statements made in 1952 and the ones after the collapse of the Hungarian revolution were quite different. While the earlier speeches carried the messages of liberation and encouragement for it, the retrospection betrays honest revelations. Ernest Lefever later on wrote: "There was a serious and unjustified hiatus between pronouncement and policy, promise and performance. We spoke loudly and carried a small stick."[233]

The chief architect of liberation policy, John Foster Dulles started realizing that the US inaction during the Hungarian crisis had left a damaging impact on the credibility of a great power. He was aware of the barrage of criticism leveled in and outside the United States on the efficacy – both theoretical and operational – of liberation policy and ethical foundation of the false propaganda aired by its media for an induced revolution. He began to disown any responsibility of the Administration in the happenings in Hungary. On December 2, 1956 he stated that the United States had been subscribing to an "an evolutionary process' of liberation. When he faced a pertinent question as to whether the US Administration now retreated to the containment policy in place of liberation policy, Dulles remarked:

> I would n't so describe it, no. In fact, the contrary. Containment implies that you accept the Soviet rule over the satellites. We believe that that rule can and must be ended. But we believe that the processes must be evolutionary processes, and not violent revolution.[234]

233 Ernest Lefever, *Ethics and United States Foreign Policy* (New York: Meridian Books, 1958) p. 151.

234 *New York Times*, December 3, 1956; and for a similar statement of December 18, 1956 see Department of State, *Bulletin*, January 7, 1957, pp. 3-9.

In order to cover up his discomfiture, Dulles took pride in the American non-intervention and expressed satisfaction over the US role in the United Nation. He said, "When Hungary was invaded and freedom crushed, we sponsored a United Nations condemnation of the Soviet Union."[235] The official statement of Dulles at a press conference in Canberra on March 13, 1957, in a reply to an often-asked but uncomfortable question as to why did his country refused to intervene in Hungary could be cited as a further realization of the US inaction:

> There was no basis for our giving military aid to Hungary. We had no commitment to do so, and we did not think that to do so would either assist the people of Hungary or the people of Europe or the rest of the world.[236]

Two days later, on March 15, President Eisenhower expressed moralist optimism on the occasion of the anniversary of the 1848 Hungarian revolution. He said that the 1956 revolution strengthened his conviction that the "process of enlightenment and justice among men and nations will triumph."[237] Similar emotional and patent sentiments continued to occupy a scheduled space in the statements of US policy and decision makers. The statement of the State Department[238] and the American Ambassador's report to the United Nations on the developments in Hungary submitted on May 2, 1957 contained similar sentiments,[239] implying thereby that there could not be better response than expression of helplessness of the protagonist of liberation of Eastern Europe.

Nonetheless, trivial matters kept the spillover bitterness between the United Nations and the Kedar Government alive. The Hungarian Foreign Ministry submitted a note to the American Legation in Budapest with a request to remove the American Minister, Edward Thompson Wailes, as he did not present his credentials to the Hungarian Government, and consequently, the US Government recalled him and kept the

235 *American Foreign Policy: Current Documents*, 1957, p. 29.

236 Department of State, *Bulletin*, April 1, 1957, p. 533.

237 *ibid*, p. 538.

238 *ibid*, April 22, 1957, pp. 654-655.

239 *ibid*, May 29, 1957, pp. 865-866.

American Legation under a Charge d' affaires.[240] The brittle relationship between Washington DC and Budapest continued unabated with a series of actions taken against the functionaries of the US diplomatic mission in Budapest. In April 1957 the Hungarian Foreign Ministry booked Captain Thomas R. Gleason, a US Military Attache at the American Legation, for his alleged involvement in an "open espionage" and demanded that he leave Hungary within 48 hours. Six days earlier Captain Gleason and Colonel J.C. Todd were halted by the Hungarian troops on a public road and were detained for six hours to which the US Government issued a note of protest.[241] Again Hungarian Government complained against the use by the United States of a postal stamp having the message "Support Your Crusade for Freedom" on private letters reaching Hungary.[242]

A line of distinction between the frenzy propaganda materials aired by the American media and the sordid solace enjoyed by US Government functionaries at the vindication of their stand on liberation can be drawn to understand the predicament of the State Department. It could correctly assess the Soviet determination to retain its hold in Eastern Europe and maintain the monolithic structure of the Warsaw Treaty Organization at all cost. This realization dissuaded the State Department from advancing any theory of military action in aid of the Hungarian rebels and towards the eventual collapse of the Warsaw strategic defence system. Robert Murphy, of course, argued that the United States could have taken military measures, without of course, making a proper assessment of the strategic situation in Europe, where the West had been facing a massive and well-equipped and well-trained Soviet army estimated to be more than 1.4 million in number. He wrote:

> Perhaps history will demonstrate that the free world could have intervened to give the Hungarians the liberty they sought, but none of us in the State Department had the skill or the imagination to devise the way.[243]

240 *ibid*, March 18, 1957, pp. 441-442.

241 *ibid*, May 20, 1957, pp. 810-811.

242 *ibid*, May 29, 1957, pp. 849-850.

243 Robert Murphy, *Diplomat Among Warriors*, p. 432.

Murphy did not spell out the possible course of action that the US Government could have taken in furthering the Hungarian quest for freedom through an armed revolt. Like him, there were many who felt erroneously and suggested that the United States could have seized the opportunity presented by the Hungarians at least for initiating negotiating the withdrawal of troops. It appeared that Robert Murphy and others probably did not try to understand the remoteness of the possibility of Soviet withdrawal without a full-scale war which would have in wildest imagination ensured a total defeat of the Soviet Union, without at the same time a total destruction of Western Europe. Probably they did not have any illusion about the impracticability of a war as a recourse to liberation, but their sentimental statements tried to soothe the wounds of inaction and moral suffering. Richard Löwenthal made an objective observation. To him the West could have proposed for a simultaneous dissolution of the NATO and the Warsaw Treaty Organization and that could have, had it materialized, set the ball of peaceful liberation to roll.[244] But such a contention was too academic and not politically charged to attract the attention of responsible quarters as the two big powers were in a belligerent mood created by the Cold War politics. This kind of suggestion, theoretically plausible notwithstanding, might be workable in an atmosphere of mutual trust only, which was a far cry in the atmosphere of a psychological warfare between the two powers. Another proposal was that at the critical juncture of Hungarian crisis, the West could have initiated steps for the reunification of Germany. Had there been a serious attempt in this direction, [in the mould of Austrian State Treaty of 1955], the Soviet leaders would have faced irresistible pressure to respond positively to a proposal of the withdrawal of troops from Hungary in return for an effective guarantee to its security interests.[245] An avowed anti-communist Dulles himself was not in favour of such a discussion, which would take up both the NATO and Warsaw

---

244 Richard Löwenthal, "Hungary – Were We Helpless?" *The New Republic*, November 26, 1956, p. 14.

245 Hugh Seton-Watson, "Hungary and Europe", *Spectator*, November 9, 1956, pp. 638-639; also *New York Times*, November 2, 1956.

Treaty Organization at par. He advocated for genuine independence of Eastern Europe and the reunification of Germany as a precondition to military disengagement rather than as a consequence of it.[246] Therefore, the whole issue remained confined to premature theoretical speculations.

It seems that everyone in the United States, the formal decision-making structure as well as the public, was aware of a grim reality – a superpower has also its limits. There is a wide gap between a cherished desire and practical politics both in the domestic and international context, and election promises and real *politik*. Consequently, the United States had an extremely limited role play in the drama that had unfolded itself in Budapest during October-November 1956. It was crystal clear that an American military adventure in aid of the Hungarian rebels would have undoubtedly entailed greater human sacrifice and catastrophe. The policy makers in Washington DC were aware of the fact that Soviet Union had massive military buildup in Eastern Europe with around 1.4 million well-trained troops backed by conventional weapons of considerable credence. Why would United States risk a major war with the Soviet Union for a cause in which there is least involvement of America's basic strategic interests? An attempt to alter the *status quo* in Eastern Europe taking the pretext of the Hungarian crisis would have been a prescription to a total war with the Soviet Union, as President Truman warned in 1952.

As the Hungarian revolution went down in history as a closed chapter and the advocates of the liberation theory silently watched the proceedings of collapse of the revolution in the face of massive invasion committed by the mighty Soviet Union, it was decided once for all that the United States would never go for a war with its strongest adversary for any cause not directly connected with America's vital interests. The sphere of influence of the two great powers remained well-defined, not to be disturbed and unsettled by violent and military means. The discourse on liberation of Eastern Europe and the question of incalculable human cost that might take

246 Department of State, *Bulletin*, January 7, 1957, pp. 3-9.

place in the pursuit of violent liberation had continued to occupy an important space in the American foreign policy making forums. Each time it was made clear that learning from the Hungarian experience the United States would not risk a war with the Soviet Union for a moralist position in international affairs. In a statement made before the Hearings of the Draft Report on Foreign Policy and Mutual Security immediately after the Hungarian crisis, Paul H. Nitze, President of Foreign Service Education, dismissed the idea of military engagement in pursuit of liberation of the people of Eastern Europe. The Hungarian episode was an eye opener. He observed:

> I don't think anything we have ever said has really committed us to go to war in a case like the Hungarian case. Even some of the statements about the bold and new foreign policy in 1952, liberation, and so forth, these were subsequently helped to make it clear we did not propose to follow that policy to that extent of being willing to go to war in support of Hungary.[247]

The US justification for its inaction could be viewed from the perspective of its oblique recognition of Soviet sphere of influence. Behind the pious utterances of Dulles from time to time hailing the thrust of the Hungarians for freedom, and his faith in the forces of freedom, there was a conscious and subtle attempt to bury the issue of America's ignominious inaction during the period of crisis. A consistent reasoning was that the US military intervention "would have torched off a third world war", as Senator Church commented later on in the Hearing of the Senate Committee on Foreign Relations.[248] If that was the position, why was the voluble incitement for a revolt to achieve the liberation of Eastern Europe, which carried the prescription of inevitable Soviet intervention? No one seems to be keen on finding a plausible answer to this unpalatable question.

---

247 US Congress, *Foreign Policy and Mutual Security: Draft Report Submitted to the Committee on Foreign Affairs*, December 24, 1956, pp. 223 and 227.

248 US Congress, Senate, Committee on Foreign Relations, *Hearings on Disarmament and Foreign Policy*, 86th Congress, 1st Session, 1959, p. 216.

The preparation for risking a war with Soviet Union for a cause like that of the Hungarian revolution presupposes a theoretical formulation of identifying America's interests gravely endangered by Soviet intervention and also a meticulous search for alternatives short of military action. In the absence of these, the rhetoric of roll back communism, massive retaliation and encouragement for liberation proved to be not only hollow but also dangerous for those who paid importance on their simplistic values and exposed these defenceless people to ruthless assault at the hands of a determined power prepared to protect its sphere of influence even at the risk of a major war. It was a war of nerves. While the United States continued to propagate liberation of Eastern Europe to dismantle the Soviet sphere of influence and thus upset the strategic *status quo* in Europe without, of course, taking recourse to a major war, the Soviet Union was determined to maintain its preeminent position in Eastern Europe at all cost, even at the cost of major military confrontation with its pronounced and powerful adversary. For the United States, a trouble in Eastern Europe far away from its territory and away from its vital interests was not too important to risk a major war, while a trouble in the Soviet backyard was too serious a problem for Moscow to be ignored. The predictable proliferation of such a trouble would shook the very foundation of communism not only in Eastern Europe but also in the USSR. There is a qualitative difference in the approach of the United States and the Soviet Union to Eastern Europe. The public as well as the policy planners and makers in the United States picked up the issue of political and strategic position of Eastern Europe for electioneering purpose, and therefore, they naturally found the Hungarian crisis was not worthy of a war with the Soviet Union. John Foster Dulles was honest enough to admit in unequivocal terms this simple truth. He reportedly said that the US military response to the Soviet invasion of Hungary would have risked "a nuclear war with the Russians, and the American government was not prepared to take this risk on the Hungarian issue."[249] To risk a nuclear war needs thorough commitment to the cause,

249 Drummond and Coblenz, *Duel at the Brink*, n. 18, pp. 180-181.

matchless political will of the decision-makers backed by unflinching public support and a robust motivation. As stated already, the Soviet Union had demonstrated all these in defence of its interests in Hungary, the United States had rhetoric only.

The Suez war was a heaven sent pretext to justify American inaction. It is understandable that the United States was fully seized with the war in West Asia. Two of its defence partners in the ambit of the NATO, Britain and France, together with Israel, a dependable ally in the oil rich region, were deeply involved in the war. The combined invasion of Egypt was committed without the knowledge of the United States. The fear of Soviet penetration in the region, which was looming large in the context of Moscow's open support for Egypt worried the Eisenhower Administration. Khrushchev tried to draw Nasser to the Soviet fold taking the advantage of the richness in the relationship between Tito and the emerging Arab leader, who had proved to be an ardent representative of Arab nationalism.[250] The US Administration was not unaware of the developments in the region. It had been monitoring these from a close range. This is evident from a significant statement made by Dulles on December 31, 1956 emphasizing the importance of the oil rich region for the American foreign policy makers, in view of the possible thrust of the Soviet Union into the region. He stated that the "United States had a major responsibility to help prevent the spread to the Middle East of Soviet imperialism...During the coming year the United States will have to accept an increasing responsibility to assist the free nations in the Middle East".[251] A similar tone was evident in the statement of Dulles issued on January 7, 1957 when he said that it would be a major disaster if the region "were to fall into the grip of international communism."[252] Six months later, he commented that had there been no crisis in

---

250 *Khrushchev Remembers*, Vol. 1, n. 7, pp. 461-62.

251 Department of State, *Bulletin*, January 14, 1957, pp. 50-51.

252 *ibid*, January 28, 1957, p. 127. Also see David Tal, *The 1956 War: Collusion and Rivalry in the Middle East* (London: Routledge, 2001) Chapter 10 and 11.

West Asia he "would have deeply loved to focus the eye of world public opinion uniquely on what was happening in Hungary."[253] One could see the helplessness of Dulles who was caught between the two grave crises – the Hungarian revolution in which he would have loved to initiate military option as a response to Soviet invasion, and the Suez War in which the United States had to oppose the combined aggression committed by Britain, France and Israel.[254] One can notice the difference of perception of the situation in Hungary in the honest revelation of Eisenhower in 1961 that under no circumstances the United States would have gone for a war with the Soviet Union and the contradictory position taken by Dulles, which, of course, confined to efforts towards creating strong public opinion against the Soviet invasion.

Robert Murphy, however, argues that the Suez War provided the Soviet Union with "an admirable distraction", but it "could not have been timed more advantageously for the Russians", because they were determined in any case to crush the Hungarian insurrection."[255] Eisenhower had something more to speak on this matter:

> Did the British and French action provide an excuse for the Russians to move with massive force into Hungary? If the Russians had moved into Hungary with no Suez problem preoccupying all Western Europe, would the reaction of the West have been more intense? To both of these questions my own answer has always been negative.[256]

The statement of Eisenhower, a military general with outstanding reputation and international standing, is a reflection of the reality obtaining at that critical moment of history. Ferenc A. Vali argues in an unconvincing manner that the division of the West on the Suez War (American opposition to the combined aggression of Egypt) "encouraged the Soviet

253 *ibid*, August 12, 1957, p. 274.

254 Richard H. Immerman, *John Foster Dulles and the Diplomacy of the Cold War* (Princeton: Princeton University Press, 1990), Chapter 5, Dulles, Suez and the British, pp. 133-158 also see Escolt Reid, *Hungary and Suez* (Oakville, Ont.: Mosaic, 1986).

255 Robert Murphy, *Diplomat Among Warriors*, pp. 430-431.

256 Dwight D. Eisenhower, *Waging Peace*, n. 97, pp. 89-99.

action" in Hungary, because the Soviet leaders did not foresee any danger of joint Western military action to rescue the Hungarian rebels.[257] Eisenhower's honest assessment of the situation of Hungarian crisis together with the Soviet military buildup in Eastern Europe backed up by massive conventional war set up and its spectacular success in liberating the entire region from the Nazi occupation reveals that his Government at no stage did consider seriously to intervene militarily to stop the Soviet invasion and in the pursuit of its own liberation policy, the Suez War being there or not. It also sent a signal in unmistakable terms that in the near or distant future the United States would not venture a war in aid of any revolt in the Soviet zone of influence. That is why a policy of 'gradualism' started emerging to replacing the liberation policy.

THE POSTSCRIPT: EXECUTION OF NAGY

Soon after the Soviet forces had crushed the revolution and established full order in the city of Budapest and a new Government headed by Janos Kadar took charge, there took place crack down of the rebels. Hundreds of participants in the revolution were arrested. Thousands escaped the country and took shelter in Austria and neighbouring countries. The swoop on the rebels did not figure immediately in the Government controlled press and radio. Only the Western press published news on the arrests of the rebels. On February 2, 1957, the Hungarian Government announced that Ersebet Manyi and Mihaly Farkas had been hanged for organizing and participating in the anti-Government riots. Two weeks later on February 18, Ilona Toth, a 25 year medical student, with ten others testified that she had assaulted and killed a Hungarian policeman. On April 8, 1957 a Hungarian court sentenced three rebels namely Ilona Toth, Miklos Gyongyoesi and Ferenc Geonczi to death for taking part in the 1956 revolt. At that time there was no certain news about Nagy, the man who declared Hungary's neutrality and appealed to the UN Secretary General for its protection. There was a rumour that Nagy escaped arrest and sneaked into the Yugoslav embassy on November 4, 1956 and remained there till November 22.

257 Ferenc A. Vali, *Rift and Revolt in Hungary*, n. 68, p. 353.

Just one month after what had happened in front of the Parliament Square on the fateful evening of October 23, 1956, Nagy emerged from the Yugoslav embassy on his *en route* to Rumania. The Hungarian police took no time to arrest him at the instance of Janos Kadar.[258] The intention of the arrest was shrouded with mystery as the new Government had assured him safe conduct and a guarantee of free passage to Romania. As confusion continued to prevail about the fate of Nagy, *New York Times* published a news item on December 19, 1957 informing the world of the secret trial on Nagy. Till that time no one including the United States seemed to be worried about him. On the next day Alsing Andersen, Chairman of the Special Committee on the Problem of Hungary, wrote to the Hungarian Minister for Foreign Affairs requesting him for information about the reported trial of Nagy and his associates, General Pal Maletor, General Istvan Kovac and Colonel Sandor Kopacsi.[259] The letter was returned to the Committee with a note that the Hungarian Government did not recognize the functioning of such a body. Being alarmed at the uncooperative gesture and also by conflicting reports about the secret trial on Nagy and his close associates, the Acting US Ambassador to the United Nations, James J. Wordsworth, wrote to the Hungarian counterpart Peter Mod requesting him to furnish information about the fate of the arrested persons.[260] The Hungarian representative decided to maintain a discreet silence. This compelled Ambassador Henry Cabot Lodge Jr. to write to Peter Mod on March 6, 1958 requesting him to reply to Wordsworth's letter.[261] The reply to this letter was quite hostile and evasive. It questioned the authority of the US ambassador in inquiring a matter that fell within the domestic jurisdiction of Hungary.[262] There was no clear indication about

258 For details see *The Secret Trial of Imre Nagy* (Westport: Greenwood Press, 1995); Melvin Lasky J., *The Hungarian Revolution*, n. 73, pp. 280-283; also see *The Truth about the Nagy Affair: Facts, Documents, Comments*, n. 66.

259 Annexure II to the *UN Document A/3849.*

260 Department of State, *Bulletin*, April 7, 1958, pp. 581-582.

261 *ibid*, p. 582.

262 *ibid*, p. 583.

the whereabout and fate of the deposed leader. However, it was not difficult to presume from the reports of hanging of a number of participants and military functionaries that the extreme punishment was awaiting Nagy.

There was some ray of hope for sparing Nagy for securing a political mileage. The Nagy trial was suspended in March 1958 when Janos Kadar paid a visit to Yugoslavia. There he apparently assured Tito that Nagy would not be put on trial "for the time being."[263] Notwithstanding the assurance, the secret trial continued. On June 16, the Hungarian radio announced the execution of Nagy (by hanging) and three of his associates.

There was a terrible shock wave throughout the world. On hearing the news, the State Department issued a strong condemnation of the extreme punishment and regarded it as shocking and cruel.[264] Dulles held a press conference on the next day and commented that the execution was a "brutal terrorist method".[265] President Eisenhower also issued a similar note of condemnation and considered the execution as a violation of good faith and adherence to a policy of terror and intimidation.[266]

It would be difficult to argue that Nagy could have been saved by the United States by any means in view of the executions of a number of rebels committed by the Kadar Government soon after the rebellion had been crushed. The reports on the Nagy trial indicated extreme punishment would be invariably inflicted on the key figures of the revolt and no leniency would be shown. What the United States could have done was that on the receipt of the news of the secret trial it could have mobilized world opinion against the secret trial in which fair justice could not be expected at all. The US Government virtually remained silent over the alarm raised in the US Congress when Congressman, Bentley, spoke on the

---

263 Ferenc A. Vali, *Rift and Revolt in Hungary*, n. 68, p. 444.

264 Department of State, *Bulletin*, July 7, 1958, pp. 6-7.

265 *New York Times*, June 18, 1957 and *ibid*, pp. 6-7.

266 *Public Papers of the Presidents, Dwight D. Eisenhower*, 1958, p. 480.

trial and expressed grave concern at the fate of Nagy and his associates. He suggested that the US Government should approach the United Nations Commission on Human Rights on the matter and should appeal to the "conscience of the entire world so that the lives of these heroes" could be spared.[267] Interestingly enough, the US Government remained insensitive to the voice of concern. Had the world opinion been mobilized and a considerable pressure generated, Nagy's life could have been saved. As the news of execution of Nagy reached the United States, the US Congress joined the public condemnation and revulsion. The Senate passed a resolution holding the Soviet Union squarely responsible for the execution and expressed sympathy with the people of Hungary on the "occasion of this new expression of their ordeal of political oppression and terror."[268] Nagy was buried along with three associates in a distant corner (section 301) of the Municipal Cemetery outside Budapest without allowing any funeral services to take place. During the era of communist rule the Government did not allow to place any mark on the grave and also access to his burial site. A cenotaph was placed in Pere Lachaise Cemetery in Paris in Latin, which read "I call the living, I mourn the dead, I chase the lighting". In 1989, with the fall of communism in Eastern Europe including Hungary, he was rehabilitated and his remains were reburied in the same plot after a funeral service organized by his admirers. In 2004 a celebrated Hungarian director Marta Meszaros produced a film on his life entitled "The Unburied Dead".[269]

Hungary was a test case to reassess and review the efficacy of the American liberation theory in the backdrop of Soviet determination to retain its hold in its sphere of influence. As indicated already, for the Soviet Union it was a robust challenge

---

267 US Congress, *Congressional Record*, 85th Congress, 2nd Session, January 8, 1958, p. 94.

268 *ibid*, p. 12035; for other details of the discussion on the execution of Nagy in both the Houses of the US Congress see pp. 114402, 11502, 11678 and 11708.

269 For details see Alajos Dornback, *The Secret Trial of Nagy* (London: Greenwood Press, 1995) and also Peter Unwin, *Voice in the Wilderness: Imre Nagy and the Hungarian Revolution,* n. 66.

to its advantage in Eastern Europe, which it earned during the final phase of World War II at enormous human and material costs, unprecedented in the recorded history of war. The US policy makers and planners underestimated the Soviet determination to hold intact Moscow's control over the region. The act of invasion is a reflection of its determination. However the Soviet military action devastated US efforts to influence the Soviet bloc as a part of America's Cold War objectives, which was tried with the help of an overt policy of liberation as a replacement to the covert policy of Truman through broadcasting channels. Looking back, it is felt that the overt policy made known to the 'captive peoples' of Eastern Europe through official statements of the President of the United States and his Secretary of State acted as a source of inspiration for a revolution spearheaded by virtually unarmed people of Poznan and Hungary.[270] The covert policy of President Truman would have avoided a massacre of several thousand people.[271] Had the Soviet sphere of influence been allowed to crumble in the face of an unorganized rebellion in Hungary, it would have definitely laid a damaging and spillover impact on the entire region. It would have initiated the process of the end of the Soviet empire. The Soviet Union successfully demonstrated its determination not only to retain its hold but also to consolidate its position by means of an agreement with the Kadar Government concluded on May 27, 1957 allowing Soviet troops to stay in Hungary for an indefinite time.[272]

The Hungarian revolution presented an opportunity to test the operational dynamics of its highly publicized liberation policy. It not only proved that there was a world of difference between what the US Government professed in theory and

---

270 The left thinkers in the United States launched frontal attack on the US Administration for inciting a violent rebellion that exposed the common citizen to death and destruction. For a representative criticism see Herbert Aptheker, *The Truth about Hungary* (New York: Mainstream Publishers, 1957).

271 Gregory Mitrovich, *Undermining the Kremlin: America's Strategy to Subvert the Soviet Bloc, 1947-1956* (Ithica: Cornell University Press, 2000) pp. 177-191.

272 *American Foreign Policy: Current Documents: 1957*, pp. 673-678.

practiced, and between the two lies the danger of exposing defenceless people to ruthless suppression by a mighty power. The US inaction also indicated that the Government accepted tacitly the Soviet sphere of influence in Eastern Europe as a *fait accompli*, going back to square to testify the merit of the containment theory once again. This provoked Raymond Aron to comment: "there existed a hidden *Russo American pact against war*, an agreement probably more binding that any other alliance."[273] Such an understanding, Aron writes, done at the cost of Moscow's victims, would have ensured peace or not, is a matter of speculation. Now it is not difficult to understand that the two superpowers had already decided to avoid any possibility of mutual destruction by engaging themselves in a war which would be undoubtedly fought with nuclear arsenals for a cause of a third party. Even in a situation like that of the Cuban missile crisis, which took place six years later, the two great powers demonstrated their capacity to use deterrent diplomacy, but not to the extent of mutual destruction. In 1956, the United States positioned itself in a strategically more advantageous power than the Soviet Union. Nonetheless, mere military superiority could not deter a motivated opponent to strike decisively in its zone of control, more so, when nuclear weapons have become increasingly unusuable liability.

Zbigniew K. Brzezniski wrote on a number of occasions that the United States never had any policy towards Eastern Europe, and therefore, it was difficult to visualize any tangible plan of action in preventing or forestalling Soviet aggressive design in the satellite nations. Yet, certain quarters tended to erroneously misconstruct the rhetoric of liberation as a concrete policy towards the Soviet sphere of influence.[274] President Eisenhower was aware of the limitations of his country in dealing with certain aspects of the Soviet external behaviour,

---

273 Raymond Aron, "The Meaning of Destiny" in Tamas Aczel (ed), *Ten Years After: The Hungarian Revolution in the Perspective of History* (New York: Rinehart and Weston, 1967) p. 21.

274 Zbigniew Brzezinski, *Alternative to Partition: For a Broader Conception of America's Role in Europe* (New York: McGraw-Hill, 1965) Chapter 1.

yet he remained as a prisoner of liberation ideas and emotions that appeared to be a catchy devise to win the presidential election. An election slogan charged with emotions eventually worked as an inducement to the defenceless Hungarian to revolt against a mighty power on a false notion that America's aid would be forthcoming in no time. It is, therefore, always dangerous to raise an impractical slogan which is likely to act as an incitement to a premature revolt, as in the case of the Hungarians which exposed them to the grave risk of ruthless killing.[275]

John Foster Dulles showed his moral and intellectual shallowness in advocating liberation theory when he himself was not sure of his role in such a crisis situation in Eastern Europe like the one that had occurred in Hungary. His rhetoric of "massive retaliation" proved to be a fiasco. Henry A. Kissinger late on wrote:

> The weakness of Dulles's "massive retaliation" strategy of the 1950s ...was not that it brought us to close to a nuclear war, but that in a crisis it gave us the choice between nuclear war and doing nothing. We ended up doing nothing...[276]

Dulles in the last stage of life realized the ground real situation in Eastern Europe. This eventually provided him the basis for advocating 'gradualism'. It was definitely painful for him to abandon the policy of liberation, which had been so dear to him for four years at least seen from his polemic perception, but to disown a part of unworkable strategy of a psychological warfare against its mighty adversary is *realpolitik* taking over *idealpolitik* quietly.

---

275 Around 2502 civilians and 720 Soviet troops were killed and several thousand were injured during the uprising. For details see Csaba Bekes and Janos Rainer, *The 1956 Hungarian Revolution: A History in Document* (Budapest: Central European University Press, 2002) Chapter 2

276 Henry Kissinger, *White House Years* (Boston: Little Brown & Co., 1979) pp. 115-116. Kissinger maintained a strong view on the efficacy of liberation policy which not only placed the United States in an embarrassing position in the community of nations but also led to the brutal repression, killing, execution, deportation of the rebels. For his excellent and philosophical observations see *Diplomacy* (London: Simon & Schuster, 1995), Chapter 22 Hungary: Upheaval in the Empire, pp. 550-567.

CHAPTER III

CZECHOSLOVAKIA 1968: ACCEPTANCE OF SPHERE OF INFLUENCE

Ever since the failed Hungarian revolution of 1956, the official position of the United States towards the policy of liberation of Eastern Europe had undergone a noticeable change in the following decade till the onset of reform movement in Czechoslovakia leading eventually to another massive Soviet invasion in 1968 to topple a legitimate government and install a puppet regime. The preparation for the obvious change was set to roll in the lifetime of John Foster Dulles, who was a silent spectator of the vivid collapse of liberation policy. It was he along with President Eisenhower who had to face the American public to explain why the US Administration failed to redeem the electioneering promises. He had to painfully accept the demand for a thorough review of his much publicized policy to weaken the Soviet hold in Eastern Europe. He could not remain unresponsive to a barrage of criticism against American show of helplessness at the onset of the Hungarian rebellion, subsequent Soviet invasion and America's dubious performance in the United Nations. In an attempt to cover up the US sordid performance during the crisis Dulles declared in a major foreign policy address on April 22, 1957: "We seek liberation of captive nations . . . but we do not ourselves incite revolt. Rather we encourage an evolution to freedom."[1] As he tried to recapitulate his dismal performance

1 Department of State, *American Foreign Policy: Current Documents, 1957* (Washington DC, 1961) p. 29 also Russell Baker, "Dulles Looks on Dulles's Policy", *New York Time*, April 28, 1957.

during the crisis period with a veil attempt to justify America's inaction for extraneous reasons like the Suez War, one could find his preparedness to accept a change in America's foreign policy towards Eastern Europe.

Various committees started reviewing American foreign policy and the efficacy of liberation policy. The Study Report of the House Committee on Foreign Affairs conceded that the Hungarian revolution was a "lost opportunity" to initiate the dismantling of the Soviet grip in Eastern Europe, and at the same breath observed that "While it was not expected of the United States to send troops or military weapons into Hungary for fear of provoking a third world war, the fact remains that we were without any means or devices at our disposal to meet the crisis."[2] Therefore, the report recommended that the United States should attempt to revitalize the United Nations to deal with similar type of crises and to seek the revision of the Charter to ensure the enforcement of resolutions taken against an interventionist country. These suggestions to every one's guess were without practical substance as long as the elite role of the five big powers exists in the Security Council. Another report of the House Committee recommended that the United States should continue to encourage the growth of nationalism in Eastern Europe in a gradual manner.[3] The Senate review report prepared by Allen J. Ellender concluded that a single and one-dimensional approach to the problem of Eastern Europe could not be adequate, and therefore, it favoured the establishment of more contact with the people if the region and pursue tract II diplomacy.[4] Senator Mike Mansfield advised the Administration to have diplomatic, cultural and commercial contacts with the governments of the region. He suggested that the Secretary of State should visit

---

2 US Congress, House Committee on Foreign Affairs, *Report of the Special Study Mission to Europe on Policy toward the Satellite Nations*, 85th Congress, 1st Session, 1957, pp. 6-7.

3 US Congress, House Committee on Foreign Affairs, *Reports on Foreign Policy and Mutual Security*, 85th Congress, 2nd Session, June 11, 1957, p. 76.

4 US Congress, Senate Committee on Foreign Relations, *A Review of US Foreign Policy and Operations*, 85th Congress, 2nd Session,, February 13, 1958, pp. 228, 232-233.

these countries from time to time to strengthen the tract I diplomacy. Such activities, he believed, would eventually enable these governments to be less dependent on the Soviet Union and would develop their own separate and independent personality. Dulles, however, rejected the second suggestion, probably on the ground that his visit would amount to a tacit recognition of the *status quo* position in Eastern Europe.[5] At the same time the Administration was uncertain about its future line of approach towards Eastern Europe, presumably it wanted to keep the matter in abeyance for consideration by the next Administration.

It is, therefore, not at all difficult to foresee the nature of US reaction to a Hungarian type situation in Eastern Europe in view of the fact that the US capacity to confront the Soviet Union militarily had been increasingly circumscribed with the passage of time mainly by the Soviet advancement of strategic defence and weaponry system.

Just after the Hungarian uprising, President Eisenhower directed the National Security Council to analyze the crisis and to draw guidelines for the Administration to meet similar situation. The report concludes that both the great powers lost the capacity to take recourse to any dangerous step affecting each other's areas of vital interests. The Hungarian crisis proved it in unmistakable terms. In future, the United States was destined to be a helpless spectator of similar events occurring in Soviet sphere of influence. Such a realization warranted the formulation of a new policy towards Eastern Europe.[6]

In the first quarter of 1958, the Senate Committee on Foreign Relations reviewed the foreign policy and arrived at a consensus that the American interest should no longer be pursued "through suicidal military adventure", and therefore, recommended in favour of resisting 'Soviet expansionism' by means other than military confrontation.[7] Dulles and

5 *New York Times*, January 30 and July 17, 1958.

6 Edward Weintal and Charles Bartlett, *Facing the Brink* (New York: Scribner's, 1967) pp. 210-211.

7 US Congress, Senate Committee on Foreign Relations, *Review of Foreign Policy, 1958*, 85th Congress, 2nd Session, February March, 1958, p. 732.

Eisenhower could construe this as an honourable retreat to containment policy, which had been abhorred during the electioneering of 1952. The American public had already been aware of the impossibility of a military showdown with the Soviet Union, more particularly, after the psychological syndrome created by the successful launching of the *Sputnik*. The Committee, while discussing the fear psychosis, maintained that the United States should avoid military confrontation with the Soviet Union and instead should settle its differences by peaceful means. Assistant Secretary of State, C. Burke Elbrich made an important observation in the Committee in the light of Soviet advancement of strategic weaponry and against the backdrop of the Hungarian uprising. While reacting to Senator Smith's contention Elbrich said that "there is the danger of fomenting some revolution which might destroy them [enslaved peoples]". Therefore, the United States should "try to give the people inside the Iron Curtain the courage to resist" the enslavement. At the same time he made it loud and clear: "We have no intention of inciting these people to rebellion."[8]

President Eisenhower's address to the US Congress in 1958 did not carry the message of 'gradualism', which meanwhile gained currency among the concerned levels of foreign policy makers. It merely dwelt with the threat to the safety and peace of the world coming from the "communist imperialism". His statement is a reflection of America's anxiety at the growing influence of the Soviet Union in the oil rich countries of West Asia. Nonetheless, he outlined his plan to meet the threat:

> Every part of our military Establishment must and will be equipped to do its decisive job with the most modern weapons and methods...we must make a candid estimate of the effect of long range ballistic missiles on the current deterrent power . . . [9]

The ideas of 'gradualism' started to secure prominence in the statement of Dulles. In his prepared speech before the Atomic Power Institute, New Hampshire, on May 2, 1958, he stated that his country would extend support to "the evolutionary

8 *ibid*, p. 748.

9 *American Foreign Policy: Current Documents, 1958*, p. 3.

forces of freedom" without the "awful horror of world war III".[10] Two weeks later he defended the shift of his thesis from liberation to evolutionary process of freedom. He said: "I have constantly said that we need to keep our foreign policy flexible and acceptable to changing situation".[11]

Meanwhile, at different levels of the United States, most notably in the Congressional committees, a psychological preparation was initiated to accept the evolutionary theory. There were alternative proposals like mutual engagement as a means to change the power position in Europe. Chester Bowles, after his meeting with Nikita S. Khrushchev in February 1957, reported that the Soviet leader found the possibility of easing the unnatural situation in Europe by giving effect to a phased and mutual withdrawal of the NATO forces from West Germany, France and Benelux on the one hand and simultaneous withdrawal of Soviet troops from East Germany and other East European countries on the other.[12] In the House Committee of US Congress, Bowles repeated his contention of peaceful disengagement of forces on mutual basis. He said that it would be unrealistic to demand the withdrawal of Soviet troops from Eastern Europe at a time when the United States was arming West Germany. He remarked:

> If I were a Soviet dictator, I would not withdraw Soviet troops from East Germany, Poland, Hungary and Czechoslovakia in the face of well armed nuclear equipped Germany in the middle of Europe.[13]

George F. Kennan, on a number of occasions, pleaded with the Eisenhower Administration to consider the proposal for mutual

---

10 *ibid*, pp. 32-33.

11 Department of State, *Bulletin*, June 9, 1958, p. 942.

12 Chester Bowles, "Our Objective in Europe – and Russia's", *New York Times Magazine*, May 12, 1957. Later on in October a Polish Minister, Adam Rapacki, told the UN General Assembly that a nuclear free zone in Central Europe covering both the German states, Poland and Czechoslovakia would contribute actively to the establishment of peace in Europe. For Details see Eugene Hinterhoff, *Disengagement* (London: Stevens, 1959) pp. 402-407.

13 US Congress, House Committee on Foreign Affairs, *Briefing on World Situation*, 86th Congress, 1st Session, January 28 and 29, 1959, p. 27.

withdrawal of forces as a step towards reunification of Germany and liberation of Eastern Europe from the Soviet sphere of influence. Most notably, he argued in the Hearings before the Senate Foreign Relations Committee on May 12, 1959, that the United States should make concession in the matter of withdrawal of US forces and should stop rearming West Germany with atomic weapons.[14] Dean Acheson, former Secretary of State, however, considered the idea of disengagement as "new isolationism" and dismissed it as an unworkable proposition.[15] The Senate Foreign Relations Committee arrived at a conclusion that it was nothing less than balderdash to expect the Soviet withdrawal of troops from Eastern Europe for economic, political and strategic reasons in the era of the Cold War confrontation. It was observed that disarmament or disengagement would eventually lead to disappearance of communism in Eastern Europe, which the Soviet leaders would never allow it to happen.[16] The Eisenhower Administration examined the conclusion of the Senate Foreign Relations Committee report and disfavoured a partial disengagement without German reunification and also without ensuring change in the political status of Eastern Europe, because mere partial disengagement would be detrimental to the Western defence system. For the West, the question of rearming West Germany was more important that the reunification of Germany and unpredictable changes in Eastern Europe aftermath the disengagement. The priority of interest was made clear in Berlin Declaration of July 29, 1957, signed by Britain, France, the United States and West Germany, which proposed a security arrangement for the Soviet

---

14 US Congress, Senate, Committee of Foreign Relations, *Informal Meetings with George F. Kennan*, 86th Congress, 1st Session, May 12, 1959, pp. 13-14. Also for details see George F. Kennan, *Russia, the Atom and the West* (London: Oxford University Press, 1958)

15 Dean Acheson, "The Illusion of Disengagement", *Foreign Affairs*, Vol. 36, No. 3 (1958) p. 378 and for the details of Kennan's reply see "Disengagement Revisited", *Foreign Affairs*, Vol. 37, No. 2, (1959) pp. 187-210.

16 US Congress, Senate, Committee on Foreign Relations, *Control and Reduction of Armaments: Final Report*, Staff Study, No. 8, 85th Congress, 1st Session, June 6, 1957.

Union and Eastern Europe in the case of a reunited Germany joined the NATO.[17] Such a proposition, to everybody's imagination was unacceptable to the Soviet Union. In this way, to advance an unacceptable and unworkable proposal became a part of the Cold War diplomacy. On this the Soviet Union offered a new proposal in December 1957 favouring disengagement, of course, without mentioning the question of reunification of Germany as well as the future of Eastern Europe, and suggested a summit meeting in 1958 in order to have a full length discussion of the proposal.[18] It was difficult for the Administration to reject the proposal outrightly, and therefore, it wanted to know the Soviet motives behind the proposal. President Eisenhower wrote back to Bulganin stating that the summit meeting should include items such as "reunification of Germany by free election" and the future of Eastern Europe.[19] In response to Eisenhower's letter Khrushchev made a hard-hitting controversial speech, known as Minsk speech of January 22, 1958, declaring that discussions in the proposed summit would collapse if the prevailing *status quo* position of Eastern Europe was not reçognized and matters relating to their internal affairs intruded upon.[20] Consequently, the prospect for a summit meeting on the question of disengagement became bleak. It received a further set back. Moscow insisted on the West's recognition of German Democratic Republic, failing which, Khrushchev declared on November 20, 1958 that the responsibility of Berlin would be handed over to East German Government.[21]

Meanwhile, on July 17, 1959 the United States Congress unanimously adopted the 'captive Nations Week' Resolution

17 Royal Institute of International Affairs, *Documents on International Affairs, 1957* (London, 1960) pp. 97-99.

18 Bulganin's letter of December 10, 1957 contained the Soviet proposals of disengagement. See Department of State, *Bulletin*, January 27, 1958, pp. 127-130.

19 *Public Papers of the Presidents: Dwight D. Eisenhower*, 1958, pp. 79-84.

20 Arnold Wolfers (ed), *Alliance Policy in the Cold War* (Baltimore: John Hopkins Press, 1959) pp. 156-157. In his letter to Bulganin, dated February 17, Eisenhower reacted sharply to Khrushchev's Minsk speech, for the text of the letter, see *ibid*, pp. 156-157.

introduced by Paul Douglas in the Senate and John McCormack in the House of Representatives.[22] Referring to the 'subjugation' of the people of Eastern Europe, the resolution held that the United States, as the "citadel of human freedom" shared the desire of these people for liberty and independence, and therefore, it resolved that the President be authorized to issue a proclamation designating the third week of July 1959 as the 'Captive Nations Week' and "inviting the people of United States to observe such week with appropriate ceremonies and activities." Accordingly, President Eisenhower proclaimed the week beginning July 13, 1959 as the 'Captive Nations Week' and urged the Americans to "study the plight of the Soviet dominated nations and to commit themselves to the support of the just aspirations of the peoples of those captive nations." He also urged upon the Americans to continue to observe the third week of July each year as the 'Captive Nations Week' until "Freedom and independence shall have been achieved for all the captive nations."[23] The joint resolution and President's declaration were widely published through the mass media, and the week was observed by holding meetings, prayers in the churches all over the country, making thereby known to all Americans the renewed desire for freedom of the peoples of Eastern Europe. While the Americans were observing the Captive Nations Week, Vice President Richard M. Nixon arrived in Moscow on July 23 to open the American National Exhibition at Sokolniky Park indicating thereby that the Cold War rhetoric and tract II diplomacy could go in a parallel way. Just a few minutes before Nixon's landing at the airport, Khrushchev addressed a rally in Moscow denouncing the American 'Captive Nations Resolution' and the renewed campaign for liberation of Eastern Europe by a week observation of activities on that line.[24] During the discussion that took place between the two leaders in the Kremlin Palace

21 *New York Times*, November 11, 1958.

22 US Congress, *Congressional Record*, 86th Congress, 1st Session, 1959, pp. 13115, 14105-106.

23 Department of State, *Bulletin*, August 10, 1959, p. 200; and also see US Congress, *Congressional Record*, *ibid*, pp. 14106-107.

24 *New York Times*, July 24 and 28, 1959.

on July 23, Khrushchev questioned the American motives behind these steps, which carried the potentiality of risking a major war. Nixon replied:

> . . . the resolution did not call for our intervention, or even for support of a revolution in the satellite nations, but only expressed moral support and asked prayers for those who want freedom in those nations.[25]

The 'Captive Nations Week' Nixon's visit to Moscow during the observance of the week and the aforementioned remark implied that the United States was intending to live with Dullesian rhetoric in a milder form and within the boundaries of hopes only. Simultaneously, it would strive to improve relations with the Soviet Union.

The gradualist approach was conceived merely as a hope of the US Administration to see greater freedom in Eastern Europe with the passage of time. Therefore, it was not conceptualized theoretically. With the death of Dulles in 1959, Andrew H. Berding, Assistant Secretary of State, used to make major foreign policy statements on Eastern Europe. His statements carried the evidence of America's acceptance of peaceful co-existence with the Soviet Union and also the hope for the evolutionary liberation of Eastern Europe. The contradictory position of the US Administration demonstrated its helplessness on the future of Eastern Europe. Neither it could declare that it was prepared to live with the *status quo* reality in Europe nor could it actively campaign for a revolutionary situation in Soviet sphere of influence. Berding's remark at the Freedom Day celebration at the base of the Statute of Liberty, New York, can be referred to here. He said:

> The United States seeks nothing itself in the Eastern Europe. It offers no threat to the security of the Soviet Union in that area...It desires for their peoples only this; they be truly free; that they be able to establish whatever form of government and whatever economic and social institutions they desire to live under. The peoples of Eastern Europe aspire

25 Richard M. Nixon, *Six Crises* (New York, Garden City: Doubleday, 1962) p. 247 and 251-252. Khrushchev's memoirs, however, referred to the kitchen debate and not about the Soviet reactions on the observance of the week. See *Khrushchev Remembers, The Last Testament*, Vol. 2 (Harmondsworth, Middlesex: Penguin, 1974), pp. 419-423.

> this freedom. Our Government and our people hope they will achieve it. Whatever this country can do by peaceful, legitimate means to help them to the end, we shall do.[26]

Khrushchev's visit to the United States and the Camp David talks created an apprehension among the East European émigrés that the United States had made a deal with the Soviet leader on the fate of Eastern Europe under the cover of peaceful co-existence. However, Andrew Berding made a statement synchronizing peaceful co-existence with the hope of gradual liberation:

> Accepting peaceful co-existence means accepting the *status quo* whereby the Soviet Union dominates a communist bloc of nations. We have given the Soviet Union solemn assurance that we have no desire to turn these nations against Moscow, that we do not seek military alliances with them, that we do not wish to impose the American way of life upon them, that we do not wish a return to their prewar process of government. But we do desire for their peoples true freedom, genuine national independence, and ability to establish whatever form of government and economic and social institutions they wish. We cannot accept a *status quo* which makes this impossible.[27]

The US Government began to experiment with its gradualist approach by enlarging the avenues for economic cooperation with most of the East European countries barring Hungary. In the assessment of the Administration, Poland could be the principal expectation and is likely to come out of Soviet domination. There are reasons for such expectation. Ever since the return of Gomulka to power, Poland appeared to have liberalizing the political control over the church for which in the election of 1957 he secured the support of the Roman Catholics. The US Administration, though unhappy with Gomulka for his support to Soviet invasion of Hungary, took the January 1957 election as a step towards political liberalization in Poland, and therefore, began to test the viability of its gradualist strategy in that country.

Soon after the elections, a Polish delegation came to the United States in February to obtain a credit of $300 million.

---

26 Department of State, *Bulletin*, July 20, 1959, p. 76.

27 *ibid*, November 2, 1959, p. 629.

The Eisenhower Administration, after an initial hesitation, agreed in June to grant $30 million Export Import Bank loan and to sell $18.9 million worth of cotton, fats and oils for Polish currency. Thereafter in August the US Congress extended the Agricultural Trade Development and Assistance Act to give coverage to Poland. Another agreement was concluded for the sale of $46.1 million worth of American cotton and wheat.[28] Moreover, a cultural agreement was reached to enable 300 Poles to visit the United States during 1957-1959 under the sponsorship of Ford and Rockefeller Foundations.

The Gomulka regime could remain content with the quantum of American aid, and therefore, on April 11, 1958, a Polish-Soviet trade protocol was announced.[29] It was a renewed expression of economic cooperation among the socialist countries under the Council for Mutual Economic Assistance (CEMA). Further, it was a message to the US Administration that Washington DC was not the only source of economic assistance to Poland. President Eisenhower was also not happy with the net result of the American aid programme and expressed his dissatisfaction in a press conference on July 18, 1958 saying that the US aid and trade concessions did not produce any evidence of increased independence in Poland and Yugoslavia.[30] The American hope for positive results in Poland was further shattered in November when Gomulka visited the Soviet Union and leveled blistering attack on the West. Nonetheless, the State Department favoured the continuation of the aid programme to Poland with an uncertain hope of gradual emergence of a more liberal political atmosphere.[31] The American aid proved to be counter-productive as the Soviet Union tried to tighten its control over the Polish economic system by way of propagating for an integrated economy.

Similar move to draw Tito, whose estranged relationship with Moscow was a *fait accompli*, closer to the United States

---

28 *ibid*, June 24, 1957, pp. 1003-09 and September 9, 1957, p.44.

29 *New York Time*, April 12, 1958.

30 *ibid*, June 18, 1958.

31 Department of State, *Bulletin*, June 29, pp. 959-961 and November 30, 1959, pp. 789-790.

proved to be a mere miscalculation as he was looking for a third front which eventually led him to become the champion of the Non-aligned Movement (NAM). It was he who hosted the first NAM Conference at Belgrade in 1961. His anti-West position was more pronounced in the Conference than his seemingly anti-Soviet stand. The US Administration missed a vital point to note. Tito at no point of time did take a pro-Western position. He sought American aid but by that he did not mean that he had changed his colour to come closer to the United States or he wanted to connive American imperialism. He made a clear declaration to that effect in the Seventh Congress of the League of Communists.[32]

In February 1960, at the request of the Senate Foreign Relations Committee, a Colombia-Harvard Research Group prepared a report on the US policy towards the Soviet Union and Eastern Europe. The report contained an exhaustive analysis of the situation in the region and the success and failure of American foreign policy. It argued that the domestic controversy in the United States over 'containment versus liberation' had remained in the realm of confusion and much of the debates had lacked real content.[33] While the Soviet Union had a major material and prestige consideration at stake on the question of Eastern Europe, and therefore, demonstrated its capacity to retain its hold over the region at any cost, the West did not have such stakes and hence proved its inability to intervene in the Hungarian crisis. It observes that there was an abortive revolt in Hungary. It seems unlikely that there would be another. This meant that the Hungarian uprising marked the end of the hope for liberation of Eastern Europe. The October revolt of 1956, according to the study, "proved the definition of limits: limits of the ability of the West to free themselves; the Soviet Union's limit of tolerance; the limit of the West's will and capacity to intervene."[34] On these

32 Milorad M. Drachkovitch, *United States Aid to Yugoslavia and Poland: Analysis of a Controversy* (Washington DC: American Enterprise Institute of Public Policy Research, 1963) p. 11.

33 A Colombia-Harvard Research Group, *United States Foreign Policy: USSR and Eastern Europe; A Study prepared at the request of the Senate Foreign Relations Committee* (Washington DC, 1960) p. 70.

34 *ibid*, p. 50.

considerations the report advanced certain guidelines on American policy towards Eastern Europe, *viz*, (i) "the US policy should not work to provoke or exacerbate crises within Eastern Europe between the people and their communist rulers", (ii) the centre of gravity of American foreign policy should be outside Eastern Europe, i.e. in the non-communist world, where the United States should build up the strength to resist communism, (iii) by means of accurate reporting of the situation in Eastern Europe, the United States could check certain excesses and abuses committed on the people.[35] In short, the report concluded that the United States was no longer in a position to break down doors, and therefore, the alternative for the West was to cultivate contacts with the peoples and governments of Eastern Europe. This contention finally found a better expression in the theory of 'peaceful engagement'.

PEACEFUL ENGAGEMENT:

The American public and the Administration had realized that there was no alternative but to accept the *status quo* position in Eastern Europe. It was reflected in the 1960 US Presidential campaign. Both the Democratic and the Republican planks gave no space for the rhetoric of containment versus liberation policy, implying thereby that liberation of the region from the Soviet control might be a desirable goal but it was unlikely to be achieved in the near future. John F. Kennedy categorically stated that he had no intention to arouse any revolutionary movement in the region. Rather he would prefer to apply peaceful economic measures to forge better relations with the region, more particularly, with Poland.[36] Richard Nixon also spoke on similar lines and promised not to incite senseless rebellion. If elected he would visit these countries in order to tell the rest of the world that ultimate freedom would come to the region at some point of time.[37]

After taking over the office of President of the United States, Kennedy began to work on better economic ties with the governments of Eastern Europe. Long before, as a young

35 *ibid*, pp. 71-72.

36 *New York Times*, October 2, 1960.

37 *ibid*, October 28, 1960.

Senator he had favoured better economic relationship with the region so that the governments in the region could be made less dependent on the Soviet aid. Participating in a debate in the US Congress on August 21, 1957 Senator Kennedy said:

> The only point I make is that we have seen, when discontent becomes too great, as in the case of Hungary, what has happened with the country when the United States has considered itself powerless to assist it. Therefore, at this time we do not wish to encourage those people to revolt, because there is nothing we can do for them, or nothing we will do for them.[38]

While accepting the truth, he argued that the United States should extend economic assistance to the East European countries when sought for, as in the case of Poland "in order to lessen their dependence on the Soviet Union". He criticized the Eisenhower Administration for "merely waiting and hoping" that caused the United States "to be caught wholly unprepared for the events in Poland and Hungary"[39] and for its "too little and too late response" to the Polish request for economic assistance. He also pleaded for the Presidential authorization to grant aids to the deserving East European countries, and to extend cultural relations with them.[40] Two years later, in 1959, he urged upon the Administration to extend economic assistance to these countries and to "recognize that there are varying shades and degrees within the communist world."[41]

President Kennedy remained steadfast to his expressed position that the United States should improve its economic and cultural relations with East European countries. In his inaugural address as well as his first message to the US Congress he referred to the historic ties of the American people

---

38 US Congress, *Congressional Record*, 85th Congress, 1st Session, August 21, 1957, p. 15450. For some details of Kennedy's ideas on peaceful engagement in Eastern Europe see "A Democrat Looks At Foreign Policy", *Foreign Affairs*, Vol. 36, No. 1, October 1957, pp. 44-59.

39 US Congress, *Congressional Record, ibid,* p. 15447.

40 John F Kennedy, *The Strategy for Peace* (New York: Harper, 1960) pp. 82-98.

41 *ibid,* p. 18.

with the peoples of the region and announced that he would request the Congress to give his special authority to develop economic relations with Poland and other countries of the region and that would obviate the politically charged contentious issues making it easier for the United States cultivate a normal relationship with these countries. In other words, Kennedy as a Senator and afterwards as the President tacitly recognized the *status quo* position in Eastern Europe and believed that economic and cultural ties of America with the peoples and the governments of the region would encourage the growth of pluralism in the communist world which would eventually help reduce their dependence on Moscow.

Meanwhile, Zbigniew Brzezniski and William Griffith published an article "Peaceful Engagement in Eastern Europe" on the line of Kennedy's thesis. They observed that the United States had never had a realistic and effective foreign policy towards Eastern Europe. Outlining a dual policy to be followed by the US Administration, they wrote:

> . . . the United States should adopt a policy that might be called peaceful engagement in Eastern Europe. This policy should: (1) aim at stimulating further diversity in the communist bloc; (2) thus increasing the likelihood that East European states can achieve a greater measure of political independence from Soviet domination; (3) thereby ultimately leading to the creation of neutral belt of states which, like the Finnish, would enjoy genuine popular freedom of choice in internal policy while not being hostile to the Soviet Union and not belonging to Western military alliance. Finally, American policy must disassociate itself from any notion that it favors a restoration in Eastern Europe of an economic system patterned on that of the West.[42]

Such a policy, they argued, would serve the long-term goals of the United States and ensure a free pluralistic world. It would minimize the Soviet domination of Eastern Europe and at the same time would not pose any threat to the "legitimate security of the Soviet Union." In the pursuit of peaceful engagement,

42 Zbigniew K. Brzezniski and William E. Griffith, "Peaceful Engagement in Eastern Europe", *Foreign Affairs*, Vol. 39, No. 4, July 1961, p. 644,

the United States should cultivate better economic and cultural relations with the region. Such relationship would strive to draw these countries closer to the rest of world. For moral consideration, they believed, the United States should continue to "insist on self-determination in Eastern Europe in order to prevent any violent anti-Western reaction there which would follow any apparent endorsement of Soviet control and any act which seemed to recognize that communist rule was permanent".[43] In other words, the theory of peaceful engagement came as an intellectual extension of Kennedy's thesis of a world of diversity and better economic engagement with Eastern Europe.

THE BERLIN WALL AND THE US RESPONSE:

The city of Berlin, after World War II, became the focal point of cold war confrontation. In pursuance of the London Protocol as amended on November 14, 1944, Britain, France, the Soviet Union and the United States divided Germany into four zones of occupation. The city of Berlin lied in the middle of the Soviet zone of occupation, 160 km away from the British zone and twice as much as from American zone of occupation. The complex nature of occupation eventually led to two grave crises, the Soviet blockade in February 1948, which, however, was made ineffectual by the massive US-led allied airlift forcing the Kremlin leaders to withdraw it in May 1949.[44] An uneasy situation continued to exist centering the political division of the city. So long as the inter-sector borders remained open, the East Germans, not happy with the socialist system, could easily opt to cross over to West Berlin. At the initial stage the "small amount of immigration might have benefited the East German Government by purifying the population of its least cooperative elements."[45] But in a period of twelve years from May 1949 to August 1961 the number of East German refugees

---

43 *ibid,* p. 645.

44 Otto M. Von der Gablentz (ed), *Documents on the Status of Berlin, 1944-1959* (Munich: R. Oldenbourg KG, 1959) pp. 17-19.

45 Richard L. Merritt, "A Transformed Crisis: The Berlin Wall" in Roy C. Macridis (ed), *Modern European Governments: Cases in Comparative Policy Making* (Englewood Cliff, New Jersey: Prentice-Hall, 1968), p. 143.

crossing over to the West was 2.7 million. Most of them were young and belonged to the productive force comprising doctors, engineers and highly trained personnel. The exodus tended to reduce alarmingly the manpower resources in East Germany.

In this background, Khrushchev reopened the question of Berlin in November 1958. He proposed that West Berlin be a demilitarized 'free city', independent of both the German States to be under the supervision of the four powers and even the United Nations. The routes of access would rest upon the arrangements made between East and West Germany. The proposal came in the form of an ultimatum that the failure of the West to initiate steps towards the settlement within six months would compel the Soviet Union to negotiate a peace treaty with German Democratic Republic and to terminate unilaterally the Western rights guaranteed by the occupation agreements on West Berlin.[46] The proposal was obviously unacceptable to the West because the idea of 'free city' would give the Soviet Union a voice in deciding everything in West Berlin, without, however, ensuring a reciprocal position for the West in matters concerning East Berlin. Being alarmed at the threat, the Council of Ministers of NATO declared on December 16, 1958 in Paris that the unilateral renunciation of the four-power agreements on Berlin by the Soviet Union could not deprive the other contracting parties of their rights. The Soviet Union must honour the terms of agreements and bear the consequences of the termination of those agreements.[47] At the same time the West did not show any intention to aggravate the situation indicating thereby that the Khrushchev's threat did not deserve hostile and sharp reaction. The Western mood was for the success of the proposed summit in Paris in May 1960, which signaled some hope for a negotiated settlement of the issue. But the summit did not take place because of the U2 espionage episode on May 1. The breakdown of the summit did not result in any significant consequence.

In the months following Kennedy's ascendancy to the White House, the Berlin issue received attention of his Administration.

---

46 *New York Times*, November 28, 1958.

47 *ibid*, December 17, 1958.

Khrushchev, on the other hand, intended to postpone the conclusion of the proposed peace treaty with the United States in order to test the conciliatory flexibility that Kennedy had shown during the election campaign. But the situation in Berlin posed to be grave because of the continuous flow of East German escapees to the West, which registered an alarming proportion in 1960 alone crossing an astounding figure of 200,000. The rate of exodus increased in the early part of 1961. It compelled Walter Ulbricht to take recourse to a strong measure.

In the Vienna meeting of June 3-4, 1961, a façade of measured goodwill was evident at the initial stage when Kennedy and Khrushchev exchanged views on Berlin. Both of them did not put forward any new proposal for discussion towards the solution of the impasse over Berlin.[48] Khrushchev reintroduced his ultimatum of 1958 and suggested a dedicated conference on Berlin in order to "formally recognize the situation which had developed in Europe after the war". He meant to recognize the existence of two German states and to transform West Berlin into a demilitarized free city, failing which, he warned, would lead to unilateral conclusion of a treaty with East Germany terminating West's rights in West Berlin, if necessary by application of force. Kennedy reaffirmed his stand adhering to three basic essentials: (i) continuation of unhindered Allied presence in West Berlin, (ii) unrestricted use of access routes to and fro West Berlin, and (iii) freedom of West Berliners to choose their own form of government.[49] Khrushchev interpreted the American stand as challenge, which he would accept even at the risk of war.[50]

President Kennedy's firm stand on the security of West Berlin within the framework of three essentials rests on the recommendations of a report prepared by Dean Acheson, former Secretary of State, who favoured the full use of American

48 *ibid*, June 5, 1961.

49 *American Foreign Policy: Current Documents*, 1961, pp. 584-586.

50 For Khrushchev's assessment of the situation and his secret plan to construct the wall see *Khrushchev Remembers, The Last Testament*, Vol. 2 n. 25, pp. 571-575.

military might in defence of the West Berliners, to ensure free access to the city of West Berlin and to protect the Western garrison located in the city.[51] Although he was not in favour of a military confrontation, Kennedy prepared a contingency plan. On July 25, in a nation-wide television address President Kennedy reiterated his willingness to consider all reasonable proposals about the future of the city, at the same time he reiterated his firmness to protect the three essentials at all cost. To strengthen his stand he announced emergency measures including the full alert of reserved and strategic air command and increase the defence expenditure to improve US military capability. He declared: "We cannot and will not permit the communists to drive us out of Berlin, either gradually or by force." He further stated:

> We recognize the Soviet Union's historical concern about their security in Central and Eastern Europe after a series of ravaging invasions and we believe arrangements can be worked out which will help to meet these concerns, and to make it possible for both security and freedom to exist in this troubled area.[52]

Meanwhile, the idea of constructing a wall on the line of control dividing the city into two parts had been working in the minds of Khrushchev and Ulbricht. They intended to stop the exodus of East Germans once for all who had been escaping to the other side at the alarming rate of 1000 daily towards the latter part of July 1961. As they started to work out the details they found two indicators working in their favour. President Kennedy's three essentials completely ignored the state of affairs in East Berlin, meaning thereby the US would remain unaffected and unconcerned at any development in East Berlin. Second, Senator William J. Fulbright, the Chairman of the Senate Foreign Relations Committee, said in a television interview: "I don't understand why the East Germans don't close their borders because I think they have a right to close it."[53] It is difficult to say now whether Senator Fulbright's

51 Theodore C. Sorensen, *Kennedy* (New York: Harper and Row, 1965), Chapter 21.

52 *New York Times*, July 25, 1961.

53 *ibid*, August 3, 1961.

comment hastened their decision to close the border by constructing a wall.

On August 3, the Warsaw Pact Council met to deliberate on the measures to be adopted for ending the human exodus. On the very next day it unanimously agreed to seal the border with West Berlin. The decision was formally announced at 1:11 am on Sunday, August 13, 1961. Thus, began the erection of the 160 km long Berlin wall along the perimeter of West Berlin.[54]

The only decision that the West took on August 13, as Richard L. Merritt writes, was not to take any action.[55] It was mainly due to the fact that the construction of the wall was an activity in the Soviet zone of occupation and in no way affected the United States or Western interest. The surgical action merely halted the refugee flight without stifling any of the Western occupation rights. As Theodore Sorensen writes: "Our contingency plans had been prepared for interference with our access to West Berlin, not emigration from the East." His concluding observation merits attention:

> Not one responsible official – in this country, in West Berlin, West Germany or Western Europe – suggested that Allied forces should march into East German territory and tear the wall down. For the Communists, as General Lucius Clay later pointed out, could have built another ten or twenty or five hundred yards back, and then another, unless the west was prepared to fight a war over extending its area of vital interest into East Berlin. Nor did any ally or adviser want an excited Western response that might trigger an uprising among the desperate East Berliners – that would only produce another Budapest massacre.[56]

Far from demonstrating any reaction to the erection of the Berlin wall, the Allied powers felt immediately a sense of relief, as the situation did not warrant any step to operationalize their feared contingency plan. President Kennedy learnt about

54 The decisions adopted by the Warsaw Pact Council and GDR Council of Ministers appeared in *New York Times*, August 14, 1961.

55 Richard L. Merritt, "A Transformed Crisis: The Berlin Wall", n. 45, p. 148.

56 Theodore Sorensen, *Kennedy*, n. 51. p. 594.

the commencement of the construction of the wall late on Saturday night and sixteen hours after the announcement of Warsaw Pact Council's decision. Secretary of State Dean Rusk informed him over telephone at Hyannis Port, where the President had been spending the weekend with his family. Max Frankel commented: "Officials who had lived with expectation of Berlin 'crisis' for three years were routed from the bed."[57] Dean Rusk made a brief statement to the press in which he protested against the unilateral decision of the Soviet backed authorities to sever the communication between the two parts of Berlin in violation of the four power agreement of 1949. He, however, said: "Available information indicates that the measures taken thus far are aimed at the residents of East Berlin and East Germany and not at the Allied position in West Berlin or access thereto."[58]

The argument was consistent with truth, because, the 1949 four-power agreement referred to the communication between the western zone of Germany on the one hand and Berlin and the eastern zone on the other hand, and not the communication between the two sectors of Berlin. Just as Kennedy did not cut short his weekend holidaying, Dean Rusk too went to a baseball game. Similarly, the NATO members, except issuing a statement deploring the erection of the wall, did not demonstrate any emotion or reaction. West German Chancellor Konrad Adenauer was posted with the fact that the United States would make no response, and hence, his Government did not attach any importance to the issue in order to avoid public unrest, in view of the ensuing election to be held in September. In West Berlin, there was an expression of a measured emotional feeling against the construction of the wall. The West Berliners under the leadership of Willy Brandt wanted to avoid any trouble in the city over the issue. A small number of them rushed to the border and shouted slogans. Certain minor incidents like pelting stones took place but the situation was brought under control. Sidney Gruson reported

---

57 *New York Times*, August 20, 1961.

58 US Department of State, *Berlin: 1961*, European and British Commonwealth Series, No. 64 (Washington DC, 1961) pp. 41-42.

that about 4,000 people assembled at 8:00 pm at Hindenburg Platz in front of Brandenburg Gate and that was the largest crowd protesting against the action of Soviet backed East German regime.[59]

Against the backdrop of the three essentials of President Kennedy, the American response to the erection of the wall, when analyzed, would mean that the Kennedy Administration had no commitment to the citizens of East Berlin for obvious reasons, and naturally when the exodus of people from Soviet sphere of influence was stopped by strong means, the Administration had little to say about it. The three essentials of President Kennedy gave a green signal to the Soviet Union to do whatever it had intended to do without directly affecting the vital interests of the Allied powers. The only accusation one could level is that the United States did not spell out the West Berliners, who were exposed to Soviet punitive measures, the extent of its commitment to them. A clear commitment would have left no scope for wild speculation and illusion created by the press on American rescue plans in the event of Soviet military incursion into West Berlin. As a result, the West Berliners, on the following days demonstrated not against the Soviet Union or the Government of GDR but against the West for its discreet silence on the question of protecting the West Berliners if they were affected by any possible Soviet action. Alarmed by this development, Willy Brandt, appealed to President Kennedy on August 16 to take some symbolic retaliatory measures. This prompted the President to act in order to save the credibility of his country and secondly to save Willy Brandt from a grave predicament. President Kennedy had, in an earlier occasion, promised the governing Mayor of West Berlin in May 1961 to defend and protect the freedom of his city to which the United States was bound by "treaty obligation and conviction". Already Brandt incurred strong displeasure of Chancellor Adenauer for writing to President Kennedy without his knowledge. In response to the letter, Kennedy sent Vice-President Lyndon B. Johnson, accompanied by General Lucius Clay, to West Berlin to deliver

59 *New York Times*, August 14, 1961.

the message to Brandt that a free West Berlin would be maintained at all costs. At the same time a contingent of 1500 soldiers was sent to strengthen the Allied garrison. One can understand that these were mere symbolic gesture to restore publi confidence in Willy Brandt and in the American promise to stand by the citizens of West Berlin.

An emotional welcome in Berlin overwhelmed Vice-President Johnson. As many as half a million West Berliners lined on the streets to greet him. In a prepared speech Johnson said:

> To the survival and to the creative future of this city we Americans have pledged, in effect, what our ancestors pledged in forming the United States: "Our lives, our freedom and our sacred honor".[60]

The presence of General Clay had a tremendous psychological effect because his name had been associated with the crisis period of Berlin Blockade, and later on he became the permanent representative of President Kennedy to the city of Berlin. General Clay initiated a policy designed to restore the city's four-power status by forcing the Soviet Union to accept the responsibility of East Berlin and to recognize the rights of three allied powers in Berlin as a whole. This policy sharply generated tension and on October 27 the Soviet and the American tanks faced an eye-ball-to-eye-ball confrontation at the checkpoint Charlie.[61] The Kennedy Administration was not in favour of a showdown, and therefore, it disapproved General Clay's confrontation. Subsequently, in April 1962 General Clay had no alternative but to leave the post.

It became clear that the erection of the wall effectively checked the alarming rate of exodus of East Germans to the other side. The wall did not pose any formidable threat to the security of West Berlin. Again, the United States did not find any threat to its interests in the city, and therefore, had found no ground to react strongly against the construction of the

---

60 *New York Times*, August 20, 1961.

61 *ibid*, October 28, 1968.

wall.[62] President Kennedy pleaded in the UN General Assembly for the relaxation of tension over Berlin and expressed his flexible approach to any formula on an honourable solution to the crisis. In a message to Britain, France and West Germany on April 12, 1962, the United States favoured normalization of relations between the two German states and also an agreement between NATO and Warsaw Pact to respect the existing borders.[63] It indirectly meant that the Kennedy Administration would not challenge the Soviet sphere of influence in East and Central Europe. Whatever unrest, political trouble or anti-government and anti-Soviet revolutions were likely to take place would be a matter of Soviet concern and would be beyond America's intervention. United States, however, would continue to improve its economic, diplomatic and cultural relations with the peoples and governments of the region.

PEACEFUL ENGAGEMENT EXPERIMENTED:

In the pursuit of peaceful engagement, William R. Tyler, Assistant Secretary of State, argued before the Subcommittee on Europe under the House Committee on Foreign Affairs favouring more normal and active trade relations of the United States with East European countries in view of the adoption of a comparatively more flexible Soviet policy to these countries and also of certain changes taking place therein like Goulka's defence for private farming and Kadar's new conciliatory slogans.[64] The Subcommittee, in its final report, supported the Administration's recent initiatives to have a mutually beneficial

---

62 A number of authors, more or less, appeared to have arrived at this conclusion. See in this connection Arthur Schlesinger Jr. *A Thousand Days: John F. Kennedy in the White House* (Boston: Houghton Miffin, 1965), Jean Edward Smith, *The Defense of Berlin* (Baltimore: John Hopkins Press, 1963); Philip Windsor, *City on Leave* (New York: Praeger, 1963) and Hans Speier, *Divided Berlin* (New York: Praeger, 1961).

63 Jean Edward Smith, *The Defense of Berlin*, *ibid*, pp. 313-315.

64 US Congress, House, Committee on Foreign Affairs, Subcommittee on Europe, *Captive European Nations: Hearings*, 87th Congress, Second Session, 1962, pp. 303-307.

trade policy towards the region.[65] At different levels in the Administration, arguments in favour of better American trade relations had been advanced in order to neutralize an anticipated Congressional opposition to it. Testifying before the House Select Committee of Export Control in October 1961, Dean Rusk once again observed that the economic system in Yugoslavia was significantly better than that of Soviet Union. Poland reflected more nationalistic sentiments than communism. Therefore, these countries deserved American aid.[66]

The Administration's peaceful engagement with Eastern Europe, as anticipated, faced serious opposition in the US Congress. A special study report on Poland prepared by Congressman Clement J. Zablocki offered negative findings on the aid programme and observed that despite the American aid to Poland, the Polish Government instead of appreciating the American gesture, indulged in virulent distortion of American image. The United States provided $2,304 million economic aid to Yugoslavia and $878 million to Poland, but both the countries were gradually coming closer to the Soviet Union and had been taking anti-American stand on Cuba and Germany. Therefore, the report concludes that there was no point of continuing the aid to these countries.[67] Kennedy's conciliatory approach to the Governments in Eastern Europe received a further set back in June 1962 when the US Congress decided to reconsider the Foreign Assistance Act of 1961. Senators Proxmire and Lausche successfully introduced an amendment intended to do away with the discretionary power of the President to allocate surplus commodities for aid. Alarmed by the possible adverse effect of the amendment, Secretary of State Dean Rusk forcefully made it clear that it was wrong to give an impression that by offering aid the US

65 US Congress, House, Committee on Foreign Affairs, Subcommittee on Europe, *Report on Captive European Nations*, 88th Congress, 1st Session, April 29, 1963, pp. 13-17.

66 Dean Rusk, *The Winds of Freedom* (Boston: Beacon Press, 1963) pp. 244-245.

67 US Congress, House, *Report of the Special Study Mission to Poland*, Prepared by Congressman Clement J. Zablocki, 87th Congress, 1st Session, July 12, 1961.

Government was "primarily writing off to Soviet domination" of the people of Eastern Europe.[68] The Congressional opposition was neutralized by the Administration's assurance that the recipients of the aid would not engage in aggressive activities against the United States and would not involve themselves in "international communist conspiracy". The President was allowed to extend agricultural surplus aid to East European countries. But almost simultaneously, the Congress included a new provision in the Trade Expansion Act denying the President the right to grant the most favoured-nations treatment to the communist countries, and thus, depriving Poland and Yugoslavia from enjoying the privilege.[69] However, President Kennedy managed to do away with the restrictions by securing a favourable amendment. In this way the tussle between the Administration and the hardliners in the US Congress continued till December 24, 1963 when the new President Lyndon B. Johnson obtained Congressional approval for a bill free of credit restrictions.[70] All this leads one to conclude that accepting the East and Central Europe as a part of the Soviet sphere of influence and intra-communist bloc relations and conflicts as matters of internal affairs, the US Administration began to improve relations with these countries including Hungary.

The United States gradualist approach to Hungary could be seen for the first time when Assistant Under Secretary of State gave an 'unofficial' memorandum to the Hungarian charge d'affaires on July 20, 1962 expressing the hope that the Kadar Government would erase the post-revolution consequences and that would eventually ease the United States to end its opposition to Hungarian representation to the United Nations.[71] The Hungarian Government announced on March 21, 1963 a general amnesty for most of the political prisoners

---

68 Department of State, *Bulletin*, July 2, 1962, p. 25.

69 For details see Milorad M. Drachkovitch, *United States Aid to Yugoslavia and Poland: Analysis of a Controversy*, n. 32.

70 *ibid*, p. 149.

71 Janos Radvanyi, *Hungary and Superpowers: The 1956 Revolution and Realpolitik* (California, Stanford: Hoover Institution Press, 1972) pp. xv-xvi.

and wished to normalize and improve relations with the United States.[72] The amnesty decision was well received in the United States. The State Department considered it to be a fulfillment of its main condition for normalization of relations and issued a statement on May 9 stating that there had been a definite improvement in the political climate in Hungary. Senator Lausche took this statement as a confirmation of the fear that his country was contemplating to bury the controversy around the Hungarian credentials to the United Nations.[73] In the House of Representatives, Edna F. Kelly also expressed concern over the change of attitude of the Administration to Hungary.[74] On June 5, 1963 the State Department, ignoring the opposition of the hardliners, reported to the UN Credential Committee the American decision to drop the credential issue and thereby allow the United Nations to restore Hungary's representation in the world body.[75] In the following month the UN Secretary General visited Budapest marking the end of Hungarian issue.[76] The United States also agreed to withdraw its restrictions on the Hungarian diplomats and agreed to sell wheat to Hungary.[77] This was the first step towards resumption of trade relations between Hungary and the United States. To state precisely, by 1963, the United States normalized its relations with all the states in Soviet sphere of influence in Eastern Europe.

Despite the progressive improvement of American relations with all the East and Central European countries, in order to satisfy the émigré of the region living in the United States, who constitutes a bulk of the American electorate, as well as the anti-communist hardliners, the Administration facilitated the celebration of the Captive Nations Week in July 1963.

---

72 *ibid.*, p. 149.

73 US Congress, *Congressional Record*, 88th Congress, 1st Session, May 15, 1963, p. 8646.

74 *ibid*, p. 10208, and for the text of the letter of Congressman Louis C. Wyman to Dean Rusk and reply of Assistant Secretary Dutton see p. 11219.

75 Department of State, *Bulletin*, July 1, 1963, p. 32.

76 Janos Radvanyi, *Hungary and Superpowers*, p. 151.

77 Department of State, *Bulletin*, December 2, 1963, pp. 860-861.

Secretary of State Dean Rusk made a confirmatory statement that the Administration was hopeful about the eventual freedom of Eastern Europe.[78] But for all practical purposes, the successive US Administration tacitly accepted the division of Eastern Europe on ideological lines. Further, the Cuban missile crisis confirmed about the inherent limits of deterrence. This provided an additional weightage on the compulsions for superpowers' mutual recognition of sphere of influence and for adopting a less expensive strategy later on popularly known as *détente* replacing the more expensive and unproductive Cold War confrontation. President Kennedy's assassination interrupted the momentum of the new strategy in the American foreign policy. All these developments imposed serious limitations on the United States to respond other than verbal condemnation to any Soviet military intervention in any part of Moscow's sphere of influence.

THE BRIDGE-BUILDING THESIS

Ever since the end of World War II every American President evolved a new thesis to the problem of Eastern Europe and communism – from containment, liberation to peaceful engagement. President Johnson, too, had a new theory on the US approach to East and Central Europe, which, however, was not a departure from Kennedy's peaceful engagement. Rather, it was a new name for the process initiated by the late President. Johnson's thesis of bridge-building came up in the wake of gradual economic liberation in the region. His administration considered the changes taking place in the Soviet controlled world to be encouraging for the United States to find the rationale in expanding cultural, economic and diplomatic relations with these countries. On February 25, 1964, Dean Rusk made a significant address covering America's positive response to the pluralist trend gaining currency in the region. He argued that although the American foreign policy objectives were to check communism, in doing so it must try to reduce the danger of war. Simultaneously, the Administration would continue "to encourage evolution within the communist world towards

78 *ibid.*, October 23, 1963, pp. 656-657.

national independence, peaceful cooperation and open societies" and it had found the conditions in East and Central Europe to be conducive to pursue this policy. He maintained that Yugoslavia's success in defending its independence had set an encouraging example for the others. Similarly, Poland had set a good example of national independence. Such instances were being followed by others like Romania and Hungary. In this way these countries had adopted more permissive policy of national reconciliation. The United States should encourage similar developments in Bulgaria and Czechoslovakia, Rusk observed.[79]

George F. Kennan, who had been pleading at different forums for the relaxation of Cold War tension, contended that only a rational approach to the Administration would encourage pluralist trends to grow in Eastern Europe. He accused the US Administration of adopting contradictory foreign policy "one aiming at coexistence, the other at victory through confrontation." He could realize how measures like the Captive Nations Resolution could complicate the task of everyone in the Government who had been trying to avoid the catastrophe of war. He felt that the economic blockade against the communist nations would not bear any significant effect on them. It would only retard the development of polycentralism.[80] Scholars like Hans J. Morganthau held the opposite view and believed that the communist countries still pursued their goal of world domination and that the measures taken by the West to normalize its relations with them would not contribute to reduce the Cold War tension.[81]

As the US Congress stood firmly against the aid programme to East and Central European countries, the Under Secretary of States Averell Harriman appeared before the Subcommittee on Europe of the House Committee on Foreign Affairs to plead in favour of establishing "every kind of peaceful

---

79 *ibid.*, March 16, 1964, pp. 390-96.

80 George F. Kennan, *On Dealing with the Communist World* (New York: Harper and Row, 1964) pp. 23-36 and 44-51.

81 Hans J. Morganthau, "Peace in Our Time", *Commentary*, Vol. 37, No. 3, 1964, p. 66.

contact available" in order to encourage the development of polycentrism in the region.[82] However, the Subcommittee concluded that "there is no indication that the process of change has altered the authoritarian nature of the Communist system" and hence cautioned the Administration that an "over optimistic interpretation of the significance and extent of change within the Soviet bloc, combined with the impact of the initial steps toward disarmament, can compound the problem by giving the United States a false sense of security." The report viewed that the United States could assist liberalization but at the same time should demand the lifting of travel restrictions and electoral reforms in these countries.[83]

While the American policy of peaceful engagement had been put under constant review, President Johnson made a major foreign policy address, which came to be known as 'building bridge' speech. Speaking at the dedication ceremony of the George Marshall Research Library at the Virginia Military Institute on May 3, 1964, President Johnson said that the "nations of Eastern Europe are beginning to reassert their own identity." He declared:

> We will continue to build bridges across the gulf, which has divided us from Eastern Europe. There will be bridges of increased trade, of ideas, of victims, and of humanitarian aid. We do this for four reasons: First, to open new relationship to countries seeking increased independence yet unable to risk isolation. Second, to open minds of new generation to the values and the visions of the Western civilization from which they come and to which they belong. Third, to give freer play to the powerful forces of legitimate national pride – strongest barrier to the ambition of any country to dominate another. Fourth, to demonstrate that identity of interest and the prospects of progress for Eastern Europe lie in a wider relationship with the West.[84]

82 US Congress, House, Committee on Foreign Affairs, Subcommittee on Europe, *Recent Developments in the Soviet Bloc: Hearing*, 88th Congress, 2nd Session, 1964, pp. 384-372.

83 *ibid.*, pp. 12-19.

84 *Public Papers of the Presidents of the United States: Lyndon B. Johnson, 1963-1964*, Vol. I, p. 709.

President Johnson was careful enough not to demand any change in the political system in Eastern Europe as a precondition for 'building bridge' connecting the West with the region because any such demand would carry adverse impact on his carefully drawn approach. Further, the US Administration had already recognized tacitly the *status quo* position in Europe indicating thereby the adoption of a policy of non-interference in the internal affairs of the communist regimes in Eastern Europe. President Johnson did not use the thesis as the Presidential electioneering issue in 1964 in order to avoid unnecessary controversy on the concept. After his massive victory, President Johnson declared in the Union of State message: "In Eastern Europe, restless nations are slowly beginning to assert their identity. Your Government, assisted by the American labour and business, is now exploring ways to increase peaceful trade with these countries and with the Soviet Union."[85] This marked the beginning of a new phase of the American economic relationship with Eastern Europe.

In order to minimize the hurdles put by a number of previous Congressional legislations on the process of US increased trade relations with the East and Central European countries, President Johnson carefully moved his steps first by announcing on February 16, 1965 the formation of a special Presidential committee headed by J. Irwin Miller, Chairman of the Board of Cumins Engine Company, to prepare a comprehensive report on the prospects of America's trade relations with the communist countries.[86] The Miller Committee report observed that the forces of nationalism in these countries had been growing and the Soviet ties with them had been weakening; hence, the United States could use "trade to influence the internal evolution and external behavior of communist countries."[87]

---

85 *ibid,* Vol. I, 1965, p. 3.

86 *New York Times*, February 12, 1965.

87 US Department of State, *Report to the President of the Special Committee on US Trade Relations with East European Countries and the Soviet Union*, presented at the White House on April 29, 1965 (Washington DC, 1966).

Although President Johnson did not initiate steps immediately on the line of recommendations of the Miller Committee, he took steps in May 1966 to send the draft of the "East-West Trade Relations Act of 1966" to the US Congress. The draft proposed to empower the President to enter into a three-year renewable commerce agreement with communist countries and to expand to them the most favoured nations treatment.[88] In his letter to the Congress, Dean Rusk wrote that in the absence of such an authority the United States would lose and continue to lose 'significant opportunities to influence the course of events in Eastern Europe."[89] The move of the Administration was stalled in the House of Representatives. The Senate Foreign Relations Committee had held hearings on the subject in 1964 and had strong reservations about the increasing US trade relations with the 'satellite' countries.[90] A survey, conducted to understand the views of 125 businessmen and 20 bankers, favoured the position of the Johnson Administration to expand the trade relations. The result of the survey did not impress the US Congress. The battle between the Administration and the US Congress continued. While the former wanted to make all efforts to expand trade relations with the East and Central European countries as a part of 'building bridges', the latter dominated by the conservatives continuously opposed it. Under the circumstances the President made a major foreign policy address in the New York City before the National Conference of Editorial Writers on October 7, 1966 in which he reiterated the thesis of 'building bridges' and announced his commitment to "seek healthy economic and cultural relations with the communist states." He referred to certain steps already taken like the conclusion of US-Soviet Cultural Agreement, and air agreement with the Soviet Union. He announced other new steps such as reduction of export controls on East-West trade with respect to hundreds of non-strategic items; permission for the Export-Import Bank guaranteeing commercial credit

88 Department of State, *Bulletin*, May 30, 1966, pp. 843-844.

89 *ibid,* pp. 839-840.

90 US Congress, Senate, Committee on Foreign Relations, *East-West Trade: Hearings*, 88th Congress, 2nd Session, 1964, pp. 31-32.

to Poland, Hungary, Bulgaria and Czechoslovakia; consideration of easing the burden of Polish debts to the United States through expenditures of America's Polish currency holdings; further liberalization of travel to communist countries; and exchange of cloud photographs taken from the weather satellites. He observed:

> . . . the Western Nations can explore the ways of inviting the Soviet Union and Eastern European countries to cooperate in tasks of common interest and common benefit. Hand in hand with these steps to increase East-West ties must go measures to remove territorial and border disputes as a source of friction in Europe. The Atlantic nations oppose the use of force to change existing frontiers. This is bedrock, too, of our foreign policy. We respect the integrity of a nation's boundary lines.[91]

The content of the speech centered around the philosophy of building bridges to stabilize the sphere of influence and to slowly westernize politically the countries in East European.

In the face of strong Congressional opposition, Johnson's 'building bridges' did not achieve tangible results in relaxing export licenses. By 1967 embargo on some 400 non-strategic items had been lifted. Poland continued to get the most favoured nations treatment. The new entrance to the fray was Romania which did not secure the same status but the volume of US-Romania trade tripled between 1964-1967 which was, however, still less than that of Poland, East Germany and Czechoslovakia.[92]

The efforts made in the framework of 'building bridges' left a clear indication that the US Government could realize the impossibility of any change of *status quo* in Europe, and therefore, through these new innovations it wanted to establish its links with the government and the peoples of the region. Already in Eastern Europe a process of liberalization of the political atmosphere had started, even in Hungary. The US

---

91 *Public Papers of the Presidents of the United States: Lyndon B. Johnson*, Vol. I, 1966, p. 1129.

92 For details see Jozef Wilczynski, *The Economics and Politics of East-West Trade* (London: Macmillan, 1969) pp. 272-276.

economic aid had no role to play in this process. The only benefit or positive result derived from the American aid, according to Brzezniski, was that it "reduced the Soviet capacity to use its economic power for blackmail purposes, and improved the East European bargaining power with Moscow, forcing Moscow to increase its economic aid to East Europe."[93] These policies, however, were not designed to create an atmosphere in which there could be repetition of a Hungarian-type rebellion against the Soviet Union, at the same time all these developments also reduced drastically the American capacity to respond to any Soviet military intervention in Eastern Europe. The US response to Soviet-led Warsaw troops intervention in Czechoslovakia has to be examined in the light of this scenario.

PRAGUE'S EXPERIMENTS OF REFORM:

Czechoslovakia was the last country in Europe to fall under communism in the post-World War II period. The road to communist take over in February 1948 had been paved a decade earlier when the Western appeasement of Hitler produced the Munich agreement, a symbol of great powers' surrender to an aggressive power with an unlimited territorial ambition. Following the entry of German troops into the Sudentenland on October 1, 1938, wrote David W. Paul, "The Czechs, who had prided themselves on their political kinship with the West, learned in 1938 that the West considered them dispensable – lesson that was subsequently confirmed in 1948 and 1968."[94] Taking advantage of the pitiable and shattered condition of this dismembered country, Poland captured Tesin (Cieszyn), and Hungary seized a strip of land in southern Slovakia and the eastern region known as Subcarpathian Ruthenia. On March 14, 1939, Slovakia seceded away to become a separate state allied to Germany. On the following day German troops occupied Bohemia and Moravia. All these had happened even before the outbreak of World War II. In this

93 Zbigniew K. Brzezniski, *Alternative to Partition: Broader Conception of American Role in Europe* (New York: McGraw Hill, 1965) pp. 119-120.

94 David W. Paul, *Czechoslovakia* (Boulder, Colorado: Westview Press, 1981) p. 27.

way Czechoslovakia was crushed into pieces while the West remained a silent spectator.[95]

During the War, various resistance movements helped the Czechoslovak Communist Party (KSC), formed in 1921 after a split of Czechoslovak Social Democratic Organization, to grow from strength to strength and to establish a special relationship with the Soviet Union including the conclusion of the Soviet-Czechoslovak Treaty of Friendship, Mutual Assistance and Post-War Cooperation. These developments eventually compelled Eduard Benes, the head of the exile government of Czechoslovakia to agree to the inclusion of the communists in the post-War coalition government on the basis of parity with other political parties. In Moscow, Benes spoke to Klement Gottwald and other exile members of the KSC, and thus, laid the foundation of mutual cooperation with the communists. Benes now began to piece together his plan: his country would be a bridge between the East and the West; its international position would be guaranteed by the alliance of socialist and the capitalist countries; and its democratic politics would be a combination of liberal democracy and socialist revolution.[96]

The course of World War II drew Czechoslovak closer to the Soviet Union. As the American troops under the command of General George Patton advanced towards Prague, Czechoslovakia came under the zone reserved for liberation to be accomplished by the Soviet forces. Therefore, the US forces did not proceed further. As Prague rose against the Germans in a well-timed uprising on May 5, 1945, it was Soviet Red Army and not the Americans, which completed the task of liberation.[97] And thus, the Soviet Union secured a position of advantage in Czechoslovakia.

---

95 John Bennet Wheeler, *Munich – Prologue to Tragedy* (London: Macmillan, 1963); Hubert Ripka, *Munich and After* (London: Gollancz, 1939); Zdenek Suda, *The Czechoslovak Socialist Republic* (Baltimore: John Hopkins Press, 1969) Chapter 1.

96 Eduard Benes, *Memoirs* (London: Allen and Unwin, 1954) pp. 264-286 and for details see Richard V. Burks, *Dynamics of Communism in Eastern Europe* (Princeton: Princeton University Press, 1961).

97 Dwight D. Eisenhower, *Crusade in Europe* (Garden City, New York: Garden City Books, 1952) p. 460; also Snell-Prague-Delzell-Lensen, *The Meaning of Yalta* (Baton Roughe: Louisiana State University Press, 1956) pp. 119-126.

In April 1945, an agreement was reached in newly liberated Kosic among the leaders of different political groups including the communists and non-communists, barring the outlawed fascist organizations. The agreement brought together loosely all the participant political organizations under the broad umbrella of the National Front. At the 1946 elections the communist emerged as the leading party securing 40.17 per cent votes, which reflected a genuine popular support in favour of the left. The results of the elections strengthened the political bargaining capacity of the communists. This enabled them to secure several strategically important portfolios like ministries of agriculture, information, finance, internal trade and more importantly the ministry of interior responsible for police and civil administration.

One year later, an important development took place. As President Benes favoured his country's international position as a bridge between the East and the West, Czechoslovakia by an unanimous decision of the Council of Ministers adopted on July 7, 1947 accepted an invitation of US Secretary of State, George C. Marshall, to participate in the European Recovery Program, i.e. the Marshall Plan. The Soviet Union forcefully intervened in the matter at the eleventh hour compelling Prague to withdraw from the preparatory conference in Paris.[98] It was undoubtedly an unwarranted interference which not only dismantled the much expected 'bridge' designs of President Benes but also set an unhealthy example of limiting maneuverability of the non-communist partners of the Government by external forces.

The end of the 'bridge episode' paved the way for the actual takeover of power by the communists in February 1948. The non-communist leaders themselves offered the opportunity on February 20 when 12 out of them resigned from the cabinet as a mark of protest against the functioning of the Ministry of Interior. They wrongly calculated that their resignation would force the communist partners to retreat to a conciliatory position. The communists reacted in an unexpected manner.

---

98 For details see Hubert Ripka, *Czechoslovakia Enslaved* (London: Gollancz, 1950).

They published their version of the situation and consolidated their position. President Benes was forced to appoint Klement Gottwald as the Prime Minister, who quickly declared a state of emergency. On February 25, Benes bowed down to Gottwald's pressure and approved a new cabinet. The only hope for the non-communists to have a say in the new government was Foreign Minister Jan Masaryk, son of Thomas G. Masaryk, the first President of the Republic, but on March 10, 1948, Jan Masaryk died in a fall from a window of his office in the Foreign Ministry. The official version of his death was that he committed suicide, but evidence disclosed twenty years later supported an earlier suspicion that he might have been murdered. Unable to proceed along with the new Government, President Benes resigned on June 6. Gottwald made quick move to install himself as the President. Thus, the process of communist takeover was complete.[99]

Benes dream that Czechoslovakia could be a bridge between the East and the West was unrealistic in the context of the post-War situation in Europe. The course of the War made Czechoslovakia a pro-Soviet country as the Red Army had liberated it. Second, the resistance movement within the country brought forward the communists as the most dominant political force. The West had no moral ground to oppose the inevitability of communist takeover of power in Prague because the infamous Munich agreement was West's handiwork, which pushed Czechoslovakia to the claws of an aggressive imperialist. Third, the West adopted an ambivalent attitude to the country in 1945 while the people were fighting against the Germans. And in February 1948, it distanced itself from the political crisis. The communist takeover confirmed that the Soviet power would be the cornerstone of Czechoslovakia's international orientation.

Klement Gottwald consolidated Prague's fraternal ties with Moscow. The political and economic system of his country had been modeled after the Soviet Union. His closer relations with Moscow and faithful adherence to Stalinist style of functioning

---

99 Pavel Tigrid, "The Prague Coup of 1948: The Elegant Takeover" in Thomas T. Hammond (ed), *The Anatomy of Communist Takeover* (New York: Yale University Press, 1975) pp. 399-432.

laid a thorough impact on the country. Even after the death of Stalin in 1953, Czechoslovakia continued to pursue a relatively more conservative approach to communism. Gottwald's successor Antonin Novotny, preserved the Stalinist conservatism through repression, purges and political trials.[100] Attempts had been made to initiate the process of de-Stalinization in 1960 and 1963 with no favourable results. The 4th Congress of Czechoslovak Writers' Union held in Prague on June 27 and 29, 1967, served as a forum for explosive criticism against the Party and the Government, marking the beginning of the end of the old guards and an onset of a new political atmosphere.[101] In October 1967 in the meeting of the Central Committee, Alexander Dubcek openly criticized Novotny for his failure on a number of fronts. The rift within the party was intensified in December 1967, which compelled Leonid I. Brezhnev to pay a personal visit to Prague to avert the ouster of Novotny.[102] Finally, the open revolt against the old guards led to the replacement of Novotny on January 5, 1968 as the party chief by Alexander Dubcek, a relatively obscure forty-six year old Slovak.[103] Novotny, however, retained

100 For details see Jiri Pelikan (ed), *The Czechoslovak Political Trials 1950-1954* (Stanford, California: Stanford University Press, 1971).

101 For details see Vladimir V. Kusin, *The Intellectual Origins of the Prague Spring: The Development of Reformist Ideas in Czechoslovakia 1956-1967* (New York: Cambridge University Press, 1971) and Galia Golan, *The Czechoslovak Reform Movement: Communism in Crisis* (London: Cambridge University Press, 1971)

102 Novotny reportedly arranged Brezhnev's visit. Although this visit averted the imminent fall of Novotny, but it failed to patch up the strong difference of political positions taken by the conservatives and the reformists. See Fritz Ermarth, *Internationalism, Security and Legitimacy: The Challenge to Soviet Interests in Eastern Europe, 1964-1968* (The RAND Corporation, RM-5909, March 1969) pp. 63-64. Also see *Newsweek*, Special Issue, July 27, 1968 on Alexander Dubcek. For more details see Alexander Dubcek, *Hope Dies Last: Autobiography of Alexander Dubcek*, Translated by Hochman, Jiri (New York: Kodensa, 1993).

103 "Czechs Turns Out Novotny", *Washington Post*, January 6, 1968; "Novotny Deposed as Party Leader: Slovak Gets Post", *New York Times*, January 6, 1968. For some details of the collapse of Novotny's repressive regime see Kenneth N. Skoug, *Czechoslovak's Lost Fight for Freedom, 1967-1969: An American Embassy Perspective* (New York: Praeger, 1999).

his other post as the President of Czechoslovakia, largely a ceremonial position, but had to resign on March 21, and thus ending the chapter of power struggle in the party which originated in 1963.

The unseating of Novotny and the emergence of Dubcek marked the beginning of a broad process of internal reform, described by the Czech intellectuals as a 'bloodless revolution'.[104] As a symbol of change, a public homage was paid to the memory of Jan Masaryk on his twentieth death anniversary.[105]

The new leadership in Prague showed restraint in spearheading the reform movement until the publication of the "Action Program" of April 5, 1968 in order to avoid any possible hostile reactions from the internal opponents which might provide them a pretext to stage a come-back and also to provide ground for external intervention. Dubcek tried to strike a balance between the demand of the intellectuals on the one hand, and the opposition to his reforms by the conservatives in the party, state bureaucracy, the army and the police on the other.[106] He promised that there would be no return to "administrative method" of governance and at the same time he expressed awareness of the danger of going too far in the process of democratization. As for the external affairs he hinted greater independence in foreign policy making process, in the formulation of its strategies on international questions, and reaffirmed Czechoslovakia's loyalty to the Soviet Union. He declared that his party "stands firmly and unshakably" linked with the Soviet Union and its "fraternal bonds with the CPSU."[107]

---

104 Dan Morgan, "Zeal of Reform Stirs Czechs", *Washington Post*, February 25, 1968; "reforms Pushed in Czechoslovakia under Dubcek", *New York Times*, March 3, 1968.

105 Henry Kamm, "Masaryk's Grave is a Shrine Again", *New York Times*, March 18, 1968.

106 Anatoly Shub, "New Czech Chief States Aims", *Washington Post*, March 17, 1968. For more details see Galia Golan, *Reform Rule in Czechoslovakia: The Dubcek Era, 1968-1969* (London: Cambridge University Press, 1973) and Harry Schwartz, *Prague's 200 Days: The Struggle for Democracy in Czechoslovakia* (New York: Praeger, 1969).

107 *New York Times*, February 23 and March 17, 1968.

Two days after Novotny's resignation as the President of the country, leaders of the East European countries, with the exception of Romania, in a move initiated by the Soviet Union, held a hastily convened meeting in Dresden, where Dubcek was called upon to explain the rationale behind introducing and activating changes towards political liberalization in his country. What went wrong at the Dresden summit was only partly disclosed in its communiqué which stressed on the danger of "militaristic and neo-Nazi activity" in West Germany. An indirect warning to Czechoslovakia not to stay way from the socialist fold issued in the said communiqué stating that the conference members expected the new Czech leadership to ensure further progress of socialist reconstruction.[108] This was the first employment of collective pressure on Dubcek and his government. It was a foretaste of a future heavy and determined punitive action taken against the Czech reformist leaders who had allegedly undermined the socialist objectives. During the first three months of 1968, the Soviet press maintained discreet silence on the developments in Czechoslovakia, but the most outspoken critics of the changes in Czechoslovakia were Walter Ulbricht and Gomulka who asserted that "counter-revolutionary" and "imperialist" forces had been active in Prague.[109] The Soviet leaders preferred to watch the situation without showing any over-pitched reaction with the hope that in due course of time the opponents in the party would restrain Dubcek. But the adoption of the "Action Program" on April 5 shattered such a hope.

The Czechoslovak Communist Party (KSC) published its "Action Program" on April 9 as the basis for reforming communism. The resolution accompanying the document said that its purpose was to purify communism of its "former aberration" and to "build socialism in this country in a way corresponding to our conditions and traditions". The 60 page document entitled "The Czechoslovak Road to Socialism" pledged among others (i) guarantee of freedom of speech for

---

108 Richard Eder, "Dresden Parley Disturbs Czechs", *New York Times*, March 25, 1968.

109 David Binder, "Events in Prague Vex German Reds", *New York Times*, March 14, 1968.

minority interests and opinion within the framework of socialist law, freedom of assembly and association and religious observance; (ii) electoral laws to provide a broader choice of candidates and greater freedom of non-communist parties within the National Front, because "socialist power cannot be monopolized by a single party or by a coalition of parties"; (iii) upgrading the National Assembly i.e. the Parliament and the Government with regard to the power of communist party apparatus; (iv) broad economic reform to accord enterprises with greater independence and to increase trade with Western countries; (v) an independent judiciary; (vi) federal status for Slovakia on an independent basis and a new constitution to be drafted by the end of 1969. "The Action Program" also outlined the international status of the country and its foreign policy within the framework of "democracy and socialism" and in the context of the struggle "against the aggressive attempts of world imperialism". The basic orientation of the Czechoslovak foreign policy shaped during the struggle for national liberation would be adhered to by way of maintaining "alliance and cooperation with the Soviet Union and other socialist states" on the basis of mutual respect for equality, sovereignty and international solidarity. The Central Committee also pledged a "full and just rehabilitation of all persons" that had been unjustly persecuted during 1949-1954. It guaranteed "moral, personal and financial compensation" to persons affected by such persecutions. It also vowed that "persons who took active" part in the persecutions would not be allowed to hold any important positions in the social and political life of the country. To state precisely, Dubcek's new programme was directed to embark upon a new experiment with "communism with a human face". [110]

The publication of the "Action Program" provoked the Soviet leaders who had been already worried about the new threats of "subversion" from the West and the "rightist

110 Robin Alison Remington (ed), *Winter in Prague: Documents on Czechoslovak Communism in Crisis* (Cambridge, Mass: MIT Press, 1969), also see Abu Nasar Saied Ahmed, "Communism with a Human Face: The Dubcek Experiment", *Journal of Politics*, Vol. VI, Special Issue, 1999, pp. 85-95.

excesses" in Prague. As a result, Dubcek had to make a hasty trip to Moscow in early May 1968.[111] Dubcek probably failed to reassure the Soviet leaders that the process of democratization in his country was under full control, and thus, could not obtain the much needed hard currency loan. At this point, the hard-core Warsaw Pact members convened a meeting in Moscow to express their anxiety over the liberalizing trends in Czechoslovakia, which had essentially an anti-communist overtone.[112] Still the Soviet leadership was not bent on a single course of hard-line approach to deal with the Czechoslovak reform movement. Therefore, Kosygin made a sudden visit to Czechoslovakia on May 17 for a ten-day "work and cure" sojourn at Karlovy Vary.[113] Simultaneously, a Soviet military delegation led by Marshall Grechko appeared in Prague for a seried of discussion with the Czech defence officials that continued for six days. It was finally agreed that a joint military exercise would take place in Czechoslovakia in June under the command of Marshall L. Kuboskii. It was a tactical mistake on the part of the Czech leaders to agree to the joint military exercise, which had far-reaching consequences. They were too fragile to oppose the Soviet move, even though they knew about the consequences. The introduction of its troop deep inside Czechoslovakia gave the Soviet Union a comparative advantage to pressurize Prague to come to Soviet terms. It also eventually made the task of military intervention in August much easier.

The process of democratization in Czechoslovakia was marked by two developments in Prague. On June 27, the National Assembly voted to abolish censorship redeeming one of the principal promises of the Party's programme of action. This created a liberal atmosphere allowing the press to express free opinion. On the same day, a manifesto entitled "2000 Words" written by Ludwig Vaculik and signed by seventy prominent scientists, artists, athletes and other public figures

---

111 Anatole Shub, "Czech-Russian Sessions End Coolly", *Washington Post*, May 6, 1968.

112 "Prague Warned", *ibid*, July 4, 1968.

113 Richard V. Burks, *The Decline of Communism in Czechoslovakia*, The RAND Corporation, P3939, September 1968, p. 4.

were published in several Prague-based newspapers.[114] Some party leaders including Dubcek deplored the publication of the document, which called for a radical speed-up of the reform programme at grassroots levels.[115] Moscow viewed these developments with grave concern and considered the manifesto "2000 Words" as evidence of "activation of right wing and counter-revolutionary forces in Czechoslovakia". It sounded essentially the same rationale for intervention as that was applied in Hungary in 1956.[116] From the early part of July, the Soviet media mounted a gradually intensified war of nerves against the Dubcek regime giving a clear forewarning of an armed intervention, should the Czech leadership continue the process of democratization. The first step in this direction was Moscow's decision to delay the withdrawal of its troops from Czechoslovakia upon the completion of the joint Warsaw troops exercise on June 30, 1968.[117]

On July 15, Bulgaria, East Germany, Hungary, Poland and the Soviet Union in a joint letter issued an ultimatum to the Prague leadership to abandon the course of reform movement or face consequences.[118] The letter enjoined the Czech leaders to impose control over the mass media and deal firmly with anti-socialist forces and organizations and to observe the principles of Marxism-Leninism. The core of the message the

---

114 Ludwik Vaculik, "2000 Words to Workers, Scientists, Artists and Everyone", see Robin A. Remington (ed), *Winter in Prague*, n. 110, Document 29, pp. 198-202.

115 Immediately after the release of the Document "2000 Words" on June 27 Dubcek censured it for trying to push the pace of democratization too rapidly. Some others like Premier Oldrich Cernik held a moderate view on it. See Henry Kamm, "Prague Spurns Plea for a Drastic Purge", *New York Times*, June 29, 1968.

116 I. Alexandrov, "Attack on the Socialist Foundation of Czechoslovakia", *The Current Digest of the Soviet Press*, Vol. XX, No. 25, July 31, 1968, pp. 3-7.

117 Warsaw Dispatch, "Poor Showing Held Cause", *New York Times*, July 17, 1968 also Raymond H. Anderson, "Moscow Continues Prague Pressure", *New York Times*, July 28, 1968.

118 "To the Czechoslovak Communist Party Central Committee", *The Current Digest of the Soviet Press,* Vol. XX, No. 29, August 7, 1968, pp. 4-6.

letter tried to convey was that Warsaw allies would not hesitate to intervene militarily in the internal affairs of Czechoslovakia. It warned:

> . . . we cannot assent to hostile forces pushing your country off the path of socialism and creating the threat that Czechoslovakia may break away from the socialist commonwealth. This is no longer your affair alone...And never will we consent to allow these historic gains of socialism and independence and security of all our peoples to be jeopardized. Never will we consent to allow imperialism, by peaceful or non-peaceful means, from within and without, to make a breach of socialist system and change the balance of power in Europe and in its favor.

The letter was in effect an ultimatum outlining the rationale for the military intervention. Considering the seriousness in the tone and the content of the letter, the Central Committee of the KSC had a thorough deliberation on it and gave a reply rejecting all the charges of counter-revolutionary activities allegedly indulged in the country. Refuting the allegation that Czechoslovakia was being pushed off from the socialist path, it recalled the pledges contained in the Soviet declaration of October 30, 1956 that the relations among the socialist countries would be based on equality, mutual respect for territorial integrity and political sovereignty, and mutual non-interference in the internal affairs. The reply of the Central Committee reaffirmed that the Czechoslovak alliance and friendship with the USSR and other socialist countries was deeply rooted in the social system, historical tradition and experience of the people, in their interests, thought and feelings.[119] At the time of releasing the joint letter on July 18, the Soviet Union made a public message to the Presidium of the KSC demanding a top level meeting of the communist parties of the Soviet Union or Czechoslovakia on either July 22 or 23 in Moscow or in Kiev or in Lvov. This summon was unprecedented. Next day *Pravda* published a "revelation" of the alleged discovery of an armed cache and secret documents

---

119 The full text of the reply was published in *New York Times*, July 19, 1968. For some details see Carol Skalnik Leff, *National Conflict in Czechoslovakia* (Princeton: Princeton University Press, 1988).

providing evidence to say that American and West German agencies were conspiring to aid subversion and counter-revolutionary elements in organizing violent uprising in Czechoslovakia.[120] This was followed by extensive movements of Soviet troops all along the western border of the USSR including the border with Czechoslovakia. East German and Polish troops also joined the exercise. There were reports that Soviet troops stationed in these countries and in Hungary were moving closer to Czechoslovakia within whose territory around 8000 Soviet troops had been encamped.[121] *Pravda* published a few letters from two groups of Czech factory workers asserting that the presence of Soviet troops in their country had made "every honest man feel more secure in his work".[122] This was done to strengthen the rationale for the movement of the Soviet troops as a prelude to the imminent invasion.

On August 3, 1968 at the peak of the Czechoslovak crisis, Leonid Brezhnev and other members of the Soviet delegation to the Cierna-Bratislava Conference together with other leaders of the Warsaw Pact appeared to have reached a modus vivendi about Dubcek's leadership.[123] Simultaneously, the movement of Warsaw troops along the Czechoslovak border was suspended leaving a scope to interpret these events as a victory for the Czechoslovak reformers. There was a short-lived truce achieved through the Cierna-Bratislava communiqué[124] and a ray of hope that the scepter of Soviet-led invasion would disappear soon. General James H. Polk, a former Commander in Chief of the US Army in Europe, noted ten years later that both the US

120 For details see *The Current Digest of the Soviet Press*, Vol. XX, No. 2, August 7, 1968, p. 7.

121 Richard Eder, "Soviet Troops in Germany are Reported Alert", *New York Times*, July 30, 1968; "Red Bloc Forces Near Czech Border", *Washington Post*, July 31, 1968.

122 *The Current Digest of the Soviet Press*, Vol. XX, No. 31, August 21, 1968, p. 9.

123 For all the details of day to day developments on the Prague Spring and eventual Soviet invasion with original documents see Jaromir Novratil, *The Prague Spring 1968: A National Security Archive Documents Reader* (Budapest: Central European University Press, 1998). See Document 85 for Cierna-Bratislava meet.

124 For the text of the communiqué see *ibid*, pp. 3-6.

Government and the NATO officials considered a Soviet invasion to be highly unlikely.[125] But it did not take time for Moscow to gear up severe criticism of Dubcek giving a clear indication that a military intervention in Czechoslovakia was imminent.[126] And on the night of August 20-21, the Soviet-led Warsaw powers invaded Czechoslovakia – the second invasion in Eastern Europe to put the theory of regime change by force into practice.

THE AMERICAN RESPONSE

The brief account of the Czechoslovak situation indicated that the reform movement was not a sudden development. All the developments leading to the invasion of August 20-21 had been made available to the West and the rest of the world through media. These had been carefully watched by responsible quarters in the US capital. The US Congress paid considerable attention to the Czechoslovak reform movement. On April 11, 1968, six days after the publication of the "Action Program" of the KSC, Congressman Gilbert Gude drew the notice of the House of Representatives to these developments. He said that the statements of Dubcek and Western reporting from Czechoslovakia suggested that the new regime was strongly committed to a liberal and reformed communism, which would have a human face. He felt that the developments were likely to lead to a break between Moscow and Prague, and any such attempt would be definitely crushed by the Soviet Union. He concluded that "these developments should be studied closely and watched", with the hope that the prevailing spark of freedom would eventually lead to reversal of the communist policy of expansionism.[127] Congressman John S. Monagan, however, cautioned against undue enthusiasm about

---

125 General James H. Polk, "Reflection on the Czechoslovakian Invasion, 1968", *Strategic Review*, Vol. V, 1977, pp. 36-37.

126 *ibid*, pp. 7-8. For a detailed analysis on the decision leading to the Soviet invasion see Jiri Valenta, *Soviet Intervention in Czechoslovakia, 1968* (Baltimore: John Hopkins Press, 1979) and Karen Dawisha, *The Kremlin and the Prague Spring* (Berkeley: University of California Press, 1985).

127 US Congress, *Congressional Record*, 90th Congress, 2nd Session, April 11, 1968, p. 9832.

these development and said that an American "over energetic endorsement of the gradualist revolutions in the Soviet bloc are likely to bring immediate reprisals from the USSR." He observed that the "Vietnam war has affected the possible American response to changing conditions in Eastern Europe."[128] Later on he cautioned once again against any "wishful interpretation of the limited details" of the situation obtaining in Eastern Europe. He believed that the United States should continue to encourage the expression of freedom in Eastern Europe, at the same time it should temper its "enthusiasm and support with a realistic respect for the economic and social facts of their [East European] situation."[129]

The State Department started watching the developments in Czechoslovakia carefully ever since the publication of the "Action Program" in April 1968, symbolically associated with the reform movement, which came to be known as "Prague Spring". A carefully drafted statement issued on May 1, 1968 revealed that the Administration was "watching with interest and sympathy recent developments in Czechoslovakia, which seem to represent the wishes and needs of the Czechoslovak people. We hope that these developments will lead to an improvement of relations between Eastern and Western Europe and between Czechoslovakia and the United States."[130] In the mean time the State Department invited the Czechoslovak Government to open negotiations on the question of latter's gold and the American claim. The return of $20 million in gold bullion held in the United States since the communist seizure of power in 1948 had been made contingent upon the compensation of $40 to 50 million to American citizens whose property had been nationalized in 1948. Within a week the US Ambassador Jacob D. Bean met foreign Minister Jiri Hajek to convey to him the American desire to reopen talks on these issues and other commercial matters. Without going providing an iota of evidence that Czechoslovakia was estranging itself

---

128 US Congress, *Congressional Record*, 90th Congress, 2nd Session, April 30, 1968, p. 11066.

129 *ibid*, May 9, 1968, p. 12614.

130 *New York Times*, May 2, 1968.

from Moscow, the KSC leaders indicated their readiness to improve their relations with the United States. They did not want to jeopardize their historic and geo-political relations with the Soviet Union. The most pressing need of Czechoslovakia at that time was US credit for revitalizing its shaky economy in view of the Soviet reluctance to grant $400 million hard currency loan requested earlier in May. The Johnson Administration was "not prepared to" accede to the Prague request for $500 million loan, probably keeping in mind about the possible Congressional opposition.[131] The Administration decided to relax export-licensing procedures in the Department of Commerce and to release to the residents of Czechoslovakia some $5 million previously blocked social security and other retirement benefits.[132]

In the US Congress some member tried to respond favourably to the changed situation in Czechoslovakia by extending economic help. Congressman Paul Findley placed a chronology of the events taking place in the country showing the progress of liberalization trend, and introduced an amendment before the Foreign Affairs Committee authorizing the President to extend the most-favoured-nation treatment to Czechoslovakia.[133] In the Senate Walter F. Mondale referred to the newspaper reporting on the Czech reform movement and considered that it was time for the United States to demonstrate a favourable response to the changes in Eastern Europe. He introduced a Czechoslovak trade bill to modify the Export-Import Bank's financing restrictions and the regulations of the Export Control Act and to extend the benefits of most-favoured-nation status to Prague.[134] But the Congressional opposition was too stiff to overcome, and as a result no swift and favourable response to the Dubcek Government could be seen at that point of time. Meanwhile, Senator Claiborne Pell returned from a visit to Prague and suggested that President

131 *New York Times*, May 26 and 27, 1968

132 Department of State, *Bulletin*, July 22, 1968, p. 91.

133 US Congress, *Congressional Record*, 90th Congress, 2nd Session, May 29, 1968, p. 15645.

134 *ibid*, May 15, 1968, p. 13378, May 17, 1968, pp. 13803-13805.

Johnson should appoint a high-level mediator to break the deadlock in the financial negotiations. But the State Department observed that the Senator should exert pressure on the US Congress on this matter and not on the White House.[135]

The Johnson Administration did not exhibit any enthusiasm in granting economic aid to Czechoslovakia not because that the US Congress would put an obvious brake on such a move, but because of a deep-rooted fear that American initiative for better contacts with Prague would reduce the chance of survival of the Dubcek Government. The past experience had made the Administration wiser. It feared that America's enthusiasm in the developments in Czechoslovakia might provoke the Soviet Union to level allegations of American complicity in the aid of the "counter-revolutionary forces". It would eventually provide a pretext for Soviet military intervention. The Administration, therefore, had been waiting till Dubcek managed to consolidate his position. There was another important reason for America's restrained behaviour. The Johnson Administration did not want to jeopardize the process of normalization of superpower relations by actively aiding the Prague leadership who had already earned Moscow's displeasure by initiating reform movement. Further, the responsible circles in the US capital did not probably foresee a preemptive Soviet strike on the Czechoslovak leadership, because it did not find anything anti-communist and anti-Soviet in the new reform programme of action initiated by Dubcek and his followers. Viewed from Washington DC, the process of *détente* appeared to have created a sense of security of the Soviet interests in Eastern Europe and the developments in Czechoslovakia should not affect adversely the Soviet interests in view of the statements and other publications of the KSC reaffirming Czechoslovakia's fraternal relations with Moscow. Even when the Czechoslovak situation became very tense and the Western media reported the ominous signs of Soviet intervention, the Johnson Administration remained silent. Its primary concern at the time was that the process of

---

135 *New York Times*, July 14, 1968.

normalization of the Soviet-American relations must not receive any setback due to the developments in Czechoslovakia.

In a commencement address at Glassboro State College, New Jersey, on June 4, 1968, President Johnson appealed to the Soviet Union to join the United States and other nations "in the spirit of Glassboro" to help achieve world peace.[136] It was at Glassboro where President Johnson had a summit meeting with Premier Alexsei Kosygin on June 23-25, 1967 and exchanged views on the current problems like the Middle East War, the Vietnam War, efforts to halt proliferation of nuclear weapons, limitations on anti-ballistic missile systems and bilateral US-Soviet relations.[137] In this address, he pointed out that despite strains in the US-Soviet relations caused by the Vietnam War, both the nations had shown high degree of bilateral cooperation on a number of areas. The President was careful enough to avoid any comment on the Czechoslovak reform movement and their future impact on the US-Soviet relations. The Soviet Foreign Minister Andre Gromyko, in his address to the Supreme Soviet in June, announced that the USSR was ready for an exchange of opinion on the question of mutual limitation and subsequent reduction of strategic vehicles for the delivery of nuclear weapons – both offensive and defensive – including anti-missile system.[138] Responding to Gromyko's announcement President Johnson declared in Nashville on June 29 that it was time to "turn to a task at least equally complex and difficult to bring under control the nuclear arm race – in offensive and defensive weapons – in ways which do not endanger the security of the US, our allies and others."[139] Both superpowers issued statements on July 1 saying that they agreed to begin talks in the nearest future on means of limiting and reducing their nuclear weapons.[140] They joined 60 other nations to sign the nuclear non-proliferation treaty on this day, i.e. July 1, 1968.[141] On the occasion of signing

136 *ibid*, June 5, 1968.

137 Department of State, *Bulletin*, July 10, 1967, pp. 35-38.

138 *New York Times*, July 28, 1968.

139 *ibid*, June 30, 1968.

140 *ibid*, July 2, 1968.

141 For the full text of the Treaty see Department of State, *Bulletin*, July 3, 1968, p. 2.

the Treaty in the East Room of the White House, President Johnson, Secretary of State Dean Rusk and Soviet Ambassador Anatoly Dobrynin spoke in a cordial atmosphere and expressed their unfailing faith in the efforts to reduce international tension.[142] Some more positive steps in improving the US-Soviet bilateral relations followed this. On July 15, the United States and the Soviet Union signed an agreement to exchange knowledge on cultural, scientific and technical fields.[143] Under the agreement a Russian ballet team was to come to the United States, which, however, could not materialize because of the Soviet invasion of Czechoslovakia a few weeks later. On this day direct air services between Moscow and New York began marking another step towards *détente*.[144]

In order to keep the process of *détente* alive, the Johnson Administration decided to watch carefully the development in Czechoslovakia without making any loose comments. The United States reportedly cautioned the Soviet Union against using forces to stage a regime change syndrome. It advised through private channels that armed invasion would imperil "President Johnson's painstaking efforts to improve American-Soviet relations". A senior diplomat said that the Administration refrained from issuing any public statement on Czechoslovak situation because that would "seriously exacerbate the situation."[145] The State Department, of course, issued a statement denying the Soviet charges that the United States was involved in aiding the insurgents in Czechoslovakia. *New York Times* reported that President Johnson and his chief advisers had earlier weighed "the advisability of quietly informing the Soviet Government of possible repercussion in the United States and internationally of armed Soviet intervention in Czechoslovakia." The idea was dropped due to the concern that the American advice might be resented by the Soviet Union as an interference in matters involving not only the strategic security of the Warsaw pact countries but

142 For the full text of the Treaty see Department of State, *Bulletin*, July 22, 1968, pp. 85-90.

143 *ibid*, August 5, 1968, pp. 154-159.

144 *ibid*, August 12, 1968, p. 170.

145 *New York Times*, July 18, 1968.

also Moscow's politically sensitive relations with its allies.[146] Since then, on the order of the President the American officials did not comment on the Czech-Soviet tension. But in private levels they remained deeply concerned as they knew it well for reasons of its own prestige and position of leadership within the communist world, the Soviet Union might decide to take a surgical step of invasion, should the Prague situation slip out of Dubcek's hand. In the United States, the Czechoslovak National Council of America expressed concern at the situation and urged Dean Rusk to place the matter of Czech-Soviet tension in the United Nations. The Council argued that if the impending intervention was allowed to happen "without effective opposition from any quarter other than some communist states and parties, the usefulness of the United Nations will be terminated, the basis of our [American] foreign policy will have been proven erroneous and the credibility of our posture will be undermined in the eyes of the world."[147]

The American officials were reportedly worried over the continuous attempts of the Soviet propaganda organs to implicate the United States in Prague's defiance of Moscow. Far from being involved, the US Administration had been taking "great pains to remain aloof from the crisis over the liberation of Czechoslovak communism, considering it an intramural communist confrontation that should not become an East-West conflict." It was revealed that early in July Dean Rusk told his chief aids that "whatever happened the United States should stay on the sidelines."[148] The only sign of reaction to the developments in Czechoslovakia was a formal protest of the United States against the repeated Soviet charges of America's involvement in the Czechoslovak affairs. Dean Rusk summoned Anatoly Dobrynin and demanded an explanation.[149] It appeared that the American policy makers discounted the likelihood of Soviet invasion on the basis of their anticipation of *détente* to be carried forward with the assumption that the

146 *New York Times*, July 20, 1968.

147 *ibid*, July 21, 1968.

148 *ibid*, July 22, 1968.

149 *ibid*, July 23, 1968.

Soviet leaders would feel secured in Eastern Europe to allow a degree of pluralism to grow. As the democratization process quickened in Czechoslovakia giving a strong credence to the common belief that the Soviet intervention was going to take place, the Johnson Administration did not show any sign of concern publicly. At his press conference on July 30, Dean Rusk revealed that he had made an oral representation to the Soviet Ambassador Dobrynin that the United States would strongly deplore the use of force to topple the legitimate regime in Prague, but at the same time gave Ambassador an impression that his country would not use its military might to counter the Soviet invasion.[150] The impression that Rusk left for Dobrynin was a reassurance on that score – the United States would do nothing more than verbal condemnation in the event of Soviet invasion of Czechoslovakia. He made it clear that the Administration did not have any contingency plan to counter the putative fear for Soviet moves to crush a fragile member of the Warsaw Treaty Organization trying to assert its new course of reform in the communist system. Refraining from making any comments on the Czech-Soviet tension Dean Rusk said: "I think it would not be prudent for me to speculate or comment on the matter at this time." In the meantime, the NATO forces were placed in a "state of limited alarm" without resorting to provocation. One NATO official commented: "NATO is not going to do anything to make the matter worse. But it's not asleep, by any means."[151]

Although the Johnson Administration decided to remain unmoved at the developments in Czechoslovakia, which signaled in unmistakable terms the high possibility of Soviet surgical strike, the US Congress watched the situation with a sense of anguish. It took up the matter for discussion in order to express its grave concern at the impending invasion and thus tried to create a strong public opinion against another military crackdown in the Soviet satellite system. Congressman Paul Findley expressed alarm at the Administration's discreet silence on the recent events and tried to wake it up:

150 Department of State, *Bulletin*, August 19, 1968, pp. 186-187.

151 *New York Times*, July 26, 1968.

> . . . administration's attitude toward the ominous developments in Eastern Europe has Alice in Wonderland overtones. At an hour when the full diplomatic and political weight of the Soviet Union in being brought to be upon the weak and defenseless nation of Czechoslovakia, the United States is welcoming the direct flight to Moscow, urging the Senate to ratify the non-proliferation treaty with the Soviet Union, and initiating arms control negotiation with the Russians.[152]

He said that the Administration should convey the message to the Soviet Union through "private diplomatic channels" that the military interventions in Czechoslovakia would arouse profound indignation amongst the people of the United States, prevent the ratification of non-proliferation treaty, accelerate arm race and reverse the prospect of relaxation of tension in Central Europe. He agued that instead of contacting the lower level of diplomatic representatives of the Soviet Union, referring obviously to Rusk's summoning of Dobrynin, President Johnson should directly warn Kosygin on Washington-Moscow hot line that the Soviet invasion would lead the world back to the hazards of the Cold War.[153] He spearheaded the attack on the Administration over the issue and raised a question as to whether the United States had "permanently written off Eastern Europe as a part of the Soviet empire." He asked the Administration to warn the Soviet Union that the US-Soviet *détente*, discussion on disarmament and consideration of the NPT would receive a setback if intervention took place.[154]

The US Senate joined the House of Representative in raising a voice of alarm at another Hungarian type of situation in making. Senator Christopher J. Dodd correctly visualized the remoteness in the US military response to the imminent Soviet invasion of Czechoslovakia. Deploring the failure of American diplomacy in restraining the Soviet Union, the

---

152 US Congress, *Congressional Record*, 90th Congress, 2nd Session, July 19, 1968, p. 22278.

153 *ibid*, p. 22279.

154 *ibid*, p. 23069.

Senator said that at least the United States could express moral condemnation of the Soviet attempts to stifle the rights of the Czechoslovak people. He felt that the US involvement in the Vietnam War had probably reduced the American will and determination to react sharply to a possible Soviet invasion.[155] The Senate took note of newspaper reports on the reform movements in Czechoslovakia and also the possibility of a Soviet-led invasion. There were two distinct views on the US inaction at the development. Senator Claiborner Pell, who had a Foreign Service career in Prague before and after the 1948 coup and recently visited the country, supported Dean Rusk's contention that the developments in Czechoslovakia had nothing to do with the United States, and hence, his country should stay on the sidelines.[156] He felt that the United States should not "provide the Soviets with even the shadow of an excuse" for intervention. The Soviet Union should alone bear the responsibility for its action. But other members severely criticized the US position of maintaining ominous silence over the situation and could read well that their concern would not lay any impact on the Administration, which had already written off Czechoslovakia to be fully nailed by the Soviet Union.

It appeared that the Johnson Administration preferred a position of silence to sharp reaction on an assumption that such a position would not aggravate the situation. Some of the US Congressmen too had faith in such a position. Congressman Jonathan B. Binghan joined Senator Mansfield in pleading for the reduction of American forces in Western Europe as a step towards the relaxation of tension. It was believed that the reduction of NATO forces would enable the Soviet Union to withdraw its troops from Eastern Europe on a reciprocal basis and contribute to East-West *détente*. They made a strong plea for an American announcement of plan to begin immediately a meaningful consultation with NATO members on the reduction of forces, which would definitely invite the Soviet

---

155 US Congress, *Congressional Record*, 90th Congress, 2nd Session, July 22, 1968, pp. 22529-530.

156 *ibid*, July 24, 1968, p. 23061.

Union to do the same in Eastern Europe. He introduced the resolution of Senator Mansfield in the House of Representatives, which called for reduction of US forces in Europe, but, to everyone's guess, failed to invoke any favourable result.[157] The atmosphere in the House was charged with emotion against the US silence and Soviet preparation for a military assault. Edna F. Kelly presented an abbreviated chronology of the recent happenings in Czechoslovakia and expressed concern at the reported remark of Dean Rusk that the United States had decided to follow a policy of non-intervention with respect of Czech-Soviet tension.[158]

In the meanwhile, Congressman John C. Kluczynski joined the Czechoslovak National Council of America to plead with the Administration to place the current Czechoslovak situation in the UN Security Council in order to forestall an impending invasion.[159] But such a plea was ignored for unexplained reasons. Under the provision of the UN Charter the situation could have been placed before the Security Council, but presuming that the result would be negative the Administration decided not to resort to what might be a futile exercise. Dean Rusk's statement of July 30 giving a clear indication that the US Government would allow the Soviet-led Warsaw invasion of Czechoslovakia without any strong opposition from the United States contained equivocation when he said: "I think it would not be prudent for me to speculate or comment on that matter at this time."[160] Dobrynin too gathered the clear impression that the United States would not intervene in the crisis to rescue Dubcek.

A report from US Ambassador in Moscow Llewellyn Thompson made it crystal clear what was going to happen in next few weeks. He sent an urgent communication to tell that the Soviet-led military invasion of Czechoslovakia was

157 US Congress, *Congressional Record*, 90th Congress, 2nd Session, July 27, 1968, p. 23887.

158 *ibid*, July 30, 1968, p. 24308.

159 *ibid*, August 2, 1968, p. 25404.

160 Department of State, *Bulletin*, August 19, 1968, p. 187.

imminent. President Johnson later on recollected that the people of Czechoslovakia themselves decided not to resist the intervention nor would they welcome any Western help. Under the circumstances, the United States had very little to do in dealing with the situation. He wrote:

> We considered what we should do if Warsaw Pact forces rolled into Czechoslovakia. We had no treaty commitments, of course. NATO would not support military action. The Czechs themselves had indicated that they did not plan to resist with military force, and they would not welcome any response from the West. We could only try to avoid any action that would further inflame the situation.[161]

The American role in the Hungarian crisis, Brzezniski wrote, conclusively proved the US inability to use its military might as a pressure tactics against the Soviet Union on behalf of the dissidents in Eastern Europe.[162] Since then the Soviet Union not only consolidated its position in the region but also immensely advanced its strategic firepower to deter any military action initiated by the West. For the Johnson Administration there was hardly anything left except maintaining silence over the situation synchronizing the East-West *détente*. It only hoped that in order to keep alive the process of *détente* the Soviet Union would not intervene, and that all the military manoeuvre were done to mount pressure on Dubcek to halt his reform movement. Such optimism had been further strengthened on August 19 when Ambassador Dobrynin delivered Kosygin's invitation to a summit conference in Moscow in October 1968. President Johnson was delighted to avail the opportunity of becoming the second American President to visit the Soviet Union after Franklin D. Roosevelt.[163] He discussed Kosygin's invitation with his senior officials and agreed to accept it, despite the fact that the

---

161 Lyndon Baines Johnson, *The Vintage Point* (New York: Halt, Rinehart and Winston, 1971) p. 486.

162 Zbigniew K. Brzezniski, "US Foreign Policy in East Central Europe: A Study in Contradiction", *Journal of International Affairs*, Vol. IX, No. 1 (New York: Colombia University Press, 1967) p. 68.

163 Lyndon Baines Johnson, *The Vintage Point,* p. 487.

invasion of Czechoslovakia had already gathered a definite momentum. On August 20, the White House press office prepared a news note on President's forthcoming visit to the Soviet Union to be released to the press on the next day.

President Johnson recorded the details of the development that took place on the eve of the Soviet invasion. At 7.06 pm on August 20, Ambassador Dobrynin informed the President that he had a message from the highest level of his Government with instruction to deliver it personally to him. The President could guess it to be on Czechoslovakia and decided to meet the Ambassador at 8:00 pm. The Soviet Ambassador appeared to be in a tense mood. President Johnson tried to relax him by narrating the meeting at Glassboro. But Dobrynin became serious and read out the message:

> The Government of the Soviet Union considers it necessary to inform, personally, President Johnson about the following: In connection with the further aggravation of the situation which was created by a conspiracy of the external and internal forces of aggression against the existing social order in Czechoslovakia against the statehood established by the constitution of that country, the Government of Czechoslovak Socialist Republic approached the allied states, the Soviet Union among them, with a request of rendering direct assistance, including the assistance by military forces.[164]

A similar Soviet message had been conveyed to the West European capitals to tell all these countries that the invasion of Czechoslovakia was purely a family affair within the Warsaw pact members and should not be mistaken as an act hostile to the West.[165] Dean Rusk at that point of time was testifying before the Democratic Platform Committee. Congressman Hale Boggs, Chairman of the Committee, passed on the news of Soviet invasion to him. He immediately rushed to the White House where President Johnson convened an emergency meeting of the National Security Council.[166] The President

164 *ibid*, p. 488.

165 David Wise, "The Twilight of a President", *New York Times Magazine*, November 3, 1968, p. 122.

166 Louis Chester *et. al. An American Melodrama: The Presidential Campaign of 1968* (New York: Viking, 1969) p. 532.

concluded that "there was nothing we could do immediately about the Czech situation."[167] He, however, instructed Rusk to call in Dobrynin immediately and tell him that there would be no announcement about the President's visit to the Soviet Union or on nuclear disarmament. He also informed Vice-President Hubert H. Humphrey and Richard M. Nixon, both candidates for the Presidential elections, about the invasion.

On the night of August 20-21, 1968 the Soviet-led Warsaw pact forces rolled across the Czechoslovak border from several strategic points, while Soviet airborne troops began landing at Prague's Ruzyne international airport in order to penetrate deep into the heart of the city, occupy the radio station, the parliament and other government buildings and installations as a part of the full-scale invasion.[168] Dubcek and his colleagues appealed to the people to remain calm and offer no resistance, understanding fully well that any attempt to resist the superior force would entail a Hungarian type bloodbath. Ludvik Svobada flew to Moscow for further consultation. Dubcek and others were reportedly arrested and then were taken to Moscow, where they were freed so that they might negotiate with the Soviet leaders. It was done so, as appeared, to cope with a situation in which the prospect of installing immediately a new government was not bright. The Soviet leaders believed that the step to free the Prague leaders and to offer them an opportunity to cool down the political temperature in their country aftermath the invasion was taken as a "protective cushion" between Moscow and Prague.[169] This calculated step

---

167 Lyndon Baines Johnson, *The Vintage Point*, n. 161, p. 488.

168 For details see Kenneth Ames, "Coup at Airport Led Invasion", *Washington Post*, August 31, 1968; also see Paul Wohl, "One of the Stealthiest Operations in Modern History", *Christian Science Monitor*, August 26, 1968; Stanislav Budin, "Czech Editors Tell of Events Leading to Invasion", *New York Times*, August 28, 1968; Harold Jackson, "A History of the Occupation", *Washington Post*, August 29, 1968. For some analytical account see Constaine Menges, *Prague Resistance, 1968: The Ingenuity of Conviction*, The RAND Corporation, P-3939, September 1968 and for latest analysis on the failure of the Czechoslovak reform movement see Mark Kramer, *Crisis in Czechoslovakia, 1968: The Prague Spring and Soviet Invasion* (London: Oxford University Press, 2001).

yielded Moscow's desired result. Dubcek concluded an agreement with the Soviet Union on August 26 and his regime was reinstalled.[170] This step marked the completion of Moscow's political control over Czechoslovakia. Moscow's apparent liberal gesture provided a breathing space to the Soviet leadership to haunt for a new leader to replace Dubcek.[171]

President Johnson's instruction to Dean Rusk to forestall the imminent announcement of the summit meeting with the Soviet leaders clearly indicated that the United States would do nothing more than expressing unhappiness at the invasion. The subsequent events, including the Administration's reaction to the Brezhnev doctrine of limited sovereignty, shows that the US response to the Soviet invasion remained limited to issuing statements of displeasure. One might begin with the reference to the nation-wide television and radio address of President Johnson 16 hours after Ambassador Dobrynin had been informed him of the invasion. Without condemning or deploring the intervention he said:

> The tragic news from Czechoslovakia shocks the conscience of the world. The Soviet Union and its allies have invaded a defenseless country to stamp out a resurgence of ordinary human freedom. . . . The action of the Warsaw Pact allies is in flat violation of the United Nations Charter. We are consulting urgently with others to consider what steps should be taken in the United Nations. Ambassador George Ball has been instructed to join other nations in the Security Council to insist upon the Charter rights of Czechoslovakia and its people...I call upon the Soviet Union and its associates to withdraw their troops from Czechoslovakia.[172]

---

169 James H. Billington, "Cost to the Soviets: Loss of their Dazzling Myth of Infallibility", *Life*, September 6, 1968, pp. 60-61.

170 The Communique of Soviet-Czechoslovak talk was published in *Pravda*, August 27, 1968. For the full text see *The Current Digest of the Soviet Press*, Vol. XX, No. 35 (September 18, 1968) pp. 3-4.

171 Kieran Williams, *The Prague Spring and Its Aftermath: Czechoslovak Politics, 1968-1970* (London: Cambridge University Press, 1997) pp. 29-30.

172 *Public Papers of the Presidents of the United States: Lyndon B. Johnson, 1968-69*, Book II, p. 905.

The State Department took some more time to react to the Soviet invasion. Dean Rusk addressed a press conference on August 22 and expressed a similar statement and dismissed any obligation to counter the Soviet-led invasion:

> This is not in a treaty sense a direct responsibility of ours, in the sense that we have no bilateral commitments to Czechoslovakia; but we have a broad interest in situation of this sort wherever they might arise where the interests of a member of the United Nations are so desperately periled as are at the present time.[173]

Sharing the hope of the President that good sense would prevail, Dean Rusk, in a reply to a question, said that the Soviet invasion would jeopardize the process of improvement in the relations between the two great powers. He said that the Czechoslovak Government had not "asked us [United States] for any specific action or steps" to meet the situation.[174] He skipped over a direct question, which wanted to know what more steps the United States would take beyond taking the matter to the United Nations, implying thereby that his country had no other plan to counter the Soviet-led invasion. A number of sources felt that the US involvement in the Vietnam War had drastically curtailed America's other tangible option to deal with the situation. The editorial of *New York Times* on August 22, soon after the invasion, commented: "The sympathy of all Americans will be with Czechoslovaks in this period of trial, but the ability of the United States to do anything beyond diplomatic protest is gravely limited by its over-involvement in the morass of Vietnam." Edwin L. Dale wrote that the Johnson Administration was determined to go ahead with the arms limitation talks with the Soviet Union despite the invasion of Czechoslovakia largely because of the growing awareness in the United States that "such talks bear a crucial relationship to the options available to the next President" for dealing with both domestic and global problems.[175] Senator Eugene J. McCarthy commented that the American

---

173 Department of State, *Bulletin*, September 9, 1968, p. 262.

174 *ibid*, p. 263.

175 *New York Times*, August 22, 1968.

involvement in Vietnam made it difficult for the United States to raise a serious protest against the Soviet-led invasion. "There is little the United States could have done to stop the intervention in Czechoslovakia."[176] In a press conference citing such opinion, a specific question was thrown to Dean Rusk as to how would he react to the suggestion that "We don't have a moral right to criticize the Russians because of the US role in Viet-nam and our role in Santo Domingo in the past." The reply, citied below, did not carry any meaning:

> There is a world of difference between black and white. Those who try to confuse it, it seems to me, are undertaking an enormous burden and, among other things, enormous disservice to the clarity which is important if we are to have peace in the world.[177]

The US media continued to publish the general impression that the United States had already accepted Eastern Europe as the Soviet sphere of influence, and therefore, did not like to react strongly to the happenings inside that zone. West European countries too squarely shared this belief. Dan Morgan wrote from Waidhaus, West Germany, that a free hand was given to the Soviet Union in Czechoslovakia because the United States still viewed this country as a part vital to the Soviet interests. He revealed that the communist sources also told him that the US Administration respected the sphere of influence of the Soviet Union in Eastern Europe.[178] Max Frankel also gave a similar account and argued that the mutual recognition of spheres of influence led to the American inaction.[179] Such an assumption was further strengthened by Dean Rusk who emerged from a cabinet meeting at the White House on August 23 confirmed that the Administration was not considering at least for the time being any "retaliatory actions or sanctions" against the Soviet Union.[180] The

176 *Washington Post*, August 23, 1968.

177 Department of State, *Bulletin*, September 9, 1968, p. 263.

178 *Washington Post*, August 23, 1968.

179 *New York Times*, August 23, 1968.

180 *idem*.

newspaper reports and the commonly held belief that the US inaction was a manifestation of its recognition of *status quo* in Eastern Europe carried the potentiality of strong public reaction to American foreign policy, and therefore, Robert J. McCloskey, the State Department spokesman, was prompted to issue a statement to disabuse such a theory. He said that the suggestion was malicious and totally unfounded. He asserted:

> The US Government has never entered into any "sphere of influence" or agreement or understandings with anyone anywhere in the world. There has been no discussion of any such idea in connection with recent developments in Czechoslovakia nor has any government attempted to elicit from the US Government any such understanding.[181]

Despite such a statement there had been widespread rumour that as the Soviet invasion took place inside Soviet sphere of influence without affecting America's vital interests, President Johnson did not abandon the idea of having a summit meeting with the Soviet leaders in Moscow. Replying to a question on this matter in the news conference Dean Rusk merely expressed his ignorance of such a plan. *New York Times* (August 24, 1968) published a similar account on the mutual recognition of spheres of influence. On August 23, President Johnson briefed twenty-seven key Congressional figures presumably on the subject matter of the Soviet invasion of Czechoslovakia. After the meeting Senator Richard B. Russell, a Democrat from Georgia, told the newsmen that "the United States was not called upon to respond to the Soviet-led invasion of Czechoslovakia by armed forces or through the North Atlantic Treaty Organization." He said that the matter would be pursued in the United Nations. He added: ". . . we've lost so much ground that we cann't even get a denunciation." But the more important part of the account was that the White House Press Secretary George Christian had declined to confirm or deny the widespread report that a summit meeting with Premier Kosygin was still high in President Johnson's list of priorities before the expiry of his tenure of office.

---

181 *idem.*

US MOVES TO THE UNITED NATIONS

The only option for the United States to express its resentment at the Soviet-led Warsaw pact intervention in Czechoslovakia was an unproductive debate in the Security Council. Ambassador George Ball joined the representatives of Canada, Denmark, France, Paraguay and the United Kingdom in requesting the Council to take up immediately the matter of Soviet intervention. The Council took up the issue in the late night of August 21 by a vote of 13-2 and overruled the Soviet-Hungarian opposition. George Ball cited the statement of the Acting Permanent Representative of Czechoslovakia, Jan Muzik, in which it had been clearly stated that the Soviet-led action was nothing but an illegal occupation of his country. Ambassador Ball assailed the Soviet act of invasion in strong terms and drew the attention of the Council to the grim parallel of the Hungarian crisis with the current situation in Czechoslovakia, and termed the Soviet contention of armed action as per the 'invitation' of the Czechoslovak Government a document of treason.[182] He said that the tragedy was particularly grievous for the people and the Government of the United States when they had been engaged with the process of reduction of superpower tension and controlling of arms race. Sponsoring a resolution in the Security Council, George Ball rejected the argument of the Soviet Ambassador Jakob Malik that only 'imperialists' opposed and decried the intervention. He said that Indian Prime Minister Indira Gandhi, His Holiness Pope Paul, President Ceausescu of Romania, President Nyerere of Tanzania, Communist parties of France and Italy and many others had disapproved the Soviet intervention, and he wondered how the Soviet Ambassador could brand all of them as imperialists.[183] A resolution was tabled in the Security Council affirming the "Sovereign, political independence and territorial integrity" of Czechoslovakia, condemning the armed intervention by the Soviet-led Warsaw pact members, and calling upon the member-states of the United Nations to exercise their

---

182 Department of State, *Bulletin*, September 9, 1968, p. 265.

183 *ibid*, p. 271.

diplomatic influence on the USSR for the implementation of the resolution which demanded immediate withdrawal of foreign troops and cessation of the intervention.[184] As visualized, the resolution was killed by the Soviet veto, which was the 105th exercise of the right by this permanent member. Immediately, a Canadian proposal in the form of a resolution was moved requesting the Secretary General U Thant to send a special representative to Prague to ensure safety of the Czechoslovak leaders.[185] Ambassador Malik frustrated the move by using veto and said it was a "trick of the NATO countries in this dirty, shoddy business." Foreign Minister Jiri Hajek addressed the Security Council of August 24 and refuted the Soviet contention that outside or counter-revolutionary forces had endangered socialism in his country. But he felt that the deliberations in the Security Council would not help their case at the on-going discussion in Moscow. Three days later he requested the Council to drop the Czechoslovak item in the agenda.[186] The Western countries expressed displeasure at the suggestion but agreed to postpone the item for further consideration, pending a clarification on the Soviet-Czechoslovak talk. They probably were reminded of the fact that just as in the case of Hungary, their quest for UN action against the Soviet Union would lead to nowhere, and therefore, decided to end the matter at this stage.[187] Later on the new US Ambassador James Wiggins in an interview with the CBS on November 17, 1968 commented: "the circumstances have not recommended themselves yet to convince the powers who are unhappy about it to think that the General Assembly could successfully take cognizance of it, as a practical matter."[188]

---

184 UN Document S/8761. The resolution was put to vote early in the morning of August 23. While 10 members were in favour of the resolution, the Soviet Union and Hungary were against it, Algeria, India and Pakistan abstained from voting.

185 UN Document S/8767.

186 *New York Times*, August 28, 1968.

187 For some details of the discussion on the Czechoslovak crisis in the UN see A.G. Mexerik, *Invasion and Occupation and the UN* (New York: International Review Service, 1968).

188 Department of State, *Bulletin*, December 9, 1968, p. 600.

The failure of the United States to do anything in the Security Council is understandable. In the face of the Soviet veto the United States could hardly do anything more than expressing condemnation of the Soviet invasion of Czechoslovakia. But America's helplessness in the world body gave credence to the commonly held view or accusation of Soviet-American complicity in the division of Europe. In Western Europe, the most noteworthy subscriber to this thesis was President Charles de Gaulle, who argued that the participants of the wartime conferences, from which he had been excluded, were to blame for the current situation obtaining in Europe. He, along with some other European critics saw in this situation a cynical understanding between the two superpowers on the respective spheres of influence.[189] Among the other rumours circulated in France after the invasion was that of a Soviet-American secret deal whereby the Soviet Union instructed the French Communist Party to back President de Gaulle by staying away from the main disturbances in exchange for American non-interference in Czechoslovakia.[190] The West European media also subscribed to the theory of American recognition of the Soviet sphere of influence and that the US involvement in the Vietnam War had drastically reduced the possibility of strong American protest against the Soviet invasion. Antony Terry reported from Bonn:

---

189 Charles Hargove, "France to Pursue Détente Policy Despite Invasion", *Times*, London, August 30, 1968; Henry Tanner, "De Gaulle Assails Soviets But Backs Policy of Détente", *New York Times*, September 10, 1968. However, W. Averell Harriman rejected the contention of de Gaulle and said that the Soviet domination of Eastern Europe came about not because of the Yalta agreements but because of the fact that the commitment were violated. See Donald H. Loucheim, "Harriman Answers de Gaulle", *Washington Post*, September 12, 1968.

190 Bennett Kovrig, *The Myth of Liberation: East Central Europe in US Diplomacy and Politics since 1941* (Baltimore: The John Hopkins University Press, 1973) p. 278; Andrew Pierre, "NATO after Czechoslovakia" in William Zartman (ed), *Czechoslovakia: Intervention and Impact* (New York: New York University Press, 1970) pp. 60-61; and Harlom Cleveland, "NATO after the Intervention", *Foreign Affairs*, Vol. 47, No. 2 (1969) pp. 251-265.

> Angry intelligence officials here allege that a general "play it down" order from the US Government, because of Vietnam, resulted in virtual early warning of the impending Czech invasion being ignored by the West.[191]

These theories of secret deal between the superpowers could not be substantiated for want of authentic evidence. Such theories, nevertheless, forced Dean Rusk to make an elaborate statement on September 12, 1968 denying the allegations that "there must have been some 'sphere of influence' agreement between us, that perhaps there was 'an agreement' made at the Yalta Conference, that perhaps the Soviet acted in Czechoslovakia with some 'carte blanche' from the United States, that we concurred or connived in that aggression." He observed:

> We recognized the reality of the Soviet military position and the existence of the Warsaw Pact. President [Johnson] like President Eisenhower, recognized that there was little we could do, through the use of military force, to assist any of these countries without automatically engaging in general war with the Soviet Union.

He made a further clarification:

> Nor did we in any way indicate that we would ignore an invasion of Czechoslovakia by the Soviet and other Warsaw Pact forces. On the contrary, ahead of time, through Ambassador Dobrynin, I protested the Soviet charge of 'complicity' by the United States in any endeavor to overthrow socialism in Czechoslovakia. For it seemed to be a chance that could be used as a pretext for a military move against that country.[192]

He dismissed in clear term the theory that the Vietnam War impeded the American action in Czechoslovakia. He added that no one suggested an open war over Czechoslovakia in the era of a thermo-nuclear warfare. This could not be a military argument, in political terms the United States was seeking freedom in Vietnam and in East and Central Europe, he added.

---

191 Antony Terry, "Early Warning on the Invasion was Ignored", *Sunday Times*, London, August 25, 1968.

192 Department of State, *Bulletin*, October 7, 1968, pp. 350-351.

No one would dispute the ground reality of avoiding a general war between the two superpowers, as testified to by the Cuban missile crisis in which their interests were directly involved. Who would really expect America to take recourse to a war with its powerful adversary for Czechoslovakia where it did not have any stake whatsoever?

RESENTMENT AND CONDEMNATION IN THE US CONGRESS

The US Congress reacted to the Soviet invasion of Czechoslovakia with condemnation and indignation. As a highly prestigious forum of the American people, without real power to exercise to handle a situation like this, it could only reflect the general American mood at the inaction of the Administration in responding to the Soviet action. Senator Thomas J. Dodd urged upon the Administration to call for a special emergency session of the UN General Assembly to take up the issue of Soviet invasion and to declare September 5 as the day of solidarity with the people of Czechoslovakia in conjunction with the anniversary of the infamous Munich agreement. While condemning the invasion, he said that despite repeated warning against the myth of *détente* and also about the impending invasion, the Administration had decided to sleep over such concern and warning. He shared the contention of the editorial of *New York Times*, September 3, which commented: "From Mr. Dubcek's triumph last January until the Soviet invasion, Washington did almost nothing to show serious goodwill toward the liberal regime."[193] Senator Roman L. Hruska echoed a similar statement. He said: "Western Europe, the United States, and the NATO were powerless to do little more than offer sympathy, express admiration for the heroic resistance by the Czechoslovak people, and issue statements criticizing the Kremlin."[194] He argued that the tenets of *détente* had been proved wrong, and therefore, demanded a full review of the American foreign policy and also a full-scale conference of NATO foreign and defence

193 US Congress, *Congressional Record*, 90th Congress, 2nd Session, September 5, 1968, pp. 257756-57.

194 *ibid*, p. 25780.

ministers. He viewed that the Czechoslovak crisis exposed the erroneous foundation of American foreign policy and thus it left a dangerous impact on the US interests.[195] Other Senators joined him in the demand for a thorough review of US 'bridge-building' policy in the context of the Soviet invasion of Czechoslovakia. The Democratic Senator from Utah, Frank E. Moss, who had been in the Soviet Union with his colleague Senator Hugh Scott during those fateful days of invasion, attending the Seventh World Power Conference in Moscow, made a sober and dispassionate analysis of the situation in which the United States had hardly any scope to react in manner other than verbal accusation of the Soviet action. He said:

> . . . in the power relationship that has taken shape between East and West during the postwar decade, Eastern Europe has come to be recognized internationally, by implication rather than by specific agreement, as a particular area of vital interest to the Soviet Union. For this reason, the United States did not intervene militarily in Hungary during the revolution of 1956; the underlying presumption was that a thrust by the United States into this area of the Soviet vital interests could trigger a third world war, and this could be a thermonuclear war.[196]

He further contended that the chance of taking any military measure was for more remote when the international situation had been made more complicated by the massive US intervention in Vietnam. Considering the Czechoslovak crisis as a "family affair' bearing, however, far reaching implications for the East-West relations, Senator Moss felt that there was every possibility of similar kind of action in Eastern Europe, should any anti-Soviet uprising take place, and except slowing down the process of *détente* the United States had little scope to react. In both the houses of the US Congress, members did not accept the theory that the US involvement in the Vietnam War acted as a restraining factor to a desired and strong reaction to the Soviet invasion; nor did they subscribe to the

---

195 US Congress, *Congressional Record*, 90th Congress, 2nd Session, p. 25781.

196 *ibid*, p. 25794.

idea of comparison and equity between the Soviet invasion of Czechoslovakia and America's war on Vietnam. Yet some members like Senator M. Young stood as exception, as he drew a remarkable parallel between two military incursions committed by the superpowers disdainfully flouting international law and world opinion.[197]

Some of the Congressmen advocated in favour of a temporary moratorium on the process of *détente*, there had been, on the other hand, deep-rooted speculation about President Johnson's visit to the Soviet Union. There had been visible concern in the US Congress at the alleged "bankruptcy of America's foreign policy". The members argued that the United States could have forestalled the invasion by telling the Soviet leaders that any military measure to crush the process of liberalization would cost the East-West relations to an irrecoverable level. They felt that the only alternative left to the Administration was to accelerate the US and NATO's strategic deterrence, and thereby, pose a perpetual threat to the Soviet defence system.

The US Congress feared another series of military incursions in Romania and Yugoslavia with a calculated framework to change the existing political order, which appeared to be less cooperative with Moscow.[198] The basis of fear rested on the reports that Nicolae Ceausescu and Marshall Tito had visited Prague just before the intervention to demonstrate solidarity with Dubcek. President Tito visited Prague from August 9-11, which was followed, by the visit of Ceausescu from August 15-17. Both expressed their support for the reform movement. After the invasion, the Soviet Union

---

197 *ibid*, October 9, 1968, p. 30020. This is the position that had been taken by the Chinese leadership, which not only found reasonable ground to argue that the two superpowers had mutual understanding about their sphere of influence but also launched severe attack on them for committing an abominable act of aggression against two sovereign countries. For details see Abu Nasar Saied Ahmed, "Chinese Response to Soviet Interventions: Hungary, Czechoslovakia and Afghanistan", *Indian Journal of Political Science*, Vol. 47, No. 1, March 1986, pp. 42-73.

198 US Congress, *Congressional Record*, 90th Congress, 2nd Session, September 5, 1968, pp. 25757.

and other Warsaw Pact members launched severe criticism of both the leaders for encouraging anti-socialist elements.[199] *New York Times* reported that the danger of yet another invasion had been looming large over Romania and Yugoslavia.[200] The report suggested that inside the Soviet Union there had been concern at the Tito-Ceausescu support to Dubcek and their criticism against the invasion had carried the potentiality of an alliance parallel to the pre-War Little Entente, and to stop such types of intra-communist contradiction, the Soviet Union might use force in collaboration with the remaining Warsaw Pact powers. In the last week of August, intelligence reports reached Washington DC informing of the movements of Soviet troops along Romania's border. Being compelled by the mounting criticism of US inaction, President Johnson issued a public statement in vague terms against unleashing the dogs of war.[201] The fact remains that the US Congress knew it well that how far the United States could go in the pursuit of doing something as a response to a similar Soviet invasion. But not to demonstrate its anger to cover its helplessness was too difficult for the Administration to reconcile with.

THE BREZHNEV DOCTRINE

The Soviet invasion of Czechoslovakia was the last military incursion committed to have regime change in the Soviet sphere of influence. Although there was no further invasion, a theory to justify the right to intervene militarily in the internal affairs of any of the socialist countries, was, however, advanced soon after the August invasion. Already it had been proved on two occasions that the Soviet Union had acquired the required credible capability to use effectively its conventional forces to protect its own interests in its sphere of influence even in the

---

199 See C.J. Czerwinski and Jaroslaw Piekalkiewicz, *The Soviet Invasion of Czechoslovakia: Its Effect on Eastern Europe* (New York: Praeger, 1972) pp. 159-168 and 172-180; and also see US Congress, Senate, Subcommittee on National Security and International Operations, *Czechoslovakia and the Brezhnev Doctrine*, 91st Congress, 1st Session, 1969, pp. 37, 43, 45 and 47.

200 See *New York Times*, August 25, 29 and 30, 1968.

201 Department of State, *Bulletin*, September 23, 1968, p.310.

face of American nuclear deterrence. A theory to rationalize and legitimize the use of massive conventional forces for international purposes, once received credence, could carry the potentiality of disarming the American strategy or propaganda for the liberation of Eastern Europe. Therefore, Pravda's editorial of August 22 justified the Warsaw pact invasion of Czechoslovakia as an "international duty" against the imperialist forces and in defence of the "gains of socialism".[202] A theoretically well-conceived article by Sergei Kovalev, which appeared in *Pravda* on September 26, 1968, followed this. Kovalev argued that the socialist countries could not remain inactive in the name of some abstract idea of sovereignty when they saw a socialist country was exposed to the danger of imperialism.[203] This article provided the outlines of the Brezhnev doctrine, which found its full expression in the speech of the Soviet leader delivered on November 12, 1968 at the Fifth Congress of the Polish United Workers Party. In defence of the right to intervene militarily in a socialist country, Leonid I. Brezhnev said:

> . . . there are common natural laws of Socialist construction, deviation from which could lead to deviation from socialism as such. And when external and internal forces hostile to socialism try to turn the development of a given socialist country in the direction of restoration of the capitalist system, when a threat arises to the cause of socialism in that country – a threat to the security of the socialist commonwealth as a whole – this is no longer merely a problem for that country's people, but a common problem, the concern of all socialist countries...military assistance to a fraternal country to end a threat to socialist system is an extra-ordinary measure, dictated by necessity: it can be called forth only by the overt actions of enemies of socialism within the country and beyond its boundaries, actions that create threat to common interests of the socialist camp.[204]

202 "Defense of Socialism is the Highest International Duty", *The Current Digest of the Soviet Press*, Vol. XX, No.30, September 11, 1968, pp. 5-14.

203 Sergei Kovalev, "Sovereignty and International Obligations of the Socialist Countries", *ibid*, No. 39, October 16, 1968, p. 10.

204 *ibid*, Vol.XX, No. 46, December 4, 1968, pp. 3-4, quotation, p. 4.

Andrei Gromyko restated the Brezhnev doctrine of limited sovereignty before the UN General Assembly on October 3, 1968.[205] This gave a clear indication that neither Romania nor Yugoslavia could escape from the pervasive application of the doctrine. As no one could discount the possibility of another wave of Soviet-led invasion to trim the assertive policy of Tito and Ceausescu, the United States could not afford to initiate any step to forestall such dangerous movers except issuing a warning that further military intervention would gravely imperil international peace and entail unmitigated consequences. Nevertheless, Dean Rusk said in an interview on December 1, 1968: "I don't have the impression that the Soviet Union is seeking a major confrontation, but what they are asking us to accept is that in this 'Socialist commonwealth' the Soviet Union has the right to use its armed forces to determine what happens inside independent countries, and that is very difficult for the rest of us to accept."[206] At the same time he reasserted that Soviet invasion of Yugoslavia or Romania would be considered as a threat to the West and could be an extremely serious setback in the US-Soviet relations. Such veil warning could hardly lay any impact on the Soviet leaders. The Soviet Union did not take recourse to apply the doctrine not because of the fact that the warning worked as a credible deterrence but because of the fact that the situation in Eastern Europe till the late 1980s did not deteriorate. When it deteriorated, starting with Poland, Mikhail Gorbachev declared that the Brezhnev doctrine would not be used to crush the revolting countries of the region and keep them under Moscow' control.[207]

The United States considered the Brezhnev doctrine as an "ominous manifestation of Soviet international legal doctrine" mainly dealing with the Soviet-East European relations. The Senate Subcommittee on National Security and International

205 *New York Times*, October 4, 1968.

206 Department of State, *Bulletin*, December 23, 1968, pp. 647-648.

207 For details see Matthew J.Ouimet, *Rise and Fall of the Brezhnev Doctrine in Soviet Foreign Policy* (Chapel Hill: University of North Carolina, 2003).

Operation viewed it as a strong warning issued to the East European nations against any adventure of asserting the right to independence and self-determination, a "double-talk about defending sovereignty by denying sovereignty."[208] The Subcommittee concluded that the Soviet invasion of Czechoslovakia proved that when unopposed the Soviet Union could do overnight what it intended to so. It added:

> The Soviet capability that was exercised so impressively in Czechoslovakia – under the protection of the powerful and expanding Russian nuclear-missile forces - is ready for employment on other tasks. An it is now clear that this Soviet military capability is available for use not only against long acknowledged adversaries in the free world, but also against communist friends and allies as well.[209]

Although the US Administration did not find reasons to react strongly against the Brezhnev doctrine taking it to be an inter-communist affair, it could foresee the wider application of the right to intervene in any part of the free world, without, however, directly affecting the US vital interests.

The Soviet invasion of Czechoslovakia did, however, reawaken the West as a whole and pumped new life into NATO members. It contributed to solidify the NATO alliance and strengthen its military capability. The Soviet demonstration of effectiveness of the use of conventional forces led to a new defence-building urge among the NATO partners. The invasion compelled some reluctant members to consider seriously contributing to NATO's military buildup. President Charles de Gaulle had to review his attitude to NATO in the backdrop of a momentary setback in his *détente* with Moscow caused by the Soviet-led invasion. He decided to cooperate with the integrated command of the NATO and impose a self-restriction on his criticism of the US Administration.[210] Prior to the

---

208 US Congress, Senate, Subcommittee of National Security and International Operation, *Czechoslovakia and the Brezhnev Doctrine*, 91st Congress, 1st Session, February 1969, pp. 5 and 8.

209 *ibid*, p. 9.

210 Charles Hargrove, n. 189; also see Drew Middleton, "France Moving to Cooperate with NATO Again", *New York Times*, November 21, 1968.

invasion of Czechoslovakia there had been a movement in Norway demanding its withdrawal from the NATO. But after the invasion the movement leaders renounced the demand. Its Foreign Minister John Lying declared that the Soviet invasion showed "the importance of our membership in NATO."[211] Similarly, the invasion temporized the debate over Denmark's continued membership in the alliance. Italy and Greece found it worthwhile to remain within the NATO defence system. The Federal Republic of Germany expressed concern over the massing of Soviet troops in Central Europe and feared the United States might not take a firm stand against the deepening Soviet pressure on Bonn, and therefore, Chancellor Kurt Georg Kiesinger urged for an immediate conference of the heads of Government of the NATO to consider measures for European security.[212] Great Britain initially was not enthusiastic about the idea of convening either a special summit or a ministerial meeting to review the security implications of the Soviet invasion, because it wanted to wait till the new US President took office. But later on it agreed to have a ministerial meeting. In the United States there was a strong plea for strengthening the NATO's strategic deterrence and to have a high level meeting of the alliance. On August 31, the United States announced that in view of the "changed East-West military situation" caused by the Soviet invasion, it had begun to review with the European allies the common defence arrangements in NATO.[213]

The NATO Defense Planning Committee issued a statement on September 4, 1968 affirming the necessity of maintaining "NATO's military capability, and of taking into account the implications of recent developments", and of reviewing its overall capabilities, but it never raised the question of possible counter-measure to be taken in the event of any Soviet intervention in future.[214] However, considering

---

211 "Crisis Strengthens Norway's NATO Ties", *ibid*, August 29, 1968.

212 "Bonn Asks Study of NATO Defenses", *ibid*, August 24, 1968.

213 Department of State, *Bulletin*, September 16, 1968.

214 Council of Foreign Relations, *Documents on American Foreign Relations, 1968-1969* (New York: Harper, 1970) pp. 137-138; also see Harlan Cleveland, "NATO After the Invasion", *Foreign Affairs*, n. 190.

the fact that additional Soviet troops were kept in full alert at NATO's backyard, the Western partners of defence decided to suspend the issue of troops withdrawal from West Germany till a full review of Czechoslovak crisis was completed.[215] In November, the NATO ministerial meeting in Brussels outlined a new military programme based on their evaluation of the post-invasion situation, which included improvement of the quality, effectiveness and deployment of the NATO forces and its alert procedures.[216] On the whole, the Soviet-led invasion injected the spirit of revitalization of NATO and that led to the formation of an action plan to that end. But such activities could neither pose any formidable problem or threat to the Soviet Union nor could it create a mechanism to deal with any such future invasion, notwithstanding the fact that no such surgical step had been taken till the demise of communism in Eastern Europe and disintegration of the Soviet empire.

The Soviet Union took recourse to movements of its troops towards the border of West Germany as a tactical measure to divert the attention of the Western powers from Czechoslovakia to their own security interests. The Soviet media added another dose of fear and apprehension when *Pravda* spearheaded a campaign against Bonn and claimed that the Soviet Union continued to enjoy a residual right to intervene in the internal affairs of West Germany under Articles 53 and 107 of UN Charter, interpreted *Ostpolitik* as a manifestation of hostility to the Soviet Union and warned Chancellor Kiesinger to give up attempts to exert influence on Eastern Europe or face consequences.[217] In order to allay the anxiety of West Germany, the United States declared that any attempt to test the theory of unilateral intervention in West Germany would lead to an "immediate allied response".[218] In the West, the Soviet threat

215 "NATO to Redeploy its Defences", *Times* (London), September 5, 1968.

216 Department of State, *Bulletin*, December 9, 1968, pp.595-597.

217 David Binder, "Moscow Cautions Bonn on Policies", *New York Times*, September 4, 1968; also A Zalyotny, "FRG and Developments in Czechoslovakia", *International Affairs* (Moscow), No. 11, November 1968, pp. 22-27.

218 Benjamin Welles, "Soviet Is Warned in West Germany", *New York Times*, September 18, 1968.

was considered as propaganda play rather than any preface to a military adventure.[219] It implies that the West was confident that the Soviet military manoeuvre would remain confined to Eastern Europe only.

The United States and the West European countries concentrated on the study of military implications of the Soviet invasion of Czechoslovakia. The Western accounts agreed that the Soviet military operation was impressively accomplished in Czechoslovakia with meticulous planning and flawless execution.[220] They also found that the introduction of the additional combat-ready Soviet theatre force supplemented by the reported induction of tactical missiles with nuclear role into Czechoslovakia had dislodged the military balance and had adversely affected the stability of strategic deterrence in Europe. The US statement of August 31 gave the first official appraisal in the West that the Soviet invasion altered the long-standing military balance in Europe.[221] However, not all in the West believe that the Soviet military buildup in the Northern Tier of the Warsaw pact had affected the military balance. Some observers held that the induction of Soviet forces in Czechoslovakia increased the degree of unreliability of Czechoslovak armed forces and vulnerability of the foreign troops stationed in that country. In other words, the balance of power remained unchanged.[222] Meanwhile, in the November most of the Soviet forces were being withdrawn from Czechoslovakia, as a result, the argument that the Soviet invasion had altered the European balance to lose credibility.[223]

---

219 "NATO Allies Doubt Russia Will Move into West Germany", *ibid*, September 20, 1968; Gromyko reportedly assured Dean Rusk that Soviet action in Czechoslovakia did not pose any threat to Berlin, *ibid*, October 16, 1968.

220 Tad Szulc, "Soviet Army in Action Impresses West", *ibid*, September 10, 1968; also see Raymond J. Barrett, "The United States and Europe", *Military Review*, December: 1968, p. 4.

221 Department of State, *Bulletin*, September 16, 1968, p. 296.

222 R.T. Rockingham Gill, "Europe's Military Balance After Czechoslovakia", *East Europe*, October 1968, pp. 17-21; and Charles Douglas-Home, *Times* (London), September 25, 1968.

223 For a critical assessment see US Congress, House, Special Subcommittee on National Defense Future of the Committee on

(*contd. . .*)

And the West was assured by this development that there would be no perceived threat to the security of West Europe out of Soviet invasion in Czechoslovakia.

Roger E. Kanet rightly predicted that the Soviet invasion of Czechoslovakia would not leave any major and lasting impact on the Soviet relation with the United States and the West European countries.[224] The United States took insignificant measures like stopping the Minnesota symphony team from visiting the Soviet Union from September 16 for seven weeks.[225] This was done as a symbolic protest against the military intervention leaving a deep-rooted impression that the US Administration had accepted the Soviet sphere of influence in Eastern Europe as a *fait accompli*. Kanet wrote: "The US Government seems to be resigned to recognizing a Soviet sphere of influence in Eastern Europe in which the Soviets have more or less free hand."[226] Senator Mike Mansfield, in his report to the Senate Foreign Relations Committee, refuted the contention of recognition of sphere of influence at any point of time by the United States. He argued that the United States did not act decisively to stop the invasion mainly because of the fact that the "Czechoslovak leaders sought no special help" from his country. Therefore, it was quite natural that the Administration could merely hope that the reform movement in Czechoslovakia continued to progress. To him, the US policy towards Czechoslovakia was effectively attuned to Administration's will and capacity to contribute constructively in the difficult situation when there were practical limitations in responding to the crisis. He concluded:

> There can be no tacit acquiescence in any Soviet right to dominate Czechoslovakia or any other independent nation in

---

Armed Services, *Review of a Systems Analysis Evaluation of NATO vs Warsaw Pact Conventional Forces*, 90th Congress, 2nd Session, September 4, 1968; also US Assistant Secretary Dr. Alain Ethoven's letter on the subject, *Survival*, September 1968, p. 308.

224 Roger E. Kanet, "Czechoslovakia and the Future of Soviet Foreign Policy" in E.J. Czerwinski and Jaroslaw Piekalkiewicz, *The Soviet Invasion of Czechoslovakia: Its Effect on Eastern Europe*, n. 199, p. 101.

225 Department of State, *Bulletin*, September 30, 1968, pp. 341-342.

226 Roger E. Kanet, n. 224, p. 101.

> Eastern Europe or any where in the world. The avoidance of bombast in present circumstances is merely a recognition of practical limitation of US action. When conflicts occur beyond the reach of our commitments, unilateral or regional, it is irresponsible and dangerously delusive to ignore the existence of these limitations. The United States has not the omnipotence to alter situation at will in Europe any more than in Asia.[227]

Undoubtedly, the recognition of practical limitation is the recognition of reality in Eastern Europe, i.e. the Eastern part of Europe came under the Soviet sphere of influence, whether or not there is a declared statement on it. Time and circumstances have incapacitated the United States to undo this historic reality, and its domestic politics and international position did not allow accepting the Cold War *status quo* in a formal form. But by implication the acceptance appears to have been pronounced and palpable.

After a brief spell of campaign against the Soviet invasion of Czechoslovakia, the Johnson Administration initiated steps towards a summit meeting of the US-Soviet leaders. At the end of November 1968 the Administration sent a message to US Ambassador Thompson authorizing him suggest the Soviet leaders the idea of a summit meeting at Geneva before Christmas, leaving enough scope to confirm that the Johnson Administration had decided much earlier to sacrifice Czechoslovakia for the SALT. But the Soviet response was cool. Thompson had difficulty in contacting Anatoly Dobrynin, who was at that time in Moscow for consultation and when he met "it appeared that Soviet interest in a meeting disappeared", wrote President Johnson. The Soviet leaders shifted their attention to the incoming Administration.[228]

---

227 US Congress, Senate, Committee of Foreign Relations, *Czechoslovakia: Confrontation and Crisis*, A Report prepared by Senator Mike Mansfield, 90th Congress, 2nd Session, September 1968, pp. 28-29. Also see Jiri Valenta and Jan Moravec, "Could the Prague Spring been Saved", *ORBIS*, No. 4, Fall 1991, pp. 581-601.

228 Lyndon B. Johnson, *The Vintage Point*, n. 161, p. 490.

CONCLUSION

The issues and the trend in US Presidential electioneering reflect the American mind. It is noteworthy that the Soviet invasion of Czechoslovakia was a non-issue in the Presidential election campaign. Both the candidates did not take it up at all as they decided to bury the past and to look forward to a future milestone, which came to be known as *détente*. The US policy towards the Soviet Union as well as Eastern Europe within the rhetoric of the Cold War secured no prominence in the campaign. While Richard M. Nixon favoured a shift from an era of confrontation to an era of negotiation, Hubert H. Humphrey advocated for a policy of reconciliation and peaceful engagement.[229] All such pronouncements carried an identical meaning and diplomatic implication for relaxation of tension, which eventually was popularized by Kissinger within the framework of *détente* and also acceptance of Soviet sphere of influence in Eastern Europe.

After assuming the office of the President of the United States, Richard M. Nixon initiated a new approach to Eastern Europe, an approach manifested in his official visits to Romania and Yugoslavia in 1970. It was an attempt to establish more contacts with the East European countries where some degree of independence from Moscow was visible. Brzezniski, however, viewed that it would be contradictory and misleading to pick up two favourites in Eastern Europe and at the same time seek "accommodation with the Soviet Union on certain other larger issues but otherwise ignoring Eastern Europe."[230] At any rate, President Nixon's approach to Eastern Europe became clear when in a report to the US Congress in February 1970 he wrote:

> We are aware that the Soviet Union sees its own security as directly affected by developments in this region. Several times, over the centuries, Russia has been invaded through

229 Lewis Chester *et. al., An American Melodrama: The Presidential Campaign of 1968* (New York: Viking, 1969) p. 532.

230 Zbigniew Brzezniski, "The Eastern Europe: Tendencies and Prospects" in Jery Lukaszeski (ed), *The People's Democracies After Prague: Soviet Hegemony, Nationalism, Regional Integration* (Brugest: De Temple, 1970) pp. 303-313, quotation p. 314.

Central Europe...It is not the intention of the United States to undermine the legitimate security interest of the Soviet Union.[231]

The same message was repeated two years later: "We do not want to complicate the difficulties of Eastern European Nations' relations with their allies; nevertheless there are ample opportunities for economic, technical and cultural cooperation on the basis of reciprocity. The East European countries themselves can determine the peace and scope of their developing relations with the United States."[232] In this way after pursuing a policy of encouraging the East European nations to revolt and then invite invasion from a determined and dominant power, the United States decided to live with the fact of life – recognition of Eastern Europe as being within the Soviet sphere of influence. The White House note prepared on the day before the invasion, as mentioned already, announcing an imminent summit of the SALT and the haste with which the Administration attempted to reschedule the talks soon after the invasion tells loudly the US recognition of sphere of influence in the Cold War era. The Kremlin leaders did correctly assess American mood and policy objectives, and took no time to accomplish their coercive action against an unwilling member of the Warsaw Pact.[233]

The developments in Poland leading to the imposition of martial law in December 1981 and the crackdown on the solidarity movement had been considered by the US Administration as a matter of the internal affairs of Soviet sphere of influence. The movement was put down by the Polish authorities and not by the Soviet army. The events in Poland

---

231 Richard M. Nixon, *US Foreign Policy for 1970's: A New Strategy for Peace*, A Report to the Congress (White House, February 1970) pp. 138-139.

232 Richard M. Nixon, *US Foreign Policy for 1970's: The Emerging Structure of Peace*, A Report to the Congress (White House, February 9, 1972)

233 For some argument on this line see Karen Dawisha, "The 1968 Invasion of Czechoslovakia: Causes, Consequences and Lessons for the Future" in Karen Dawisha and Philip Hanson (eds), *Soviet-East-European Dilemmas* (London: Heinmann, 1981) pp. 9-11.

once again exposed the fragility of the Soviet-led commonwealth, despite the fact that the all the revolts were crushed brutally by the state power in collusion with the dominant power. However, Moscow could not retain its hold on Eastern Europe permanently, despite the existence of the Brezhnev doctrine.[234] It is a matter of history that the Soviet authority in the region collapsed like a house of cards. Despite the presence of the robust and highly trained Soviet forces equipped with all modern sophisticated conventional weapons, things went out of Moscow's grip. The state apparatus, however powerful might be, when acts oppressively against the masses, its fall is eminent.[235] The revolt against the Soviet Union was not aided by the United States, which witnessed from a safe distance the entire proceedings of the decline of the Soviet power and eventually the disintegration of the empire in less than four months without getting involved in the situation even indirectly.[236] Now it is a part of history that the *raison dé etre* for a single party system to achieve complete victory of socialism and to strengthen its dictatorship was riddled by factionalism and opportunism. It was not unnatural to witness an unprecedented collapse of an over-extended empire.[237]

---

234 There was a widespread speculation that the Brezhnev doctrine would be used to crush the Solidarity movement spearheaded by Lech Valesa. The Kremlin leadership thought it otherwise. For an interesting analysis on the issue see Peter Summerscale, "The Continuing Validity of the Brezhnev Doctrine" in Karon Dawisha and Philip Hanson (eds), *ibid*, pp. 26-40. Also see Renée De Never, *Comrades No More: The Seeds of Change in Eastern Europe* (Cambridge, Mass.: Harvard University Press, 2003) Chapter 3 pp. 77-118 and Grezegorz Ekiert, *The State Against Society: Political Crises and their Aftermath in East Central Europe* (Princeton: Princeton University Press, 1996) pp. 215-222 on the Solidarity movement.

235 For a philosophical interpretation of the end of communism in Eastern Europe see Grezegorz Ekiert, *The State Against Society: Political Crises and their Aftermath in East Central Europe* (Princeton: Princeton University Press, 1996) pp. 305-321

236 For some of the chapters covering the issue see Michael Mandelbaum (ed), *The Rise of Nation in the Soviet Union: American Foreign Policy and the Disintegration of the USSR* (New York: Council of Foreign Relations, 1991).

237 Richard Sakwa, *The Rise and Fall of the Soviet Union 1917-1991* (London: Routledge, 1999) p. 165.

A superpower has its limitations, which are relegated to sidelines when rhetoric overwhelms them for political reasons. In retrospection, the liberation policy was an election gimmick, which has a narrow perspective of hoodwinking the electorate for achieving quick victory over the political adversary. Such a policy could possibly be tried by application of military might to dislodge a comparatively smaller power occupying foreign land, as it was done in the case of liberating Kuwait from Iraqi occupation. Even it might be possible for a country without a superpower status to take recourse to war to liberate a physically separated wing from the oppressive and dominating wing as had been done by India in 1971. But to think of liberating Eastern Europe at that point of history when the Cold War was in full motion was not only unthinkable but dangerous too. The American policy makers who spearheaded the campaign for liberation did realize the remoteness of engaging their strategic power to achieve it. But to experiment with the idea of liberation of Eastern Europe as a part of psychological warfare against the Soviet Union and to demonstrate its seriousness on the matter proved to be highly costly in terms of human sacrifice and America's credibility as a great power. The myth of liberation policy haunted not only the soil of Eastern Europe but also the US policy makers for more than a decade till both the superpowers decided to opt for a low cost engagement called *détente* in an attempt to marginalize highly expensive politics of the Cold War. The process of *détente* received a jolt in the wake of the Soviet invasion of Afghanistan in December 1979[238]. The invasion, committed outside the orbit of Soviet sphere of influence, received worldwide condemnation. Although President Jimmy Carter imposed economic sanctions against Moscow and stalled the ratification of the SALT II by the Senate to demonstrate America's strong disapproval of the Soviet action, his successor

238 For details of the process of *détente* since the Nixon era see Raymond L. Garthodd, *Détente and Confrontation: American-Soviet Relations from Nixon to Reagan*, Revised Edition (Washington DC: The Brookings Institution, 1994) Chapter 2, pp. 27-57 and Chapter 26 pp. 977-1046, Coral Bell, *The Diplomacy of Détente: The Kissinger Era* (London: Martin Robertson, 1977) and Marvin Kalb and Bernard Kalb, *Kissinger* (New York: Dell Publishing Co. 1972).

Ronald Reagan initiated its rebirth after a long acrimonious accusation of the Soviet leadership for its hegemonic and expansionist designs in international politics. The Soviet Union had a long and perilous stay in Afghanistan before it unilaterally started withdrawing in April 1988, when the Kremlin leadership found it too expensive to continue the occupation.[239]

At any rate the Soviet empire crumbled like a house of cards in 1991. Many empires have come and gone, but the process of disintegration of the Soviet empire had a matchless speed and precision, which no one had anticipated. Before the disintegration of the USSR, one after another all the countries in Eastern Europe within the ambit of the Soviet sphere of influence not only withdrew from the Warsaw Treaty Organization but also renounced communism. The Berlin Wall fell in a lightening speed.[240] Till 1987, there was no symptom of dissolution of the Warsaw Treaty Organization.[241] Now, it is a different chapter of history that tells about the disappearance of communism from Eastern Europe. The multi

---

239 The Soviet withdrawal started from April 1988 and was completed in February 1989. Abu Nasar Saied Ahmed, "US Response to Soviet Invasion of Afghanistan", forthcoming.

240 Abu Nasar Saied Ahmed, "Germany: From Division to Reunification", *Economic and Political Weekly*, October 6, 1990, pp. 2242-2244. also see Tom Heneghan, *Unchained Eagle: Germany After the Wall* (Princeton: Princeton University Press, 2000).

241 For an excellent discussion see Aurel Braun, "Whither the Warsaw Pact in the Gorbachev Era?", *International Journal*, Winter, 1987-88, pp. 63-105.

242 Graeme Gill, *The Collapse of a Single-Party System: The Disintegration of the Communist Party of the Soviet Union* (New York: Cambridge University Press, 1994). David R. Marples rejects the Cold War explanation for the collapse as well as the economic collapse from within theory and believes that the rise of nationalities question lies at the heart of a convincing explanation for the demise of the Soviet Union combined together with related competition between Gorbachev and Boris Yeltsin. See his *The Collapse of the Soviet Union, 1985-1991* (London: Longman, 2004).

party democracy has replaced one party rule[242]. The Soviet forces withdrew from the region. Following that historic process the USSR also disappeared. All the 15 Union Republics under its orbit became independent countries. By December 1991 the mighty Soviet Union vanished from the map of the world. It took hardly four months to witness such a speedy process of dissolution of a superpower. Many would like to blame Mikhail Gorbachev for the sudden fall of the empire.[243] But the process had started much earlier as George Kennan could foresee in 1947 itself. An over extended empire has its own life span. It is a self-ordained manifestation of history, which he could predict so prophetically.[244] Had Dulles been alive at this historic juncture he would have celebrated pompously the end of the Soviet empire. The end was more or less peaceful except a few violent deaths of civilians and political leaders including Nicolae Ceausescu and his wife who were done to death as they tried to escape from Romania[245]. The United States witnessed the entire proceeding of disintegration of the USSR and also the Warsaw Treaty Organization from a safe distance, without sending any force or firing a single bullet. Thus, a peaceful liberation of Eastern Europe took place without America's role to play whatsoever.

With the collapse of the Soviet empire the old concept of sphere of influence did not hold good. The former Soviet power was restricted to the geo-political boundary of former Russian Republic. At the same time, the idea of Commonwealth of Independent States could not be fully operationalized and

---

243 For some details see Allen Lynch, "Does Gorbachev Matter Any More", *Foreign Affairs*, Summer, 1990, pp. 19-29, Robert English, *Russia and the Idea of the West: Gorbachev, Intellectuals, and the End of the Cold War* (New York: Colombia University Press, 2000) also Abu Nasar Saied Ahmed, "Gorbachev and Dissolution of the Soviet Union", *Journal of Politics*, Vol. II, March 1995, pp. 41-60.

244 Mr. X, "The Sources of Soviet Conduct", *Foreign Affairs*, July 1947, pp.566-82.

245 For details of Peter Siani-Davies, *The Romanian Revolution of December 1989* (Ithaca: Cornell University Press, 2005) Chapter 2, pp. 67-96.

institutionalized. Similarly, America's identical sphere of influence evaporated in no time. Today's European Union takes care of economic, political and strategic interests of all the members of the continent, notwithstanding the presence of the NATO. Today Europe faces no danger of overlordship of a distant power, nor does it face any threat of external aggression.

The US liberation policy and the two Soviet invasions committed in Eastern Europe are the products of a complicated interface of external and internal developments that had taken place inside the two superpowers in the Cold War era. The search for security created spheres of influence for the two great powers, apparently legitimizing their interventionist paradigm in handling conflict ridden situations in their respective zones of influence. At the same time, it rationalized their limited response to coercive measures taken by an adversary of equal status to bring smaller nations to submission. Nevertheless, the leaders of the both powers tried to avoid a war, which would have been perilous not only to them but to the entire world. In doing so and in retaining a position not to abandon the path of demonstrating mutual hostility, they made resolutions to conflicts and differences totally impossible. The resolution did appear after forty-five years of profound Cold War hostility, when one of the superpowers collapsed without giving considerably advance warning.

BIBLIOGRAPHY

OFFICIAL DOCUMENTS:

ADELPHI PAPERS, No. 58, *The Evolution of Warsaw Pact*, June 1969.

American Foreign Policy: 1950-1955: Basic Documents.

American Foreign Policy: Current Documents, 1956.

American Foreign Policy: Current Documents, 1957.

American Foreign Policy: Current Documents, 1958.

American Foreign Policy: Current Documents, 1961.

Documents on American Foreign Relations, 1956.

Council on Foreign Relations, *The United States in the World Affairs, 1948-1949* (New York: Harper, 1949).

Council on Foreign Relations, *The United States in the World Affairs, 1951* (New York: Random, 1952)

Council on Foreign Relations, *Documents on American Foreign Relations* (New York: Harper, 1953).

Council on Foreign Relations, *Foreign Relations of the United States, 1945: The Conferences of Malta and Yalta* (Washington DC, 1955).

Council on Foreign Relations, *Berlin 1961*, European British Commonwealth Series, No. 64 (Washington DC, 1961).

Council on Foreign Relations, *Report to the President of Special Committee on US Trade Relations with East European Countries and Soviet Union*, Presented to the White House on April 29, 1965 (Washington DC, 1966).

Department of State, *Bulletin* (Relevant Years).

Nixon, Richard M., *US Foreign Policy for 1970's: A New Strategy for Peace*, A Report to the Congress (The White House, February 1970).

Nixon, Richard M., *US Foreign Policy for 1970's: A New Strategy for Peace*, A Report to the Congress (The White House, February 9, 1972).

Public Papers of the Presidents: Harry S. Truman.

Public Papers of the Presidents: Dwight D. Eisenhower.

Public Papers of the President: Lyndon B. Johnson.

United Nations, General Assembly, *Official Records*, 561st meeting (First Special Emergency Session, 1956).

United Nations, General Assembly, *Official Records*, Eleventh Session, Supplement No. 17 (A/3572) 1956.

United Nations, General Assembly, *Official Records*, Emergency Special Session, Supplement No. 1 (A3535) 1956.

United Nations, General Assembly, *Official Records*, 561st meeting, 1956.

United Nations, General Assembly, *Official Records*, 570th meeting, Second Emergency Special Session, 1956.

United Nations, Security Council, *Official Records*, 752nd meeting, 1956.

United Nations, Security Council, *Official Records*, 753th meetings, 1956.

United Nations, Security Council, *Official Records*, 754, meetings, 1956.

United Nations, Security Council, *Official Records, S/3691.*

UN Document, A/3403.

UN Document, A/3485.

UN Document, S/3692-S/3699.

UN Documents, S/8761.

UN Documents, S/8767.

UN Document S/3251, November 1, 1956.

UN Documents, S/3726, November 2, 1956.

UN Document, A/3592, "Report of the Special Committee on the Problem of Hungary", June 1957.

United Nations, General Assembly, *Official Records*, Eleventh Session, Supplement No, 17A(A3572 Addl 1) 1957.

US Congress, *Congressional Record: Appendix*, 82nd Congress, 1st session, 1951.

US Congress, *Congressional Record,*(Relevant Years).

US Congress, House, Committee on Foreign Affairs, *The Mutual Security Program: Hearings,* 82nd Congress, 1st Session, 1951.

US Congress, House, Committee of Appropriation, Mutual Security Appropriations for 1956: *Hearings*, 84th Congress, 1st Session, 1955.

US Congress, House, Committee on Foreign Affairs, *Hearings on Foreign Policy and Mutual Security*, 84th Congress, 2nd Session, 1956.

US Congress, House, Committee on UN-American Activities, *International Communism: Revolts in Satellites*, 84th Congress, 2nd Session, 1957.

US Congress, *Foreign Policy and Mutual Security: Draft Report submitted to the Committee on Foreign Affairs*, December 24, 1956.

US Congress, House, Committee on Foreign Affairs, *Report of the Special Study Mission to Europe on Policy toward the Satellite Nations*, 85th Congress, 1st Session, 1957.

US Congress, House, Committee on Foreign Affairs, *Report on Foreign Policy and Mutual Security*, 85th Congress, 2nd Session, June 11, 1957.

US Congress, House, Committee on Foreign Affairs, *Briefing on World Situation*, 86th Congress, 1st Session, January 28 and 29, 1959.

US Congress, House, Committee on Foreign Affairs, *Report of the Special Study Mission to Poland*, Prepared by Congressman Clement J. Zablocki, 87th Congress, 1st Session, July 2, 1962.

US Congress, House, Committee on Foreign Affairs,

Subcommittee on Europe, *Report on Captive European Nations*, 88th Congress, 1st Session, April 29, 1963.

US Congress, House, Committee on Foreign Affairs, *Recent Developments in the Soviet Block: Report on Hearings*, 88th Congress, 2nd Session, 1964.

US Congress, Senate, Committee on Foreign Relations, *The Mutual Security Act 1953*, 83rd Congress, 1st Session, 1953.

US Congress, Senate, Committee on Foreign Relations, *Nomination of John Foster Dulles Secretary of State-Designate*, 83rd Congress, 1st Session, 1953.

US Congress, Senate, Committee on Foreign Relations, *Hearings on S.Res. 166 Favoring Discussion at the Coming Geneva Conference on the Status of Nations under Communist Control*, 84th Congress, 1st Session, June 21, 1955.

US Congress, Senate, Committee on Foreign Relations, *Hearings on Control and Reduction of Armaments*, 84th Congress, 1st Session, February 1956.

US Congress, Senate, Committee on Foreign Relations, *Control and Reduction of Armaments: Final Report*, Staff Study, No. 8, 85th Congress, 1st Session, June 6, 1957.

US Congress, Senate, Committee on Foreign Relations, *A Review of US Foreign Policy and Operations*, 85th Congress, 2nd Session, February 13, 1958.

US Congress, Senate, Committee on Foreign Relations, *Review of Foreign Policy, 1958*, 85th Congress, 2nd Session, February-March, 1958.

US Congress, Senate, Committee on Foreign Relations, *Hearings on Disarmament and Foreign Policy*, 86th Congress, 1st Session, 1959.

US Congress, Senate, Committee on Foreign Relations, *Informal Meetings with George F. Kennan*, 86th Congress, 1st Session, May 12, 1959.

US Congress, Senate, Committee on Foreign Relations, *East-West Trade: Hearings*, 88th Congress, 2nd Session, 1964.

US Congress, Senate, Committee on Foreign Relations,

Subcommittee on National Security and International Operation, *Czechoslovakia and the Brezhnev Doctrine*, 91st Congress, 1st Session, February 1969.

US Congress, *Hearings on Review of United States Information Agency Operation*, 85th Congress, 2nd Session, September-October, 1958.

US Congress, "Report on the Changing Situation in Hungary", *Congressional Record*, 88th Congress, 1st Session, May 15, 1963.

US Congress, *Congressional Almanac, 1952.*

The Geneva Conference of the Heads of Government (Washington DC, 1955).

Royal Institute of International Affairs, *Documents on International Affairs, 1957* (London, 1960).

World Peace Foundation, *Documents on American Foreign Relations* (Princeton, New Jersey: Princeton University Press, 1949).

ARTICLES:

Acheson, Dean, "The Illusion of Disengagement", *Foreign Affairs*, Vol. 36, No. 3 (1953).

Ahmed, Abu Nasar Saied Ahmed, "Chinese Response to Soviet Interventions: Hungary, Czechoslovakia and Afghanistan, *Indian Journal of Political Science*, Vol. 47. No. 1, March 1986, pp. 42-73.

Ahmed, Abu Nasar Saied Ahmed, "Germany from Division to Reunification", *Economic and Political Weekly*, October 6, 1990, pp. 2242-2244.

Ahmed, Abu Nasar Saied Ahmed, "Gorbachev and the Dissolution of the Soviet Union", *Journal of Politics*, Vol. II, March 1995, pp. 41-60.

Ahmed, Abu Nasar Saied Ahmed, "Dulles and Eastern Europe: A Retrospection", *Journal of Politics*, Vol. III, December 1996, pp. 93-104.

Ahmed, Abu Nasar Saied Ahmed, "US Policy Toward Eastern Europe: A History Revisited", *Journal of Politics*, Vol. IV, March 1997, pp. 15-32.

Ahmed, Abu Nasar Saied Ahmed, "Communism with a Human Face: The Dubcek Experiment", *Journal of Politics*, Vol I, Special Issue, 1999, pp. 85-95.

Aron, Raymond, "The Meaning of Destiny" in Tamas Aczel (ed), *Ten Years After: The Hungarian Revolution in the Perspective of History* (New York: Rinehart and Weston, 1967).

Békés, Csaba, "The 1956 Hungarian Revolution and the Great Powers" in Terry Cox (ed), *Hungary 1956: Forty Years On* (New York: Routledge, 1997) 51-66.

Billington, James H., "Cost of the Soviets: Loss of their Dazzling Myth of Infallibility", *Life*, September 6, 1968, pp. 60-61.

Boyle, Peter G., "The Hungarian Revolution and the Suez Crisis", *History*, Vol. 90, October 2005, pp. 550-565.

Bowles, Chester, "Ojectives in Europe and Russia, *New York Time Magazine*, May 12, 1957.

Braun, Aurel, "Whither the Warsaw Pact in Gorbachev Era?", *International Journal*, Winter 1987-88, pp. 63-105.

Brzezniski, Zbigniew K., and William E. Griffith, "Peaceful Engagement in Eastern Europe", *Foreign Affairs*, Vol. 39, No. 4, July 1961, pp. 642-654

Brzezniski, Zbigniew K., "The Eastern Europe: Tendencies and Prospects" in Jery Lukaszeski (ed), *The People's Democracies After Prague: Soviet Hegemony, Nationalism, Regional Integration* (Brugest: De Temple, 1970) pp. 303-13.

Cleveland, Harlom, "NATO After the Intervention, *Foreign Affairs*, Vol. 47, No. 2, January 1969, pp. 251-265.

Coste, Brutus, "Propaganda to Eastern Europe", *Public Opinion Quarterly*, Vol. 14. Winter, 1950/51, pp. 643-658.

Davis, Paul C., "The New Diplomacy: The 1955 Geneva Summit Meeting" in Roger Wilman and Robert C. Goods (eds), *Foreign Policy in the Sixties* (Baltimore: John Hopkins Press, 1965) pp. 165-168.

Deutscher, Isaac, "October Revolution, New Style", *The Reporter*, November 15, 1956.

Dulles, John Foster, "A Policy of Boldness", *Life*, May 19, 1952.

Gaskill, Gorden, "Time Table of a Failure" *Virginia Quarterly Review*, Vol. 34, No. 2, Spring 1958, pp. 162-190.

Granville, Johanna, "Radio Free Europe and international Decision-making during the Hungarian Crisis of 1956" *Historical Journal of Films, Radio and Television*, Vol. 24, No. 4, October 2004, pp. 589-611.

Hegedus, Andras B., "The Petoffi Circle: The Forum of Reform in 1956" in Terry Cox (ed), *Hungary 1956: Forty Years On* (New York: Routledge, 1997) pp. 108-133.

Kanet, Roger E., "Czechoslovakia and the Future of Soviet Foreign Policy" in E.J. Czerwinski and Jaroslaw Piekalkiewicz (ed), *The Soviet Invasion of Czechoslovakia: Its Effects on Eastern Europe* (New York: Prager, 1972).

Kennan, George F., "Disengagement Revisited", *Foreign Affairs*, Vol. 37, No. 2, 1959, pp. 187-210.

Kennedy, John F., "A Democrat Looks at Foreign Policy", *Foreign Affairs*, Vol. 36, No. 1, October 1957, pp. 44-59.

Lynch, Allen, "Does Gorbachev Matter Any More", *Foreign Affairs*, Summer 1990, pp. 19-29.

Merritt, Richard L., "A Transformed Crisis: The Berlin Wall" in Roy C. Macridis (ed), *Modern European Governments: Cases of Comparative Policy Making* (Englewood Cliff, New Jersey: Prentice-Hall, 1968). pp. 140-151.

Morganthau, Hans J., "Peace of Our Time", *Commentary*, Vol. 37, No. 3, 1964, pp. 79-83.

Pierre, Andrew, "NATO After Czechoslovakia" in William Zartman (ed), *Czechoslovakia: Intervention and Impact* (New York: New York University Press, 1970).

Rainer, Janos M., "The Life Course of Imre Nagy in Terry Cox (ed), *Hungary 1956: Forty Years On* (New York: Routledge, 1997) 141-151.

Summerscale, Peter, "The Continuing Validity of the Brezhnev Doctrine" in Karen Dawisha and Philip Hanson (eds), *Soviet-East-European Dilemmas* (London: Heinmann, 1981) pp. 26-40.

Taylor, Edmund, "The Lessons on Hungary" *The Reporter*, December 27, 1956.

Taylor, Edmund, "RIAS: The Story of an American Psychowar Outpost" in William Daugherty (ed), *A Psychological Warfare Casebook* (Baltimore: John Hopkins University Press, 1958).

Tigrid, Pavel, "The Prague Coup of 1948: The Elegant takeover" in Thomas T. Hammond (ed), *The Anatomy of Communist Takeover* (New York: Yale University Press, 1975) pp. 399-432.

Valenta, Jiri, "The Bureaucratic Politics Paradigm and the Soviet Invasion of Czechoslovakia", *Political Science Quarterly*, Vol. 79, No. 1, Spring 1979, pp. 55-76.

Valenta, Jiri and Jan Moravec, "Could the Prague Spring been Saved", *ORBIS*, No. 4, Fall: 1991, pp. 581-601.

Zalyotny, A, "FRG and Developments in Czechoslovakia", *International Affairs* (Moscow), No. 11, November 1968, pp. 22-27.

BOOKS:

Aczel, Tamas and Tibor Meray, *The Revolt of Mind: A Case History of Intellectual Resistance Behind the Iron Curtain* (London: Tames and Hudson, 1960)

Adams, Sherman, *Firsthand Report* (New York: Harper, 1961).

Anderson, Ernest T., *Hungary 56* (London: Solidarity, 1964).

Anonymous, *The Dark Side of the Moon* (New York: Scribner, 1947).

Aptheker, Hubert, *The Truth About Hungary* (New York: Mainstream Publishers, 1957).

Beal, John R., *John Foster Dulles 1888-1959* (New York: Harper, 1961).

Békés, Csaba and Janos Rainer, *The 1956 Hungarian Revolution: A History in Document* (Budapest: Central European University Press, 2002).

Bell, Coral, *The Diplomacy of Détente: The Kissinger Era* (London: Martin Robertson, 1977)

Benes, Eduard, *Memoirs* (London: Allen and Unwin, 1954).

Bethell, Nicholas, *Gomulka: His Poland, His Communism* (New York: Holt, Rinehart and Winston, 1969).

Brzezniski, Zbigniew K., *Alternative to Partition: Broader Conception of American Role in Europe* (New York: McGraw-Hill, 1965).

Brzezniski, Zbigniew K., *The Soviet Bloc: Unity and Conflict* (Cambridge, Mass: Harvard University Press, 1971).

Brant, Stefan [pseud], *The East German Rising* (London: Thames and Hudson, 1955).

Burk, Richard V., *Dynamic of Communism in Eastern Europe* (Princeton: Princeton University Press, 1961).

Chester, Louis *et al.*, *An American Melodrama: The Presidential Campaign of 1968* (New York: Viking, 1969).

Conant, James B., *My Several Lives* (New York: Harper and Row, 1970).

Copp, DeWitt and Marshall Peck, *Betrayal at the UN* (New York: Devin-Adair, 1961).

Cox, Terry (ed), *Hungary 1956: Forty Years On* (New York: Routledge, 1997).

Czerwinski, C.J. and Jaroslaw Piekalkiewicz, *The Soviet Invasion of Czechoslovakia: Its Effect on Eastern Europe* (New York: Praeger, 1972).

Davidson, Eugene, *The Death and Life of Germany* (New York: Alfred A. Knopf, 1959).

Dawisha, Karen, *The Kremlin and the Prague Spring* (Berkeley: University of California Press, 1985).

Dawisha, Karen and Philip Hanson (eds), *Soviet-East-European Dilemmas* (London: Heinmann, 1981).

Dornback, Alajos, *The Secret Trial of Nagy* (London: Greenwood Press, 1995).

Drachkovitch, Milorad M., *United States Aid to Yugoslavia and Poland: Analysis of a Controversy* (Washington DC: American Enterprise Institution of Public Policy Research, 1963).

Drummond, Roscoe and Gaston Coblentz, *Duel at the Brink* (London: Doubleday, 1961).

Dubcek, Alexander, *Hope Dies Last: Autobiography of Alexander Dubcek*, Translated by Hochman, Jiri (New York: Kodensa, 1993).

Dulles, John Foster, *War or Peace* (New York: Macmillan, 1950).

Eisenhower, Dwight D., *Crusade in Europe* (Garden City, New York: Garden City Books, 1952).

Eisenhower, Dwight D., *Mandate for Change* (Garden City, New York: Doubleday, 1963).

Eisenhower, Dwight D., *Waging Peace: The White House Years 1956-1961* (New York, Garden City: Doubleday, 1963).

Ekiert, Grezegorz, *The State Against Society: Political Crises and their Aftermath in East Central Europe* (Princeton: Princeton University Press, 1996).

English, Robert, *Russia and the Idea of the West: Gorbachev, Intellectuals and the End of the Cold War* (New York: Colombia University Press, 2000).

Finer, Herman, *Dulles over Suez* (Chicago: Quadrangle, 1964).

Fleming, D.F., *The Cold War and its Origins 1917-1950*, Vol. I and II (New York: Doubleday, 1961).

Fryer, Peter, *Hungarian Tragedy: And other Writings on the 1956 Hungarian Revolution* (London: Index Books, 1997).

Fritz, Ermath, *Internationalism, Security and Legitimacy: The Challenge to Soviet Interests in Eastern Europe, 1964-1968* (RAND Corporation, RM-5909, March 1969).

Garthodd, Raymond L., *Détente and Confrontation: American-Soviet Relations from Nixon to Reagan*, Revised Edition (Washington DC: The Brookings Institution, 1994).

Gerson, Louis L., *The Hyphenate in Recent American Politics and Diplomacy* (Lawrence: University of Kansas, 1964).

Gill, Graeme, *The Collapse of a Single-Party System: The Disintegration of the Communist Party of the Soviet Union* (New York: Cambridge University Press, 1994).

Golan, Galia, *The Czechoslovak Reform Movement: Communism in Crisis* (London: Cambridge University Press, 1971).

Golan, Galia, *Reform Rule in Czechoslovakia: The Dubcek Era,*

1968-1969 (London: Cambridge University Press, 1973).

Good-Adams, Richard, *A Time of Power* (London: Weidnfeld and Nicholson, 1962).

Graebner, Norman A., *The New Isolationism* (New York: Ronald, 1956).

Halt, Robert T., *Radio Free Europe* (Minneapolis: University of Minnesota Press, 1958).

Hammand, Thomas (ed), *Anatomy of Communist Takeover* (New York: Yale University Press, 1975).

Hammarskjold, Dag, *The Servant of Peace: A Selection of the Speeches and Statements of Dag Hammarskjold* (London: Bodley Head, 1962).

Heneghan, Tom, *Unchained Eagle: Germany After the Wall* (Princeton: Princeton University Press, 2000).

Hinterhoff, Eugene, *Disengagement* (London: Stevens, 1959).

Huges, Emmet John, *The Ordeal of Power* (New York: Atheneum, 1963).

Immerman, Richard H., *John Foster Dulles and Diplomacy of Cold War* (Princeton: Princeton University Press, 1990).

Johnson, Lyndon Baines, *The Vintage Point* (New York: Halt, Rinehart and Winston, 1971).

Kennan, George F., *Russia, the Atom and the West* (London: Oxford University Press, 1958).

Kennan, George F., *On Dealing with the Communist World* (New York: Harper and Row, 1964).

Kennedy, John F., *The Strategy for Peace* (New York: Harper, 1960).

Khrushchev Remembers, Vol. 1 (Harmonsworth, Middlesex: Penguin, 1971).

Khrushchev Remembers, The last Testament, Vol. 2 (Harmonsworth, Middlesex: Penguin, 1974).

Kissinger, Henry, *White House Years* (Boston: Little Brown, 1979).

Kissinger, Henry, *Diplomacy* (London: Simon and Schuster, 1995).

Kovacs, Imre (ed), *Facts about Hungary: Fight for Freedom* (New York: Hungarian Committee, 1956).

Kovig, Bennett, *The Myth of Liberation: East and Central Europe in US Diplomacy and Politics since 1941* (Baltimore: John Hopkins University Press, 1973).

Kramer, Mark, *Crisis in Czechoslovakia, 1968: The Prague Spring and Soviet Invasion* (London: Oxford University Press, 2001).

Kusin, Vladimir, *The Intellectual Origins of the Prague Spring: The Development of Reformist Ideas in Czechoslovakia 1956-1967* (New York: Cambridge University Press, 1971).

Lane, Arthur Bliss, *I Saw Poland Betrayed* (Indianapolis: Bobbs Merrill, 1948).

Lash, J.P., *Dag Hammarskjold* (London: Cassell, 1962).

Lefever, Ernest, *Ethics and the United States Foreign Policy* (New York: Macmillan, 1958).

Leff, Carol Skalnik, *National Conflict in Czechoslovakia* (Princeton: Princeton University Press, 1988).

Lippmann, Walter, *The Cold War* (New York: Harper, 1947).

Lipta´k, Be´la, *A Testament of Revolution* (Texas: A&M University Press, 2006).

Litvan, György (ed), *The Hungary Revolution of 1956: Reform and Repression, 1953-1963*, Translated by Janos M. Bak and Lyman H. Legters (London: Longman, 1996).

Macmillan, Harold, *Tides of Fortune, 1945-1955* (London: Macmillan, 1969).

Mandelbaum, Michael (ed), *The Rise of Nation in the Soviet Union: American Foreign Policy and the Disintegration of the USSR* (New York: Council of Foreign Relations, 1991).

Marples, David R., *The Collapse of the Soviet Union, 1985-1991* (London: Longman, 2004).

Melvin J., Lasky (ed), *The Hungarian Revolution: A White Book* (New York: Books of Library Press, 1957).

Memoirs of Cordell Hall (New York: Hodder and Stoughton, 1948).

Menges, Constaine, *Prague Resistance, 1968; The Ingenuity of Conviction* (RAND Corporation, P-3939, September 1968).

Meray, Tibor, *Thirteen Days that Shook the Kremlin* (London: Thames and Hudson, 1959).

Meray, Tibor, *That Day in Budapest, October 23, 1956* (New York: Funk and Wagnalls, 1969).

Michie, Allen A. *Voices through the Iron Curtain: The Radio Free Europe Story* (New York: Dodd and Co, 1963).

Mikes, George, *The Hungarian Revolution* (London: A Deutsch, 1957).

Mikolajczyk, Stanislaw, *Rape of Poland* (New York: Whittlessey House, 1948).

Miller, Richard I., Dag Hammarskjold and Crisis in Diplomacy (New York: Oceana, 1961).

Mitrovich, Gregory, *Undermining the Kremlin: American Strategy to Subvert the Soviet Bloc, 1947-1956* (Ithica: Cornell University Press, 2000).

Molner, Miklos, *Budapest 1956: A History of Hungarian Revolution* (London: George Allen and Unwin, 1968).

Morganthau, Hans J., *American Foreign Policy: In Defense of the National Interest* (London: Mathuen, 1952).

Murphy, Robert, *Diplomat Among Warriors* (Garden City, New York: Doubleday, 1964).

Nagy, Imre, *On Communism: In Defense of the New Course* (New York: Praeger, 1957).

Navratil, Jaromir, *The Prague Spring 1968: A National Security Archive Documents Reader* (Budapest: Central European University Press, 1998).

Nevers, Renée De, *Comrades No More: The Seeds of Change in Eastern Europe* (Cambridge, Mass.: Harvard University Press, 2003).

Nixon, Richard M., *Six Crises* (New York, Garden City: Doubleday, 1962).

Ouimet, Mathew J., *Rise and Fall of the Brezhnev Doctrine in Soviet Foreign Policy* (Chapel Hill: University of North Carolina, 2003).

Paul, David W., *Czechoslovakia* (Boulder, Colorado: Westview Press, 1981).

Pelikan, Jerry (ed), *The Czechoslovak Political Trials 1950-54* (Stanford, California: Stanford University Press, 1971).

Radvanyi, Janos, *Hungary and Superpowers: The 1956 Revolution and Realpolitik* (California, Stanford: Hoover Institution Press, 1972).

Reid, Escolt, *Hungary and Suez* (Oakville, Ont.: Mosaic, 1986).

Remington, Robin Alison (ed), *Winter in Prague: Documents on Czechoslovak Communism in Crisis* (Cambridge, Mass: MIT, Press, 1969).

Ripka, Hubert, *Munich and After* (London: Gollancz, 1939).

Ripka, Hubert, *Czechoslovakia Enslaved* (London: Gollancz, 1950).

Rkei, J.G. and M. Horvath, *Soviet Military Intervention in Hungary, 1956* (Budapest: Central European University Press, 1999).

Rovere, Richard, *Affairs of the State: The Eisenhower Years* (New York: Farrar, Straus, 1956).

Rusk, Dean, *The Winds of Freedom* (Boston: Beacon Press, 1963).

Sakwa, Richard, *The Rise and Fall of the Soviet Union 1917-1991* (London: Routledge, 1999).

Schlesinger Jr., Arthur, *A Thousand Days: John F. Kennedy in the White House* (Boston: Houghton Miffin, 1965).

Schwartz, Schwartz, *Prague's 200 Days: The Struggle for Democracy in Czechoslovakia* (New York: Praeger, 1969).

Siani-Davies, Peter, *The Romanian Revolution of December 1989* (Ithaca: Cornell University Press, 2005).

Skoug, Kenneth N., *Czechoslovak's Lost Fight for Freedom, 1967-1969: An American Embassy Perspective* (New York: Praeger, 1999).

Sorensen, Theodore C., *Kennedy* (New York: Harper and Row, 1965).

Stearman, William Lloyd, *The Soviet Union and the Occupation of Austria* (Bonn: Siegler and Co. 1960).

Stevenson, Adlai, *Major Campaign Speeches* (New York: Random, 1953).

Suda, Zdenek, *The Czechoslovak Socialist Republic* (Baltimore: John Hopkins University Press, 1969).

Tal, David, *The 1956 War: Collusion and Rivalry in the Middle East* (London: Routledge, 2001).

The Truth About Nagy Affair: Facts, Documents, Comments (London: Cecker and Warbur, 1957).

Theoharis, Arthur G., *The Yalta Myth: An Issue in US Politics, 1945-1955* (Colombia: University of Missouri Press, 1970).

Tökes, Rudolf L. *Hungary's Negotiated Revolution: Economic Reform, Social Change and Political Succession* (Cambridge: Cambridge University Press, 1996).

Ulam, Adam, *Titoism and Cominform* (Cambridge, Mass.: Harvard University Press, 1952).

Unwin, Peter, *Voice in the Wilderness: Imre Nagy and Hungarian Revolution* (London: Little, Brown, 1991).

Valenta, Jiri, *Soviet Intervention in Czechoslovakia, 1968: Anatomy of a Decision* (Baltimore: John Hopkins Press, 1979).

Vali, Ferenc A., *Rift and Revolt in Hungary* (Cambridge, Mass.: Harvard University Press, 1961).

Weintal, Edward and Charles Barlett, *Facing the Brink* (New York: Scriber's, 1067).

Wheeler, John Bennet, *Munich: Prologue to Tragedy* (London: Macmillan, 1963).

Wilczynski, Jozef, *The Economics and Politics of East-West Trade* (London: Macmillan, 1969).

Williams, Kieran, *The Prague Spring and its Aftermath: Czechoslovak Politics, 1968-1970* (London: Cambridge University Press, 1977).

Wolfe, Thomas W., *The Evolution of the Warsaw Pact* (RAND Corporation Memorandum, December 1965).

Wolfers, Arnold, *Alliance Policy in the Cold War* (Baltimore: John Hopkins Press, 1959).

Zinner, Paul E. (ed), *Nationalism and Popular Revolt in Eastern Europe: Selected Documents on Events in Poland and Hungary, February-November 1956* (New York: Colombia University Press, 1956).

Zinner, Paul E., *Revolution in Hungary* (New York: Colombia University Press, 1962).

NEWSPAPERS AND MAGAZINES:

Economist

Guardian

International Herald Tribune

Newsweek

New York Times

Time

Washington Post

Index